WITHDRAWN
COMMUNICA'
CULTURAL AND DIA
STUDIES: THE KEY CONCEPTS

This book provides a topical and authoritative guide to Communication, Cultural and Media Studies. It brings together in an accessible form some of the most important concepts that you will need, and shows how they have been - or might be - used. This third edition of the classic text *Key Concepts in Communication and Cultural Studies* forms an up-to-date, multi-disciplinary explanation and assessment of the key concepts and new terms that you will encounter in your studies, from 'anti-globalisation' to 'reality TV', from 'celebrity' to 'tech-wreck'.

This new edition includes:

- Over 70 new entries,
- Most entries revised, rewritten and updated,
- Coverage of recent developments in the field,
- Coverage of new interactive media and the 'new economy',
- An extensive bibliography to aid further study.

John Hartley is Professor and Dean of the Creative Industries Faculty at Queensland University of Technology, Australia. He is author of many books and articles on television, journalism and cultural studies. His most recent books are: *Popular Reality* (1996), *Uses of Television* (1999), *The Indigenous Public Sphere*, with Alan McKee (2000), *American Cultural Studies: A Reader*, edited with Roberta E. Pearson (2000) and *A Short History of Cultural Studies* (2003).

ROUTLEDGE KEY GUIDES

Routledge Key Guides are accessible, informative and lucid handbooks, which define and discuss the central concepts, thinkers and debates in a broad range of academic disciplines. All are written by noted experts in their respective subjects. Clear, concise exposition of complex and stimulating issues and ideas make *Routledge Key Guides* the ultimate reference resources for students, teachers, researchers and the interested lay person.

Ancient History: Key Themes and Approaches
Neville Morley

Business: The Key Concepts
Mark Vernon

Cinema Studies: The Key Concepts (second edition)
Susan Hayward

Cultural Theory: The Key Concepts
Edited by Andrew Edgar and Peter Sedgwick

Cultural Theory: The Key Thinkers
Andrew Edgar and Peter Sedgwick

Eastern Philosophy: Key Readings
Oliver Leaman

International Relations: The Key Concepts
Martin Griffiths and Terry O'Callaghan

Key Writers on Art: From Antiquity to the Nineteenth Century
Edited by Chris Murray

Key Writers on Art: The Twentieth Century
Edited by Chris Murray

Popular Music: The Key Concepts
Roy Shuker

Post-Colonial Studies: The Key Concepts
Bill Ashcroft, Gareth Griffiths and Helen Tiffin

Social and Cultural Anthropology: The Key Concepts
Nigel Rapport and Joanna Overing

Sport and Physical Education: The Key Concepts
Timothy Chandler, Mike Cronin and Wray Vamplew

Sport Psychology: The Key Concepts
Ellis Cashmore

Television Studies: The Key Concepts
Neil Casey, Bernadette Casey, Justin Lewis, Ben Calvert and Liam French

Fifty Eastern Thinkers
Diané Collinson, Kathryn Plant and Robert Wilkinson

Fifty Contemporary Choreographers
Edited by Martha Bremser

Fifty Contemporary Filmmakers
Edited by Yvonne Tasker

Fifty Key Classical Authors
Alison Sharrock and Rhiannon Ash

Fifty Key Contemporary Thinkers
John Lechte

Fifty Key Figures in Twentieth-Century British Politics
Keith Laybourn

Fifty Key Jewish Thinkers
Dan Cohn-Sherbok

Fifty Key Thinkers on the Environment
Edited by Joy Palmer with Peter Blaze Corcoran and David A. Cooper

Fifty Key Thinkers on History
Marnie Hughes-Warrington

Fifty Key Thinkers in International Relations
Martin Griffiths

Fifty Major Economists
Steven Pressman

Fifty Major Philosophers
Diané Collinson

COMMUNICATION, CULTURAL AND MEDIA STUDIES

The Key Concepts
Third Edition

John Hartley

With additional material by
Martin Montgomery, Elinor Rennie and Marc Brennan

Routledge
Taylor & Francis Group

LONDON AND NEW YORK

First published 2002
by Routledge
11 New Fetter Lane, London EC4P 4EE

Simultaneously published in the USA and Canada
by Routledge
29 West 35th Street, New York, NY 10001

Routledge is an imprint of the Taylor & Francis Group

© 2002 John Hartley

Typeset in Bembo by Taylor & Francis Books Ltd
Printed and bound in Great Britain by Biddles Ltd, Guildford and King's Lynn

British Library Cataloguing in Publication Data
A catalogue record for this book is available from the British Library

Library of Congress Cataloging in Publication Data
A catalog record for this title has been requested

ISBN 0–415–26888–5 (hbk)
ISBN 0–415–26889–3 (pbk)

CONTENTS

PREFACE TO THE THIRD EDITION

This is the third edition of a book first published in the early 1980s, followed by an enlarged and revised edition in the 1990s. It has remained in print and in demand for all of the intervening time. It has also been translated into Chinese, Spanish, Korean and Bahasa Malaysian.

Now here it is again, spruced up for a new century. For this edition it has been revised from top to bottom, has come under single authorship, with crucial input from Martin Montgomery, Elinor Rennie and Marc Brennan, and it has been redesigned. Some concepts survive from earlier editions, but for the most part this is an entirely new work. The entries now include many that relate to new interactive media and the 'new economy', developments that were not even on the horizon when the first edition was published.

The first edition was published in 1982 with the title *Key Concepts in Communication Studies*. The second edition was *Key Concepts in Communication and Cultural Studies*, published in 1994. This edition is called *Communication, Cultural and Media Studies: The Key Concepts*, the change in form of the title reflecting this volume's alignment with Routledge's 'Key Guides', of which it was the prototype. Cultural and media studies have also been successively added, in recognition of their importance both within these covers and in the world.

INTRODUCTION

In 1969, computers were the size of rooms; computer disks the size of woks. Time spent on them was so valuable you had to hire it by the hundredth of an hour (0.6 of a minute). These impressive machines, however, had about as much computing power as the old PC that people now pass on to the kids because it is too slow. But those behemoths – the IBM 360s – were used in 1969 to send people to the moon. In the same year, the year of the Woodstock music festival and the first episodes of *Sesame Street*, the first Boeing 747 jumbo jet rolled out of its Seattle hangar. It was in 1969 also that, using the resources of a military budget distended by Cold War fears and the continuing Vietnam War, the US Defense Department's Advanced Projects Research Agency invented a 'packet switching' technology – better known now as the Internet.

Communication was entering an unprecedented phase of intensification; culture was flowering; information was valuable and the sky was the limit. The media, communications and culture were moving centre stage, becoming among the most dynamic areas of contemporary life.

Since 1969 computing, communication, media and the field of popular culture have changed and burgeoned. Computing is many times faster and now much more socially pervasive. International transport is now a mass medium in its own right. The Internet grows exponentially each year. The new economy has made its presence felt. But things have not changed out of all recognition. The USA is still the engine of innovation and growth, and simultaneously a source of anxiety and hostility. Jumbos are still flying. And some of Woodstock's greatest hits are still playing. People don't go the moon any more, but they do go to Disney World, which also began life in 1969.

Communication, cultural and media studies are also of this vintage; relatively young by academic standards. They grew out of the period in the 1960s and 1970s when higher education began to take modern communication, culture and media seriously. This was also the time when universities in Europe, Australia and elsewhere began to open their doors to people whose families had never before sent a daughter or son to university. The combination – new ideas, new objects of study, new students – has made this field very dynamic, very interesting to work in and also controversial.

As relatively new areas of study, communication, cultural and media studies have been characterised by fast-moving and innovative research work; by the attempt to say new things in new ways. At the same time, they have borrowed widely from a variety of established academic disciplines and discourses. As a result, there is often an uneasy period for the newcomer to the area, until you get your bearings.

What follows is a field guide. It is designed to put together in an accessible form some of the most important concepts that you will encounter, and to show some of the ways in which these concepts have been (or might be) used. The book is not a dictionary – it does not claim to treat concepts 'definitively'. The entries are not destinations but starting points for further intellectual and practical work.

Communication, Cultural and Media Studies: The Key Concepts is designed to help students and teachers new to the area find their way about. It may be that getting to know a new area of study is best done by the usual method: crashing about in the dark and bumping into things. This was certainly the case was for me when I started trying to understand communication, culture and media back in 1969, the year I went to university (the first member of my family to do so). And it still is, really, given the speed and scale of change in all of these domains. Always there is something new to discover, and people keep moving the furniture around when you're not looking. I thought at the time that a guide would be handy, and still do. I hope that what follows helps you to shed a little light on your chosen topics.

Using a book like this might seem cumbersome to begin with, but as you struggle with the clumsy technology of knowledge, remember those computer disks the size of woks. Clumsy indeed – but they got us to the moon.

ACKNOWLEDGEMENTS

This couldn't have been done without Ellie Rennie and Marc Brennan – research assistants maybe; 'killer apps' (q.v.) certainly. Thanks to you both.

- Thanks to Martin Montgomery, without whose language concepts this edition would have been poorer.
- I want to thank John Fiske, Tim O'Sullivan, Danny Saunders and Martin Montgomery – co-authors of the first and second editions – it has been a privilege, snuggling between the covers with you for nearly twenty years.
- My thanks are due to Queensland University of Technology, for material assistance towards research for the book.
- As always, Rebecca Barden has made a book appear where none was expected.
- And my family – Tina Horton, and Karri, Rhiannon and Sophie Hartley – thanks for waiting!

John Hartley
QUT
March 2002

LIST OF CONCEPTS

Aberrant decoding
Accessing
Actuality
Aesthetics
Analogue
Anti-globalisation
Applications
Art–science interface
Articulation
Audiences
Author/ship
b2b
Bardic function
Bias
Binary opposition
Biotechnology
Bricolage
Broadband
Broadcasting
Celebrity
Class
Cluster
Code
Collocation
Communication
Communication design
Connectivity
Consumer sovereignty
Content analysis
Content industries
Convergence
Conversation analysis

Copyright
Creative industries
Cultural capital
Cultural citizenship
Cultural populism
Cultural studies
Culture
Culture as service industry
Culture jamming
Culture wars
Customisation
Cyberdemocracy
Cybernetics
Cyborg
Datacasting
Diexis
Democratainment
Deregulation
Diachronic
Dialect
Dialogic
Diaspora
Diegesis
Difference
Digital/analogue distribution
Digital divide
Diglossia
Discourse
Diversity
DIY culture
Dot.com crash
Dumbing down

E-commerce
Edutainment
Effects
Entertainment
Ethnic/ethnicity
Ethnography
Ex-nomination
Foregrounding
Frankfurt School
Games (computer/video)
Gatekeeper
Gender
Genre
Globalisation
Hegemony
ICT
Identification
Identity politics
Ideological state apparatuses
Ideology
Image
Impartiality
Implicature (conversational)
Independence
Individual
Individualism
Information society/information
economy
Infotainment
Infrastructure
Innovation
Intangibles
Intellectual property
Interactivity
Internationalisation
Internet
Interpellation
Intertextuality
Kinesics
Knowledge
Knowledge economy
Language

Language, functions of
Langue
Lifestyle
Literacy
Localisation
Mass communication
Mass society/mass society theory
Meaning
Media law
Mediasphere
Medium/media
Metaphor
Methodology
Metonymy
Mode of address
Moral panic
Motivation (of the shot)
Modern/modernism/modernity
MP3
Multi-accentuality
Multiculturalism
Multimedia
Myth
Nanotechnology
Napster
Narrative
Nasdaq
Nation
Naturalising
Naturalism
Nature
Net radio
Network society
New economy
New media policies
New media technologies
News values
Noise
Objectivity
Online
Online music distribution
Orality

Orientalism
Paradigm
Parole
Participant observation
Performance
Persuasion
Phatic communication
Phonemic/phonetic
Phonology
Pidgin
Polysemy/polysemic
Popular/popular culture
Post-broadcast media
Postmodern/postmodernism/post-modernity
Power
Pragmatics
Privatisation
Propaganda
Proxemics
Public
Public service broadcasting
Public sphere
Race
Reader/readership
Realism
Reality TV
Rearviewmirrorism
Redundancy
Referent
Register
Regulation
Rhetoric

Representation
Semantics
Semiosphere
Semiotics/semiology
Sign
Signification
Sit up/sit back
Speech act
Speech community
Spin
Standard language
Star/stardom
Stereotype
Streaming
Structuralism
Style
Subculture
Subjectivity
Symbol
Syntagm
Synchronic
Technological determinism
Text/textual analysis
Textual system
Textuality
Transitivity
Virtual communities
Virtuality
Violence
Walled garden
World Trade Organisation
World Wide Web

ABERRANT DECODING

A concept originating with Umberto Eco, identifying a mismatch of meaning between sender (encoder) and receiver (decoder) of any message, from ancient art to contemporary media. Eco himself used the term in a 'semiotic inquiry into the television message', first published in 1965 in Italian, a pioneering attempt to apply semiotics to mass communication (Eco, 1972). He suggested that 'aberrant decoding' was an accident in pre-industrial societies, an exception to the expectation of speakers and artists that their own communities would normally 'get' what they were talking about. There were four classes of exception to this rule:

- people who didn't know the language (what meanings did the Greeks, and then everyone till Jean-François Champollion, ascribe to Egyptian hieroglyphics?);
- people from future generations (what meanings did medieval Christians ascribe to Greek and Roman art?);
- people from different belief systems (what meanings do modern tourists ascribe to the stained glass windows of cathedrals such as Chartres?);
- people from different cultures (what meanings do white people ascribe to Aboriginal art?).

However, and herein lies the importance of the concept, Eco argued that contemporary media such as television are communicative codes in which aberrant decoding is the norm, not the exception. TV communicators know *a priori* that their code is not shared by all the receivers.

Eco proposed therefore that research into television required three phases:

- a semiotic analysis of television 'messages' to establish the codes used by the transmitting organisation and producers, and the references audiences were expected to have in order to decode them;
- field research into 'how the messages, previously analysed, have in fact been received in selected sample situations';
- a comparative analysis to determine the extent to which the two sets of results tally.

Eco speculated: 'We could discover that the community of the users has such freedom in decoding as to make the influencing power of the organisation much weaker than one could have thought. Or just the opposite' (1972: 107). This research agenda proved remarkably stable. Its combination of textual (semiotic) and audience (sociological) analysis designed to assess the ideological power of media and the room for manoeuvre of audiences remains to this day at the core of academic media research.

Eco's article was translated (by Paola Splendore) and published in the journal of Birmingham Centre for Contemporary Cultural Studies (CCS), *Working Papers in Cultural Studies*, in 1972. It was a source of influence for Stuart Hall's 'encoding/decoding' thesis and for much subsequent work by media researchers at the CCCS, for instance, Charlotte Brunsdon and David Morley, Ian Connell and Lydia Curti, and thence made its way into the mainstream of media studies.

ACCESSING

The practice of including verbal quotations and film/tape interviews or statements (in news/current affairs coverage) which originate from people or groups not directly employed by the media organisation itself. Access is a serious matter in broadcasting organisations, because scarcity of airtime means that it has to be heavily rationed, which is why for such organisations it is a political issue. In post-broadcast media such as the Internet, access does not need to be rationed and therefore is not an issue.

Demands for broadcast access are based on a reflection theory of the media – that is, that the media *ought* to reflect the plurality of different groups, politics or lifestyles that can be identified outside the media in social life. Many groups argue that their access to television is blocked and that as a result they are unable to establish their point of view in the public mind. The assumption often is that the blockage is caused by a more or less deliberate conspiracy by the media to exclude them.

Even when access is achieved, 'minority groups' are often disappointed with the coverage they receive. Commercial and industrial organisations with an extensive division of labour and an occupational ideology of professionalism won't let you simply appear on television or radio and state your case or tell your story. Despite the media's centrality to public life and to citizenship, there is no *right* of access. Whether you get on air depends on the professionals' assessment of your talent, newsworthiness or representative status, and what you say is mediated through their professional codes and production processes.

The professional mediation of accessed voices extends to the message. Even when you have your say on television, you won't speak for yourself. What you say becomes what television says, and television discourse has its own peculiarities. When a newsreader quotes or an interviewer questions you, your utterance becomes a discursive element which is subordinate to the narrative flow and visual codes of the item as a whole. Its meaning is not self-contained, but depends on what is said and seen before and afterwards. You become, in effect, one actor in a drama, and even if you're lucky enough to be playing the lead, it is still the case that what you say is significant only in the context of what all the others say, and of what the drama is about. Further, one aspect of your role is entirely at odds with your own purposes. For simply by accessing you, the institutional discourse is able to claim authenticity and credibility for itself. You become the means through which the *legitimacy* of media representations can be established – irrespective of what you actually say.

There is, then, a conflict of interest between professional media discourses and the demands for access that various groups express. The way this has been handled in practice takes two forms. First, news and current affairs subscribe to the principle of impartiality, thereby ensuring that a (narrow and 'balanced') range of voices is accessed on any one topic. Second, specialist 'access programmes' have been established on many networks. In these off-peak slots media professionals may relinquish control of the programme content, but retain control of the production process. Unfortunately, both these well-intentioned practices have negative consequences. Impartiality legitimates the mainstream bipartisan form of politics at the expense of the various single-issue groups (e.g. environmental campaigns), ethnic 'minority' groups, radical or feminist groups and community groups that tend to end up having to make do with the marginal access slots. For such groups, the very fact of winning access results in representations that seem 'naturally' to confirm their marginal status. This is why they've all migrated to the Internet.

Further reading: Glasgow Media Group (1982); Hartley (1982, 1992a); Willis and Wollen (1990)

ACTUALITY

Professional term for film/tape footage used in news and current affairs broadcasts that records events as they happen. Contrasted with studio presentation (talking heads) and with archive (stock) footage.

In semiotic analysis, actuality is seen as a key device in producing ideological closure, by anchoring the preferred reading on the apparently unarguable 'facts' of the event-as-filmed. Actuality is presented as self-evident; the production processes are rarely shown, so that viewers are encouraged to make sense of the footage in terms of the event, and not the way in which it is represented. However, actuality rarely appears on the screen without an accompanying commentary – and considerable professional skill is expended on contextualising it for the 'benefit' of viewers. As Peter Sissons, a British news presenter has put it: 'Let's remember that although a picture can tell the story, only a word can put it into its historical perspective, can caution against gullibility, can weigh the true significance of the event' (*Independent Broadcasting*, 1982). In short, actuality is a device for naturalising meaning (it proposes the cultural as natural).

AESTHETICS

A term deriving from the philosophical analysis of art, aesthetics refers to insight, expressiveness and beauty in creativity. The use of the term was popularised in the nineteenth century as a means of separating art from craft. In this tradition, aesthetics provided a paradigm for talking about texts as art, and art as humanising civility, not mere decoration. The theory of aesthetics understood its practice as objective. The properties of artworks were expressions of universal values, open to the same interpretation by all who were free. The theory relied on the assumption that aesthetic criteria lay within the work itself, negating the need to consider issues of context and the means of production ('art for art's sake').

Aesthetic judgements in Marxist theory are considered a form of ideology. Whilst this is certainly a valid point, attempts by, for example, Marxists, feminists and queer theory to subvert aesthetic practice have arguably continued the tradition. Attempting to replace 'universal' assumptions about taste with subcultural categories creates many splinter aesthetic theories that, although speaking on behalf of smaller groups, continue to imply a set of common beliefs around notions of truth, beauty and art.

The term aesthetic gained some currency in semiotic analysis, especially in the notion of an 'aesthetic code', in which the production of meaning is not the aim but the starting point of a given message. It prioritises the signifier over the signified, and seeks to exploit rather than confirm the limits and constraints of the form, genre or convention within which it operates. Hence aesthetic codes put a premium on innovation, entropy and experimentation with the raw materials of signification (words, colours, composition, sequence), and evoke pleasurable responses for that reason. Semiotics goes beyond idealist aesthetics in its attempt to find a value-free and culturally specific description of aesthetic codes, and thence to find such codes operating in discourses or media not usually associated with the category 'art': advertising copy, political slogans, graffiti, and the output of consumer and entertainment media.

Further reading: Barrell (1986)

ANALOGUE

Analogue information works by resemblance, as opposed to *digital* information, which works by fixed code, especially the zeros and ones of computer code. Thus, a painting or photograph is analogue, while videotape, computer display and digital 'photography' are digital. Analogue visual images may display infinite gradation of tone, colour, hue, line, grain, etc., whereas digital images break down such variation into standard blocks of information, such as pixels.

It is possible to identify the late twentieth century as an era passing from analogue to digital. Broadcasting, mass communication, cinema, illustrated newspapers and magazines and the recorded music industry were based largely on analogue media technologies. In cinema, for example, analogue cameras and tape recorders gathered the action, and reproduction (screening) was also done via photographic film and optical soundtracks. New interactive media, on the other hand, were entirely digital, including cameras, sound recording and playback devices, computers, etc., all the way through the production chain from image- and sound-gathering to eventual consumer/user download and interaction. Even forms of larceny shifted from 'analogue' (stealing books or magazines from retailers, for instance) to 'digital' (downloading music or pictures via Napster before its demise, for instance).

Analogue artforms retained a nostalgic aura of authenticity, both artistic and legal. A 'metaphysics of presence' (see **difference**) made artists feel better about analogue images that you could actually see in their material form, on film, canvas or paper, unlike the entirely virtual digital images. Although paintings were faked and photos doctored throughout the analogue era, digital images could be manipulated more readily than analogues, i.e. more cheaply, and without lifetime professional skills, using commercially available software. A consequence of this is that greater sophistication is required of readers and users – the naive (analogue) idea that photos depict some actually existing scene is a matter for scepticism, not least because increasingly users have the digital means to manipulate, improve, subvert and embellish information for themselves.

On the flip side, it is still the case that one of the triumphs of digital art is to make the result look like analogue, so that extensive press coverage is given to advances that allow a digitally animated movie/games heroine to look like a real woman, or a hairy monster to look truly hairy. This is the phenomenon that Marshall McLuhan called '**rearviewmirrorism**', when a new medium copies the one it is destined to supplant – for now at least, digital is copying analogue.

See also: **Digital/analogue distribution**

ANTI-GLOBALISATION

The word globalisation suggests an image of a world that is becoming whole, where borders are being dismantled and where no country will be excluded – a smooth, homogenous sphere without nationalist conflicts or class stratification. But globalisation has not shown itself to be a system of fair or complete distribution. The speed of technical diffusion depends upon the knowledge, economic circumstances, government and cultural character of a time and place. The flows of resources and capital occurring as a result of globalisation are strategic, discriminatory and influenced by countries, industries and individuals with power. Some are able to use the processes of globalisation to their advantage while others become increasingly marginalised and are excluded economically.

Resistance to globalisation has manifested in a number of forms, out of disparate and sometimes conflicting interests. Early anti-globalisation sentiments focused on the loss of jobs for workers in industrially advanced societies as corporations increasingly sought offshore product manufacturing in areas where labour was less expensive and where industrial laws were lax or non-existent. This concern waned, however, and it became apparent that forces other than globalisation were largely responsible for unemployment (Castells, 2000). A new group of activists took up the anti-globalisation banner, this time out of concern for workers and communities experiencing economic inequality and political disenfranchisement as a result of globalisation.

Much of the movement's initial attention was focused on the 'sweatshop' issue that gained prominence in the mid-1990s and singled out the Nike brand as being hypocritical in its marketing strategies (that promoted freedom and agency) and its exploitative manufacturing practices. The movement escalated in 1995 around a separate issue, when Ken Saro-Wiwa, a Nigerian writer and environmental leader was imprisoned by the Nigerian military government for leading a campaign against Royal Dutch Shell's oil drilling in Niger Delta. Saro-Wiwa and eight other Ogoni activists were executed by the military later that year. In both instances, the unethical alliances formed between multinational corporations and oppressive regimes were seen to be a central negative consequence of globalisation (Klein, 2000: 331).

These specific protests, designed to expose the practices of some as an example to the world, later joined together in a more generalist campaign through a series of large demonstrations. Gathering outside the conventions of the world's political and business leaders in Seattle (1999), Melbourne (2000), Prague (2000), Quebec City (2001) and Genoa (2001), groups ranging from anti-capitalists, environmentalists, anarchists and human rights campaigners brought the anti-globalisation movement to the global stage.

In many respects, the 'anti-globalisation' tag of this particular social movement is misleading. If there is a key demand from the activists it is to see the establishment of international laws, democratically organised institutions capable of regulating the global capital, and for some international trade union solutions to rectify the inequality of distribution. The concerns of the movement are not so much about stopping globalisation, but finding more equitable solutions for a globalised society. And, as the champion of the anti-globalisation movement, Naomi Klein, has pointed out, 'the triumph of economic globalisation has inspired a wave of techno-savvy investigative activists who are as globally minded as the corporations they track' (Klein, 2000: 327). Indymedia (www.indymedia.org) is one such network of global resistance, a collectively run web-based media outlet that has spawned local sites and centres throughout the world.

A separate wave of anti-globalisation sentiment has manifested as a conservative scepticism about the rapid increase and hybridity in cultural choice, brought about by forces described as globalisation. Localism is upheld as possessing authenticity and 'natural' community, and face-to-face relations are privileged over mediated communication. The prescription underpinning this stream of anti-globalisation thinking is a return to smaller, geographically centred communities. Critics have seen this revival of the local as a nostalgic yearning for a mythical past that overlooks the benefits of an extended and diverse cultural field. It is a vision reminiscent of 1950s' America but without the necessary acknowledgement of how such societies have been constrictive of peoples' rights and suspicious of difference.

See also: **Culture jamming, Globalisation**

Further reading: Barret-Lennard (2001)

APPLICATIONS

Software comprising the electronic instructions used to direct computers to perform certain functions. Software is divided into two categories: 'systems software', which enables the computer to operate; and 'applications software', which serves the end user. An application requires systems software in order to exist. Examples of applications include e-mail, browsers, word processors and spreadsheets. The expression 'killer application' (or 'killer app') describes software applications that are highly sought after.

Applications, together with **infrastructure** and **connectivity**, make up the information communications technologies, or ICT. Applications are set to become more important economically, as ICT infrastructure and connectivity mature.

ART–SCIENCE INTERFACE

Modernity was characterised by the ascendancy of useful over fine arts; technology over old master. Eventually, following a book by novelist C. P. Snow, it was widely accepted that contemporary societies had fractured into 'two cultures', one based on science, the other on the arts and humanities. But the tension and mutual incomprehensibility of these two cultures was productive and necessary. Meanwhile, engineering vied with artistic movements to define the era. This applied equally to spectacular, fatal constructions such as bridges and skyscrapers, airships and ocean liners, and to mundane, banal machines from railways to jumbo jets, automobiles to kitchenware. Indeed, engineering (steel-frame buildings) combined with artistic movements (art-deco) in an art–science interface to build the icon of modernity itself, New York City.

Modern communications media combine technology with artistic and aesthetic content. Such media include cinema, radio, television, publishing, computer software and games, recorded music and photography. Like architecture and engineering, but in forms that compete directly with more traditional arts, these are true art–science interfaces, since they cannot exist without scientific inventions but would find no public without their artistic content.

Popular aesthetics was always an art–science interface. The idea that truth could be revealed by technological means, rather than by a shaping artistic vision that was always in the end ideological or manipulative, was inherent in the popularity of aestheticisations of science itself, whether via photos from outer space, wildlife documentaries on TV or the entire dinosaur industry (see Mitchell, 1998). The human condition (previously the domain of literature, painting and the pursuit of 'beauty') became a province of science. Beauty was found in truth, not imagination.

On the other hand, some popularisations of scientific advance displayed nostalgic sentimentality about the human condition amounting to serious bad faith. A paradigm example of this was the Steven Spielberg movie *ET: The Extra-Terrestrial*. This fable used the latest hi-tech scientific cinematic equipment to propose a world where technology (in the form of government agencies on the lookout for ET) was the enemy of the values embodied in the human child (equipped with a heart and sentiment). The movie used science to condemn it.

Recently, the art–science interface has extended the challenge, moving from architecture, engineering and media to scarier territory, notably that of **biotechnology**. Cultivated, organic, self-reproducing objects have been produced for non-utilitarian purposes: for example, skin-graft technology applied to artistic ends. But the biosciences didn't really need to commission specialist artists. Sometimes they appeared to be enacting the darker nightmares of modern art entirely by themselves, for instance via the widely circulated photograph of a rodent with a human ear grafted on its back in a ghoulish reminder of surrealism. Other bioscientific advances, such as cloning, seemed to be vying successfully with science fiction fears of genetic manipulation. Cultural theorists such as Donna Haraway explored the human–science–technology interface in work on the **cyborg**.

See also: **Aesthetics**

ARTICULATION

In cultural studies, articulation doesn't carry its most familiar sense of 'uttering clearly'. It is used in the sense you may recognise from 'articulated truck' – where articulation denotes the joining of two things together. In cultural studies, what may be articulated are not two components of a truck but large-scale social forces (especially *modes of production*), in a particular configuration or *formation* at a particular time, called a *conjuncture*, to produce the structural determinants of any given practice, text or event. Just as an articulated lorry has a prime mover and a trailer (where the prime mover, although smaller and lighter, determines the movement of the trailer – it provides motive force *to* the trailer), so articulation describes not simply a combination of forces but a hierarchical relationship between them. Forces aren't simply joined or jointed, they are '*structured in dominance*'.

The term derives from Marxist analysis, where it refers to the articulation of different modes of production. The economic and social relations of a society during a given epoch will display an articulation of different modes of production – capitalist, feudal and even communal, all at once – but one of these modes of production is *structured in dominance* over the others or '*overdetermines*' them and obliges them to adapt to its needs, or integrates them into the mechanisms of its reproduction. Hence the *feudal* monarchy survives into the *capitalist* epoch, but is adapted to its purposes; or an industry such as publishing retains feudal relations between author and publisher within the overall capitalist mode of production of books; or a social institution such as the family allows for communal modes of production to be exploited by a capitalist economy. These are classic articulations.

The term has been extended in use to include articulations of other social forces. You might read, for instance, of the articulation of race and class in an analysis of subcultural music, or of the articulation of gender and nation in an analysis of sport.

The term peppers the writings of analysts who are not only Marxist but who are also connected with the Birmingham Centre for Contemporary Cultural Studies in Britain. Elsewhere it has been used to account for certain problems in cultural anthropology, especially the specific forms of, say, Asian or pre-conquest American modes of production within a Marxist (i.e. Eurocentric and modernist) framework of analysis.

See also: **Ideological state apparatuses, Interpellation**

AUDIENCES

The term audience is used to describe a large number of unidentifiable people, usually united by their participation in media use. Given the varying demographics of this group, not to mention variations between nations, the concept itself is a means by which such an unknowable group can be imagined. Naming an audience usually also involves homogenising it, ascribing to it certain characteristics, needs, desires and concerns. The audience is a construction motivated by the paradigm in which it is imagined. This construction serves the interests primarily of three 'producer' groups:

- media institutions
- media researchers (including critics)
- regulatory (governmental) bodies.

Audiences enable media organisations to sell advertising or to fulfil their public and statutory obligations, whether for television, radio, magazines or the press. It is important to know the size, quality (demographic composition) and characteristics of audiences for this purpose – these data relate directly to revenue. This accounts for the continual measurement of viewers, listeners and readers. For media institutions, the concept of audience allows the exchange of information and entertainment to become commodified.

For media researchers, audiences may be studied as a 'whole' if the purpose is to generate general sociological data, as for example in the work of Pierre Bourdieu on taste distinctions in French culture. But very large-scale statistical techniques nowadays are beyond the reach of most academic researchers, and are found only among commercial audience research and polling organisations (see Morrison, 1998). In media and cultural studies, researchers have turned to the study of selected groups, identities or constituencies among the overall audience. They make such selections according to their own research and political priorities (this is why audiences are a 'construct' in media research). What is of interest is not the self-understanding of the audience as a collective 'knowing subject', if such a thing could exist, but answers to questions generated by the intellectual agenda. In particular, media ethnography has concentrated on the way that social variables such as class (Morley, 1980), gender (Ang, 1985), age (Buckingham 2000), family circumstance (Morley, 1986), ethnicity (Gillespie, 1995), etc., cause audiences to interact variously with media texts.

For regulatory bodies, media audiences (unlike those for 'cultural pursuits' such as live theatre) are normally equated with the public at large. They are at once consumers in need of both exploitation and protection, citizens (voters!) and 'society' – subject to moral, welfare or educational policies. Regulators therefore occupy a *governmental* position in relation to audiences (see **power**). Legislation may be restrictive (censorship, pornography) or enabling (freedom of speech). It may be conducted at the highest level of national policy (Rupert Murdoch deals with prime ministers and presidents) or much lower (an usherette enforcing age restrictions in cinemas). But in all of this, audiences do not *self-regulate* in any organised way.

For all of these institutional bodies, the audience is the 'imagined community' that enables the institution to operate. It is rare to see or hear the views of the audience 'itself', except in letters pages and on talkback radio. Semiotic versions of audiences are included in entertainment formats, where they act as a kind of guide to the appropriate or desired response – enjoyment, laughter, applause, euphoria. These include game show participants, studio audiences, laughter/applause tracks on sitcoms, etc.

Notably absent from the formal process of gaining, and *gaining from*, knowledge of audiences are 'consumer' groups – the audiences themselves. People rarely self-identify as audiences, and are only thinly represented directly by their own organisations, which are normally single-issue associations devoted to, for instance, 'cleaning up' the apparent propensity for sex, violence and bad language on the TV (Hartley, 1992a: 105).

See also: **Discourse, Effects, Meaning, Public**

Further reading: Ang (1996); Hartley (1992b)

AUTHOR/SHIP

A common-sense concept which accounts for meaning by ascribing it to a creative, individual source. In such a context, an author's intentions govern and warrant a particular reading for texts, the meanings of which are taken to be a form of private property, belonging to the author (even though the text itself, in the form of a book, may belong to the reader). Meaning is deemed to be a creation of individual genius or experience, which is then transferred in a linear way directly to the brain of the reader. The activity of reading is reduced to that of a receiver, more or less finely tuned to pick up the already fished meanings sent down the channel by the author. This common-sense approach to authorship has its origins in medieval religious reading, where the 'author' of a sacred text such as the Bible was thought to be divine, and thus there was nothing for readers to do but work out the *authorial intentions* from the clues in the text, and then to obey them. The idea that readers might 'make' meanings for themselves was, literally, blasphemy.

Authorial intentionalism has become controversial in modern, secular textual criticism, because it takes the obvious fact that texts are written or scripted by a human agent (or agents) and uses this fact to underpin the highly ideological theory of meaning outlined above.

An author is not 'one who writes'. Only some writers and writings 'count' for the purposes of authorship. For instance, private, ephemeral and functional writings usually don't count as authored: that is, letters, diaries, shopping lists, school exercises, notes in the margins of books, telephone messages and even 'creative writing' – the things that most people actually write. In the public domain the same applies. It would be hard to find an author for labels, advertisements, news, posters, street and shop signs, graffiti, junk mail, technical instructions, etc. – possibly the majority of reading matter encountered on a day-to-day basis.

Authorship can no longer be found readily in creative and fictional writing. Much of the fiction circulating in modern societies comes in the form of television and movies, where the concept of authorship is very hard to sustain, given the input of so many people in the production process. Other creative works circulate orally and aurally – stories, jokes, songs. These too escape the traditional definition of authorship, even when they can be traced to an individual writer.

Authorship is a creation of literary culture and the marketplace; it is one of the great markers of 'high' as opposed to 'popular' culture, and it is invoked to ascribe not just meaning but value – aesthetic or moral as well as monetary – to works and authors identified by literary criticism (and marketing managers) as 'significant'. Once an author's name has been established, then potentially any writing under that name counts as authored – even down to shopping lists, if any were to turn up that had been penned by, say, Shakespeare. Such are the ironies of 'significance'.

Authorship is, then, a social system imposed on the domain of writing; it is not the act or trade of writing. It is a system for producing hierarchies within that domain. Authors are the product of a social division of labour, and authorship is an ideological notion which functions to privilege not only certain kinds of writing and writers, but also, more importantly, certain ways of thinking about the meaning of texts.

The ideology of authorship locates the source of literary quality not in aspects of writing itself – the exploitation of genre, convention, rhetoric, intertextuality and so on – but in the bodies of writers. Creativity, inspiration, experience, the ability to 'express' thought, emotion and truth, these personal attributes are supposed to emanate from a free-floating individual consciousness which is assumed to the source of meaning, with writing merely a transparent medium through which the great thoughts can flow to the reader's equally free-floating consciousness.

The ideology of authorship leads, for example, to the fruitless search for 'what Shakespeare *really* meant' – an impossible quest which leads inexorably to the imposition of authoritarian meanings on a given work by a critic who seeks to establish *one* reading as the only or *true* reading. In other words, any appeal to 'the author's intentions' is coercive – it seeks to impose ideological closure on a text, to minimise its polysemic potential. It is also dishonest, imputing to the author meanings that are necessarily the creation of the critic. 'Intentionalist' criticism is reduced to second-guessing an author who is conveniently absent, often dead, so that it is impossible to verify what his or her intentions were.

Moreover, an author's intentions do not account for the meaning of a text. Even if the author can be interrogated, as, for example, in an interview, what results from this process is not a direct account of his or her intentions, but merely *another text*. Authors always work within the domain of writing, which is an autonomous domain with its own history, modes of production, genres, conventions and established practices. Writers are to a large extent at the mercy of the discursive resources available to them, and creativity comes not from abstract 'genius' but from an ability to exploit these resources. Once written, a text takes on a life of its own, and what it means depends on the conditions of its circulation and the uses to which it is put in different places and times. Its meanings are always plural, and always exceed what the writer thought was going on, intentionally or otherwise.

However, so established has the concept of authorship become that it has achieved a kind of hegemony. It seems to represent a pathological desire for an ultimate origin, a god who will finally limit the infinite potentiality of **meaning**.

The desire for a singular origin for meaning has proved strong enough to infiltrate areas of culture hitherto regarded as too lowbrow to warrant authors, especially cinema, where the 'auteur' approach seeks to account for certain films by conferring author-status on their director. Naturally, auteur directors are credited with 'significance', which may be traced across a number of films, and their 'genius' is seen as an individual 'vision'.

However, the source of meaning in cinema is notoriously hard to pin down, which is to say that there is no single source, even at the point of production, let alone once a film is released into the cultural sphere at large. Auteur theory fixes upon just one person to represent the creative input of the whole cast and crew – often hundreds of people working on and off for months or even years, all of whom may change with the director's next project. In the history of cinema it has never been clear who, of all these people, should be treated authorially – the screenwriter has never enjoyed this status, but it has been conferred not only on directors but also on stars and, more recently, even on producers.

It seems in cinema, as in literature itself, that authorship is more a way of organising marketing strategies and conferring value on intellectual property than a way of accounting for meaning.

The general reader or viewer approaches authors not as persons at all but *textually*; either solely by engagement with a text, or additionally by knowledge gained *intertextually* about the author. The author is 'implied' in the writing itself. Hence, for readers, authors are not persons but an ensemble of rhetorical and narrative ploys, dedicated to hooking and drawing them into the writing. Throughout any discursive text or fictional story there are devices which 'guide' the reader as to its preferred reading and direction. Such devices may also be more intrusive or coercive – an authorial introduction telling readers how to read what follows, or a cover blurb which seeks to sell the writing on the basis of the author's name, institutional clout or biographical credibility.

See also: **Meaning, Subjectivity, Text/textual analysis**

Further reading: Barthes (1977); Caughie (1981); Foucault (1984)

B2B

Term meaning 'business-to-business'. Not exactly a concept, but an important element of the current architecture of interactive communication, especially in multimedia applications. 'Horizontal' b2b commerce has proven more important than 'vertical' b2c (business-to-consumer) interactions thus far in the new interactive economy. In fact b2b is now an identifiable business sector in its own right, sustaining a vibrant culture of Internet sites and portals devoted to assisting, exploiting and expanding this sector (see, for example, *http://www.communityb2b.com/* or *http://www.b2btoday.com/*)

Among the reasons why b2b matured more rapidly than the potentially much larger-scale b2c are:

- businesses invested in interactive technologies to a much higher degree than individuals, resulting in a widespread availability of fast, networked systems in many businesses large and small;
- the 'new economy' applications of IT spawned many micro-businesses and SMEs (small and medium-sized enterprises) able to compete with established dinosaur corporations online – the base of business itself broadened (at least temporarily);
- digital and broadband infrastructure was slow to roll out in most countries, making household connection to the Internet both slow and expensive;
- retail consumers proved reluctant to divulge their personal and credit details online, and may also have had qualms about the extent to which their actions could be tracked and exploited.

A 2002 search for b2b on Google yielded 2.2 million sites.

BARDIC FUNCTION

A comparative concept, proposing a similarity between the social role of television and that of the bardic order in traditional Celtic societies. The concept was suggested by Fiske and Hartley (1978) to emphasise the active and productive signifying work of television. The idea is that, like the original bards in medieval Celtic societies, the media are a distinct and identifiable social institution, whose role it is to mediate between the rulers and patrons who license and pay them, and society at large, whose doings and sayings they render into a specialised rhetorical language which they then play back to the society. The concept seemed necessary in order to overcome previous conceptualisations of the media, which concentrated on the way they were/are meant to reflect society. The notion of the bardic function goes beyond this, first in its insistence on the media's role as manipulators of language, and then in its emphasis on the way the media take their mediating role as an active one, not as simply to reproduce the opinions of their owners, or the 'experience' of their viewers. Instead, the 'bardic' media take up signifying 'raw materials' from the societies they represent and rework them into characteristic forms which appear as 'authentic' and 'true to life', not because they are but because of the professional prestige of the bard and the familiarity and pleasure we have learnt to associate with bardic offerings.

One implication of this notion is that, once established, bardic television can play an important role in managing social conflict and cultural change. Dealing as it does in signification − representations and myths − the ideological work it performs is largely a matter of rendering the unfamiliar into the already known, or into 'common sense'. It will strive to make sense of both conflict and change according to these familiar strategies. Hence bardic television is a conservative or *socio-central* force for its 'home' culture. It uses metaphor to render new and unfamiliar occurrences into familiar forms and meanings. It uses binary oppositions to represent oppositional or marginal groups as deviant or 'foreign'. As a result, it strives to encompass all social and cultural action within a consensual framework. Where it fails, as it must, to 'claw back' any group or occurrence into a consensual and familiar form, its only option is to represent them as literally outlandish and senseless. Bardic television, then, not only makes sense of the world, but also marks out the limits of sense, and presents everything beyond that limit as nonsense.

Further reading: Fiske and Hartley (1978); Hartley (1982, 1992a); Turner (1990); Williams (1981)

BIAS

Bias is a concept used to account for perceived inaccuracies to be found within media representations. The term is usually invoked in relation to news and current affairs reporting in the print media and television, and occasionally in talkback radio. Accusations of bias assume that one viewpoint has been privileged over another in the reporting of an event, inadvertently leading to the suggestion that there are only two sides to a story. This is rarely the case.

Claims of bias can be understood as relying on the assumption that the media are somehow capable of reflecting an objective reality, especially in discussions of news reporting. But news, like any other form of media representation, should be understood as a 'signifying practice' (Langer, 1998: 17). It is better understood by analysing selection and presentation rather than by seeking to test stories against an abstract and arguable external standard such as 'objectivity'. Indeed, while there is no doubt that both news reporters and media analysts can and do strive for truthfulness (much of the time), nevertheless it is difficult to 'envisage how objectivity can ever be anything more than relative' (Gunter, 1997: 11). It is better to understand the news not as the presentation of facts, but rather as the selection of discourse through which to articulate a particular subject matter or event. Thus, understanding the representations contained within the news can be achieved by, for example, discursive analysis rather than accusations of bias. As McGregor (1997: 59) states, it 'is not a question of distortion or bias, for the concept of "distortion" is alien to the discussion of socially constructed realities'.

In his study of HIV/AIDS and the British press, Beharrell manages to avoid claims of biased reporting in his analysis, providing a more meaningful way of examining why certain discourses are more favoured in news reporting than others. He notes that proprietorial, editorial/journalist and marketing strategies all act as key influences on news content covering AIDS (1993: 241). But he is able to explain why certain approaches are taken within these stories without accusing the media of deliberately distorting the facts (something that is central to many accusations of bias). Beharrell demonstrates a method that improves understanding of the nature of media representation *without* resorting to the concept of bias. Studies such as this also avoid another implicit weakness of the 'bias' school of media criticism, namely that such accusations are traditionally levelled at viewpoints that fail to concur with one's own.

See also: **Content analysis, Ideology, News values, Objectivity**

Further reading: McGregor (1997); Philo (1990)

BINARY OPPOSITION

The generation of meaning out of two-term (binary) systems; and the *analytic* use of binaries to analyse texts and other cultural phenomena. In contemporary life, it may be that the most important binary is the opposition between zero and one, since this is the basis of computer language and all digital technologies. But in culture, binaries also operate as a kind of thinking machine, taking the 'analogue' continuity of actuality and dividing it up in order to be able to apprehend it.

Thus binary opposition is used as an analytic category (this occurred first in structural anthropology and then in structuralism more generally). Basic propositions are as follows.

Meaning is generated by opposition. This is a tenet of Saussurian linguistics, which holds that signs or words mean what they do only in opposition to others – their most precise characteristic is in being what the others are not. The *binary* opposition is the most extreme form of significant difference possible. In a binary system, there are only two signs or words. Thus, in the opposition LAND : SEA the terms are mutually exclusive, and yet together they form a complete system – the earth's surface. Similarly, the opposition CHILD : ADULT is a binary system. The terms are mutually exclusive, but taken together they include everyone on earth (everyone can be understood as either child or adult). Of course, everyone can be understood by means of other binaries as well, as for instance in the binary US : THEM – everyone is either in or not in 'our nation'.

Such binaries are a feature of culture not nature; they are products of signifying systems, and function to structure our perceptions of the natural and social world into order and meaning. You may find binaries underlying the stories of newspaper and television news, where they separate out, for example, the parties involved in a conflict or dispute, and render them into meaningful oppositions.

Ambiguities are produced by binary logic and are an offence to it. Consider the binaries mentioned so far:

LAND : SEA

CHILD : ADULT

US : THEM

These stark oppositions actively suppress ambiguities or overlaps between the opposed categories. Between land and sea is an *ambiguous category*, the beach – sometimes land, sometimes sea. It is *both* one and the other (sea at high tide; land at low tide), and *neither* one nor the other. Similarly, between child and adult there is another ambiguous category: youth. And between us and them there are deviants, dissidents, and so on. Figure 1 offers a graphic presentation of the concept.

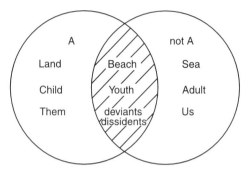

Figure 1

The area of overlap shown in Figure 1 is, according to binary logic, impossible. It is literally a scandalous category that ought not to exist. In anthropological terms, the ambiguous boundary between two recognised categories is where taboo can be expected. That is, any activity or state that does not fit the binary opposition will be subject to repression or ritual. For example, as the anthropologist Edmund Leach (1976) suggests, the married and single states are binarily opposed. They are normal, time-bound, central to experience and secular. But the transition from one state to the other (getting married or divorced) is a *rite of passage* between categories. It is abnormal, out of time (the 'moment of a lifetime'), at the edge of experience and, in anthropological terms, *sacred*. The structural ambiguity of youth is one reason why it is treated in the media as a scandalous category – it too is a rite of passage and is subject to both repression and ritual.

News often structures the world into binarily opposed categories (US : THEM). But it then faces the problem of dealing with people and events that don't fit neatly into the categories. The structural ambiguity of home-grown oppositional groups and people offends the consensual category of 'us', but cannot always be identified with foreigners or 'them'. In such cases, they are often represented as folk-devils, or as sick, deviant or mad – that is, they are tabooed.

Binary oppositions are structurally related to one another. Binaries function to *order* meanings, and you may find *transformations* of one underlying binary running through a story. For instance, the binary MASCULINITY : FEMININITY may be transformed within a story into a number of other terms:

MASCULINITY : FEMININITY
OUTDOORS : INDOORS
PUBLIC : PRIVATE
SOCIAL : PERSONAL
PRODUCTION : CONSUMPTION
MEN : WOMEN

First, masculinity and femininity are proposed as opposites which are mutually exclusive. This immediately constructs an ambiguous or 'scandalous' category of overlap that will be tabooed (e.g. trans-gender phenomena including transsexuality and transvestism). The binaries can also be read downwards, as well as across, which proposes, for instance, that men are to women as production is to consumption, or MEN : WOMEN :: PRODUCTION : CONSUMPTION. Each of the terms on one side is invested with the qualities of the others on that side. As you can see, this feature of binaries is highly productive of ideological meanings – there is nothing natural about them, but the *logic* of the binary is hard to escape.

The ideological productivity of binaries is enhanced further by the assignation of positive : negative *values* to opposed terms. This is guilt by association. For instance, Hartley and Lumby (2002) reported on a number of instances where the events of September 11, 2001 were used by conservative commentators to bring the idea of 'absolute evil' back into public discourse. They associated this with developments within Western culture of which they disapproved, including (strangely) postmodernism and relativism, on the grounds that these had been undermining belief in (absolute) truth and reality. So they invoked Osama bin Laden to damn the postmodernists:

GOOD : EVIL
'ABSOLUTE' : RELATIVISM
'TRUTH' : POSTMODERNISM
POSITIVE : NEGATIVE

See also: **Bardic function, Orientalism**

Further reading: Hartley (1982, 1992a); Leach (1976, 1982); Leymore (1975)

BIOTECHNOLOGY

The use of biological molecules, cells and processes by firms and research organisations for application in the pharmaceutical, medical, agricultural and environmental fields, together with the business, regulatory, and societal context for such applications. Biotechnology also includes applied immunology, regenerative medicine, genetic therapy and molecular engineering, including *nanotechnology*. This new field is at the chemistry/biology interface, focusing on structures between one nanometre (i.e., a billionth of a metre) and one hundred nanometres in size, from which life-building structures ranging from molecules to proteins are made – and may therefore be engineered. Bio- and nanotechnology bring closer the possibility of 'organic' computers, self-built consumer goods and a result in a much fuzzier line between human and machine.

Biotechnology has been hailed as a successor to the telecommunications and computer revolutions, especially in terms of its potential for return on the investment of 'patient capital' (unlike the boom and bust economy of the dot.coms). By the year 2000, there were over a 1000 biotech firms in the USA alone, with a market capitalisation of $353.5 billion, direct revenues of $22.3 billion, and employing over 150,000 people (see *http://www.bio.org/er/*).

The importance of biotechnology for the field of communication is that it is an industry based on '**code**' – notably the human genome. This field has transformed the concept of 'decoding' from one associated with linguistic (cultural) or social information to one based in the physical and life sciences. Biotechnological developments in relation to DNA diagnostics or genetic modification, for instance, have implications for society and culture, as well as for science and business. DNA testing has already had an impact on family law because paternity is now no longer 'hearsay' (for the first time in human history). This in turn will influence familial relations and structures. Biotechnological developments in agriculture, and the 'decoding' of the human genome, have radical implications for the relationship between nature and culture, and where that line is thought to be drawn.

BRICOLAGE

A term borrowed from the structural anthropologist Claude Lévi-Strauss to describe a mode of cultural assemblage at an opposite pole to *engineering*. Where engineering requires pre-planning, submission to various laws of physics and the organisation of materials and resources prior to the act of assembly, bricolage refers to the creation of objects with materials to hand, re-using existing artefacts and incorporating bits and pieces. Lévi-Strauss used the term to denote the creative practices of traditional societies using magical rather than scientific thought systems. However, bricolage enjoyed a vogue and gained wide currency in the 1970s and 1980s when applied to various aspects of Western culture. These included avant-garde artistic productions, using collage, pastiche, found objects, and installations that re-assembled the detritus of everyday consumerism. They also included aspects of everyday life itself, especially those taken to be evidence of **postmodernism** (see Hebdige, 1988: 195).

Western consumer society was taken to be a society of bricoleurs. For example, youth subcultures became notorious for the appropria-tion of icons originating in the parent or straight culture, and the improvisation of new meanings, often directly and provocatively subversive in terms of the meanings communicated by the same items in mainstream settings. The hyper-neat zoot suit of the mods in the 1960s was an early example of this trend. Mods took the respectable business suit and turned its 'meaning' almost into its own opposite by reassembling its buttons (too many at the cuff), collars (removed altogether), line (too straight), cut (exaggerated tightness, slits), material (too shiny-modern, mohair-nylon), colour (too electric). The garb of the gentleman and businessman was made rude, confrontational and sartorially desirable among disaffected but affluent youth. Bricolage was made 'spectacular' in the 1970s by punk, under the influence of Vivienne Westwood, Malcolm McLaren and others in the fashion/music interface such as Zandra Rhodes. Punk took bricolage seriously, and put ubiquitous 'profane' items such as the safety pin, the Union Jack, dustbin bags and swastikas to highly charged new 'sacred' or ritualised purposes (see Hall and Jefferson, 1976; Hebdige, 1979).

Architecture also used bricolage as it went through a postmodern phase. Buildings began to quote bits and pieces from incommensurate styles, mixing classical with vernacular, modernist with suburban, shopping mall with public institution, and delighting in materials and colours that made banks look like beachfront hotels, or museums look like unfinished kit-houses (from different kits). Much of this was in reaction to the over-engineered precision and non-human scale of 'international style' modernist towers. Bricolage was seen as active criticism, much in the manner of jazz, which took existing tunes and improvised, syncopated and re-assembled them until they were the opposite of what they had been. Borrowing, mixture, hybridity, even plagiarism – all 'despised' practices in high modernist science and knowledge systems – became the bricoleur's trademark, and postmodernism's signature line.

BROADBAND

Broadband can refer to a range of technologies intended to provide greater bandwidth (data capacity) within a network. Narrowband – broadband's predecessor – utilised dial-up connection via telephone lines without the capacity for multiple channels of data transmission, making it slow in comparison. It has been estimated that about one third of narrowband users' time is spent waiting for content to download (Office of the e-Envoy, 2001), earning the World Wide Web the reputation of the 'Word Wide Wait'. Available via upgraded telephone and cable lines as well as wireless transmission, broadband provides high-speed Internet access. With greater bandwidth, users are able to access and distribute video, audio and graphic-rich applications.

It is hoped that by replacing narrowband with broadband, higher rates of connectivity will be achieved – that people will spend more time online with permanent and time-efficient connection. Broadband is also expected to encourage **e-commerce** through new application possibilities offering a wider range of services.

Although bandwidth may have greater capacities, concerns have surfaced in the US that the introduction of broadband will mean more limited choices for the Internet community. Cable companies who also own or are in partnership with particular Internet service providers (ISPs), or who have specific contractual obligations to an ISP, are capable of dominating the broadband market by not providing free access to unaffiliated ISPs. Internet users who wish to use an alternative ISP could potentially be made to pay for both the cable company's ISP as well as the ISP of their choice. This issue came to a head in the US in 1998 with the merger of AT&T and TCI. The independent regulator (the Federal Communications Commission) had the opportunity to impose open access stipulation. However, it was deemed at the time that such an imposition would inhibit the roll out of the costly infrastructure which was being driven by the private investment. This remains a contested issue.

See also: **Internet**

Further reading: Egan (1991)

BROADCASTING

Jostein Gripsrud (1998) writes that the original use of the word 'broadcasting' was as an agricultural term, to describe the sowing or scattering of seeds broadly, by hand, in wide circles. This image of distributing widely and efficiently from a central point, as far as the reach will allow, is also present within the term's technological meaning, as a distribution method for radio and television. Broadcasting is over-the-air transmission, whereby signals (analogue waves or digital data) are emitted from a central transmitter in the AM, VHF/FM and UHF bands. The power of the transmitter determines how far that signal will reach.

Implicit within broadcasting is the idea of distribution from the central to the periphery. The historically dominant, one-to-many structure of television and its capacity to distribute information efficiently to large numbers of people imply that broadcasting is essentially a modernist device. It is seen as an instrument with the capacity to organise and to commodify which is based in large, centralised industry structures. The characteristics of the technological and industrial distribution of television has, in this way, given rise to analysis of broadcasting that sees it as purely one-way communication, a central voice communicating to the masses with an authoritative or controlling capacity. However, this conception of television has been revised by theories that explore the capacity of the viewer to actively engage with television, to bring their own self-knowledge and experience to interpretation of the television text and to make cultural and identity choices through viewing.

Technological changes in broadcast technology are also challenging our assumptions about the nature of broadcast media. Digital compression technology has enabled a greater amount of channels, increasing viewer choice and encouraging programming for niche, rather than mass, audiences. In many respects narrowcasting and community broadcasting have always rejected the assumption that television was intended for large audiences of common interest. Furthermore, digital technology allows for two-way communication through broadcasting, enabling interactivity (with the programme or with other people) through the television set.

'Broadcasting' also describes an industry, funded through subscriptions, advertising, sponsorship, donations, government funding or a combination of these sources.

The radio broadcasting industry, which preceded TV as *the* home-based entertainment and information medium, now displays interesting differences from television. Radio has niched, with significant activities that are not common in television, for instance, local programming (including rural and remote), youth and music programming (where different stations have very specialised playlists), and broadcasting for minority or community groups. At the international level, radio broadcasting is still supported by national governments for development and propaganda purposes. The latter is dominated by the 'big five' organisations: the BBC, Voice of America, Deutsche Welle, Radio France International, and Radio Netherlands, although most countries add their voice to the global conversation, often via shortwave.

See also: **Convergence, Datacasting, Digital/analogue distribution, Post-broadcast media**

CELEBRITY

Celebrity is the semiotics of identity. It is found only in societies in which identity is a major socio-cultural and political issue. It has become more important as contemporary Western societies have evolved towards the status of 'entertainment cultures', where identity is seen as more significant than decision-making, action or faith, and the celebrity supersedes the leader, hero or holy-person.

Celebrities are individuals who are noted for their identity in the media. Generally speaking they can come from any walk of life – musicians, sports stars, models, criminals, film, television and radio personalities as well as participants in **reality TV**. As a descriptive category, celebrity would not usually include, for example, politicians currently in power or members of royal families. This is because celebrity is concerned more with the representation of individualism in all of its forms than with the coverage of people associated with particular institutions.

The concept of celebrity differs from that of the **star**, in that the latter is understood as being a product of a particular medium, the Hollywood film industry. Celebrity, in comparison, is understood to have arisen under the conditions of postmodernity whereby the hyper-production of images leads to some faces and bodies being more recognisable than others. Tracing what he calls a 'history of fame', Braudy (1986: 4) notes that as 'each new medium of fame appears, the human image it conveys is intensified and the number of individuals celebrated expands'. The promise of photography and theatre in the construction of fame in previous eras has certainly now been realised with the increase in media forms that include tabloid newspapers, magazines and entertainment-focused TV networks such as *E* in the US, not to mention a myriad official and unofficial celebrity websites.

Although stars and celebrities have subtle differences in their creation, the purposes they serve for their audiences or fans are similar. Celebrities act as signs or media texts in that they provide a means by which media consumers can negotiate and work towards articulating personal subjectivity. Wark (1999) and Lumby (1999a), for example, claim that unlike the construction of stars, the construction of a celebrity is reliant on matters that would be considered everyday or ordinary. One aspect of the appeal of celebrities is that they *perform the ordinary*. Stories involving celebrities will often involve these *extra*ordinary people in everyday/ordinary contexts of divorce, drug abuse, weight issues and romance. This desire to 'separate celebrities from their images' (Lumby, 1999a: 139) is explicitly revealed in some of the tabloid's most often-used headlines – 'Stars without their makeup' and 'So-and-so at home'.

The ordinary value embodied in celebrities has caused some to comment that they are 'the ideal representation of the triumph of the masses' (Marshall, 1997: 6). Others suggest that celebrities do little more than contribute to a continued dumbing down of societal values, distracting populations from matters of importance such as politics, economics and religion. But this is to ignore the changing aspects of the public sphere, where important civil discourses are being challenged, discussed and debated via the bodies of celebrities. Celebrities do not represent the triumph of the ordinary; rather, they represent the possibility of popular representations concerning private/ordinary matters in a sphere long dominated by outdated models of civility.

See also: **Dumbing down, Identification, Star/stardom, Subjectivity**

Further reading: Braudy (1986); Gamson (1994); Lumby (1999a); Turner *et al.* (2000); Wark (1999)

CLASS

Class serves as a means of understanding the economic and cultural divisions that exist between individuals in society. In its common-sense usage, class articulates social to economic positions. People are sorted into groups on the basis of economic factors (income or wealth), but the groups or classes are then made to explain matters external to economics, including social values, politics, beliefs and culture.

Pre-modern (feudal) societies sorted people by rank in a society based on birth and land tenure. This conception was overturned by the Industrial Revolution and its sweeping social reforms. 'Classes' came to refer to the groups produced by the relation of people to the industrial mode of production.

It was this particular formation that was of great interest to Karl Marx, who is regarded as the instigator of class analysis. Marx identified two new and fundamental classes: those who owned the means of production (the bourgeoisie); and those without ownership, who had to sell their capacity to work (the proletariat). He argued that while both groups were bound by their **ideologies**, it was the ruling (owning) class who were also the intellectual force (Milner, 1999: 26). This structure of **power** was supplemented by surplus production that resulted in the accumulation of material wealth by the bourgeoisie at the expense of the working or 'productive' class. In Marx's analysis this situation could be resolved only by proletariat revolution. It is this aim that he understood as driving historical and social change.

Weber, who wanted to draw attention to other stratifications within society, took the theories of Marx further. While he found no reason to disagree with Marx's fundamental classes, Weber argued that the privileged class could be broken down into another subset that acknowledged status rather than simply ownership. Managers, intellectuals and journalists were privileged over other types of workers in the skills they could offer the market. In this conception, it is skills and their relation to the market, rather than ownership of the modes of production, that group together individuals. In Weber's analysis, it is relevant to include differences such as education and race in analysing the ideological construction of class.

While the concept of class continues to have importance in some branches of sociology (see for example, Crompton *et al.*, 2000), its usefulness in cultural and communications studies has been re-assessed. One reason is that cultural and communication studies have tended to focus on national cultures and various identity groups, rather than on the global economy. But the traditional two fundamental classes are now globally separated – the owners of wealth overwhelmingly living in the US, while the workers who make products for the companies in which they hold shares are located in cheap-labour countries such as Indonesia and China.

Another reason for the re-assessment of class relates to post-modernity. The reconfiguration of markets, globalisation, and the shift from material production to the trading of information, have all played a part in the reconceptualisation of class. Within the new economy it may no longer make sense to speak of owners and workers. Referring to 'information-rich' and 'information-poor' may be more relevant when considering new power arrangements; here it is not class division but the **digital divide** that is of significance, although new hierarchies of opportunity often map fairly directly onto existing ones.

Frow has attempted to reconsider the usefulness of contemporary class identity and analysis. He argues that class should no longer be understood as dependent on economic structures; rather, it should be understood as relational among the economic, political and ideological spheres (1995: 104). This position recognises the place other subjectivities have in the construction of identity, and displaces the grand, modernist narrative of class. Identities based on gender, nation, ethnicity and sexuality form part of the petit-narratives that inform the subjectivity of groups of individuals. Contemporary analysis of this kind avoids essentialist claims, recognising not only the differences between classes, but also within them.

See also: **Cultural capital, Hegemony, Ideology**

Further reading: Edgell (1993); Milner (1999); Pakulski and Waters (1996)

CLUSTER

Districts with a concentration of a single or closely related industries. If the resources you require are close at hand, and if there are others doing similar work in your local area who can assist you, then your work will be easier and more productive. If you are surrounded by people attempting to outdo you – competing for sales or attention – you are likely to work harder. The economist Alfred Marshall wrote of 'industrial districts' in 1890: cutlery production in Sheffield, cotton in Manchester and coal in Newcastle (Marshall, 1961). These are clusters. When there is such a critical mass of related industries, educational institutions, government agencies and community associations located in the same place, innovation and productivity are stimulated. The result is greater prosperity. As Michael Porter points out, competitive advantages in a global economy lie increasingly in local things – knowledge, relationships and motivation (Porter, 1999).

Localisation and industry clusters are proliferating in what US federal banker Alan Greenspan described as the 'weightless' **new economy** (see **intangibles**). No longer are the raw materials of a Newcastle essential for cluster formation. The miniature (practically weightless) microchip, creativity, information, research, talent and networks have replaced coal or steel, manual labour and machinery as components of the majority of clusters.

In 1939 two Stanford University students started an electronic measuring device company out of a car garage in Palo Alto, California. By 1999 their company, Hewlett-Packard, was one in a cluster within the area, now called Silicon Valley, that had a combined revenue of US$47.1 billion. A large number of the companies that make personal computers, circuits, software, 3D graphics and that pioneered Internet search engine technology can be found in Silicon Valley. It is also the home of Stanford University, which educates people to become researchers and workers. It is 'an entire environment, or habitat honed for innovation and entrepreneurship' (Lee *et al.*, 2000: 1).

Cluster research has expanded and challenged previous economic theories. New findings on the importance of cooperative relationships between research, private industry and third-sector organisations are arising out of cluster research. Although primarily an economic concept, clusters are focusing attention back on place, lifestyle, localism and community. The assumption that 'nations are the salient entities for understanding the structure of economic life' (Jacobs, 1984: 30) is being disproved at a macro level through globalisation and at the micro level through clusters.

See also: **Creative industries, Globalisation, Localisation**

CODE

Tacit or underlying rules of combination of recognised elements in any communication system, from language to computer code. Code is a term originating in communication science, which over the years divided into areas that had little to do with each other (see **art–science interface**). Sciences based on 'code' include mathematical and computer sciences, e.g. programming, signal processing and cryptography; communication science as applied to telecommunications, etc.; and biotechnology, in which genetic codes have become a major international focus.

The work of US information theorists led to the idea that communication was a mechanical transfer process and that code was simply the form messages would take for transmission through a channel. Clearly that model was based on telegraphy (Morse code) and telephony, where the code comprised not what was said by the caller, but the electronic form taken by soundwaves through the telephone wire. This scientific/mechanical notion of code has driven developments in computing, notably the writing of code for software applications, and in telecommunications (mobiles, G4).

Code was taken up in linguistics, media studies and semiotics. An early pioneer in the field was the Swiss linguistic theorist Ferdinand de Saussure in the first decade of the twentieth century. Saussure wanted to study language scientifically, but was faced with an almost infinite jumble and variety of actual speech. Instead he looked for whatever it was that enabled utterances to be produced – and 'decoded' – in a coherent and systematic form. Listeners needed to be able to understand sounds in a given combination that they'd never heard before, and to bypass the fact that everyone's voice is unique (including accent, intonation, speed, clarity of diction, etc.), so that *physically* the sounds heard are always unique too. The key was 'code': the generative system of rules of combination (grammar) that allowed elements (lexical items such as words) to be selected, combined and used to produce new, hitherto unuttered speech. Hearers, sharing the code, 'hear' what the code says rather than merely what the speaker says, so variations can simply be filtered out.

Codes allow both combination and organisation – words chosen from a **paradigm** or list of possible choices can be strung together in a **syntagm** or chain, but that string is itself rule-governed as to its organisation. In a standard sentence a subject, verb and object are the minimum requirement. You can choose between different words, but the lexical items chosen have to do the right work in the right order. You can say 'I love you'. But you can't say 'You love I' or 'Love you I': they don't mean the same even though the same words are chosen. Proper 'coding' requires attention to the organisation of elements chosen.

Taking that notion a stage further, many socially organised practices can be referred to as a code: there are *a*esthetic codes, *b*ehavioural codes, codes of *c*onduct, *d*ecency codes ... all the way down to *z*ip codes. In each case what is referred to is an established (shared) understanding of what is appropriately associated with what, according to rules of choice and chain.

It may be that some of these codes – codes of conduct for example – are so called because of their *codification* into tabular form, in which case the term 'code' derives from *codex* (Latin: tablet, book).

COLLOCATION

The tendency of words to co-occur in everyday discourse. Thus, *dark* collocates strongly with *night*, in so far as they tend to co-occur. The same could be said of the relationship of *deadly* to *nightshade* or *nuclear* to *weapon*. The study of **meaning**, using this approach, investigates the meaning of a word in terms of its patterns of collocation, on the principle (enunciated by R. Firth, a British linguist who first formulated the notion of collocation) that 'you shall know a word by the company it keeps'. (Compare Wittgenstein: 'the meaning of a word is its use in the language'.) Collocation does, however, imply statistical profiles of patterns of co-occurrence. These have proved notoriously difficult to produce until recently when it has become possible to apply sophisticated computational techniques to a very large corpus of data. Recent dictionaries – for instance, the *Collins Cobuild English Language Dictionary* – have been developed using such techniques.

See also: **Semantics**

Further reading: Halliday and Hasan (1975)

COMMUNICATION

Interaction by means of mutually recognised signals. Communication enjoyed great vogue in the mid to late twentieth century as a 'master discipline'. Since it was an aspect of virtually all human and quite a bit of non-human activity, it seemed appropriate for an academic discipline founded in its name to harbour similar ambitions. Thus the study of communication began to assume some of the mantle of philosophy, seeking to explain humanity to itself. Numerous strands of otherwise disconnected thought contributed to this process:

- From European *structural linguistics* and Russian formalism came the idea that there were fundamental structures underlying *all* human language. Attempts were made to theorise how signifying elements were combined *in general*, not just in a given language (Saussure). Such an approach to language was soon extended to other 'signifying systems', such as literature (Jakobson and the Russian formalists), the narrative structures of folk tales and narrative cinema, etc. (Propp, Todorov), and thence to culture in general (Lotman).

- Meanwhile, American *comparative linguistics*, under the influence of Benjamin Lee Whorf and Edmund Sapir, proposed the notion of 'linguistic relativity', suggesting that language organised perception, and different languages organised it differently. Thus, reality was a *product* of how communicative systems ordered the world. Different cultures – Hopi Indians compared with 'standard average Europeans', for instance – therefore experienced different realities.

- The French *structural anthropologist* Claude Lévi-Strauss connected communication with two other fundamental aspects of culture – marriage and money – suggesting that the *circulation* of signs (in language and art), women (in kinship systems) and money (in the economy) revealed fundamentally similar structures, which Lévi-Strauss believed revealed universals of the human mind.

- American *social-science* empirical research into the micro-processes of modern life brought communication into the purview of formal study for the first time. It concentrated on the practical details of how mass society communicated with itself, starting with the unresolvable problem that such a society comprises masses who are anonymous to each other and to commercial and political elites, but who are constitutionally and commercially sovereign as citizens and consumers. In such a paradoxical situation, *mass communication* became of strategic importance, especially the role of advertising (Vance Packard), journalism, public relations or PR, and political propaganda (Michael Schudson). The effects of 'mass' entertainment on unknowable but sovereign individuals was also seen as an important issue.

- It followed that *business* needed communication, the more scientific (i.e. using easily replicated methods to produce findings that were generalisable across large populations), the better. Consumer optimism and behaviour, maximised by the most scientific means possible, were key to the rise and continuing success of the post-World War II economic boom in the US, Japan and Europe. In the US Schools of Communication, founded on the need to train citizens in the public arts of rhetorical persuasion so as to democratise the public life of the Republic, prospered as they added media, PR, journalism and advertising to their repertoire.

- The Canadian literary historian *Marshall McLuhan* (1962, 1964), combining his own discipline with cognitive psychology and the communication philosophy of Harold Innes, was also influential in the exorbitation of communication. His aphoristic style appealed not only to many academics, but to people in the business community also, including those in the industries McLuhan seemed to be putting at the centre of the human condition – the media, advertising and television.

- But on the dark side, *governments* were interfering with communication in a major way. Contending ideologies were never more seriously at odds, both in the Cold War's 'mutually assured destruction', and in national liberation struggles from Africa to Vietnam. A serious understanding of how communication worked in practice within and between militarily formidable states seemed timely.

- Raymond Williams (1968) and others, including Herbert Marcuse and Hans Magnus Enzensberger (1970), brought to communications a *critical* perspective that – whatever the virtue of the argument advanced by any one theorist – ensured an important and permanent place for communication on the intellectual and academic agenda.

- Communication *science* gained ground enormously after World War II, when inventions ranging from radar to the 'Enigma' code-breaker had shown how important information was in warfare. The invention and commercialisation of computers took that national-military energy and redirected it both to business/ government and to imaginative ends: both the IBM 360–50s and 360–65s that sent humanity to the moon and safely back, and Stanley Kubrick's not-so-imaginary red-shifted computer 'Hal' ('IBM' minus one letter of the alphabet spells 'HAL') in *2001: A Space Odyssey*, which did not. Science had the imagination and the means, it seemed, to cause machine originated communication to transform human life.

- Communications *technologies* for mass commercial and residential uptake proliferated throughout the twentieth century. Several distinct global industries were sustained by them, including telcos, and the media **content industries**.

These different tendencies swirled around each other throughout the latter part of the twentieth century, sometimes connecting but never fully integrating. The earlier ambition of finding a unified science of communication in which they might all cohere was never realised. Instead, communication has reverted to 'small c' status: it is an aspect of incommensurable work carried out in many specialist areas, as appropriate to their needs.

COMMUNICATION DESIGN

An extension of Information Technology (IT) into the creative or content area. Communication design combines elements of IT science (programming) with the creativity of the visual and sound artist (e.g. animation). Production skills and team-based processes of the kind associated with media production (film and TV) are also needed. The output of communication design is therefore a hybrid of creativity and technology.

As the IT sector matured around the turn of the twenty-first century, it became clear that in order to continue growing, the new knowledge-based economy needed to focus not only on IT infrastructure and connectivity, but more on applications. Computers and the Internet needed to be simple and robust to operate and navigate, and commercial sites in particular needed to exploit the games and entertainment appeal of computers in order to attract and hold customers. Communication design became more prominent. Its importance was that it took creativity into areas of the economy that were not traditionally understood as having any creative 'content', such as banking, education, health, etc. As these service industries went online, they needed to harness the design flair, the information architecture and the interactive techniques that communication design had pioneered in such leisure areas as computer games and entertainment websites.

CONNECTIVITY

The use of communication technologies for interaction, and a society so characterised. The connectivity industry incorporates numerous technologies and involves the creation of networks between personal computers and other devices such as printers and modems, and with other networks such as satellite systems. The word 'connectivity' was used by IBM as a name for their proprietary service of coordinating and bringing about communication between computers, a system that inevitably tied users into IBM's own closed network of products. In 1977 the International Standards Organisation (ISO) established a committee to set standards to enable interoperability between computers manufactured by different companies. Out of this process the Open Systems Interconnection (OSI) specification was created, extending the possibilities for connectivity. As the computing industry has grown, competition between manufacturers has encouraged connectivity and compatibility with a resulting decrease in the need for regulatory intervention.

Connectivity also describes the aspect of society that ties us together through complex flows of inter-relationship and dependency (see Mulgan, 1998). A city exists in a state of connectivity. In order to live in a city we must depend upon resources brought into the city by others – our water, energy, food and entertainment. We use transport that connects us between destinations, powered by machinery that is constructed and maintained by others and organised by complex systems of timetables and signals that tell us when to connect and where. Cameras monitor our movements in shops and electronic networks allow us to withdraw money from numerous locations and record what we purchase. People come together in the city from different cultures and communities. We create places where we can meet others who share our values and at other times travel through places where we will encounter difference through other cultures, tastes and ideas, and create meanings even in the patterns of pedestrian 'connectivity' through the network of streets (de Certeau, 1984). Connectivity is a state of interdependence, of links that tie us together, allow us to communicate, and of systems that coordinate separate parts to perform functions more easily or at a greater rate and speed. It can denote a particular cosmopolitanism, a sense of 'being connected' rather than being isolated or restrained by parochialism.

Social connectivity is amplified by globalisation (and vice versa). The pathways through the city that we follow and create in order to meet others, to seek out and acquire what we want, to engage in earning and spending, which enables others to do the same, are spread across the globe. They move in irregular flows that are sometimes directed by business or government but are often organically created by peoples' tastes and interests. Our connectivity is apparent in environmental crises, when actions in one country affect the quality of life in others. In 1986 the Soviet Union's Chernobyl nuclear reactor exploded, contaminating people in three (now) republics and causing farming restrictions as far away as the UK. As with the story of IBM, our social connectivity may at times require intervention in the form of regulation and laws in order to be resolved.

See also: **Internet, Network society**

CONSUMER SOVEREIGNTY

Rule by consumption. The citizen and the consumer have largely been pitted against each other in discussions of competition policy and deregulation over the past decade. Citizenship is the framework for membership within a political community, providing us with entitlements as members and requiring that we maintain a level of participation within that community in order to sustain it. In democratic nations, citizens are sovereign, as they are the principal decision-makers who decide on the governance and rule of the state through voting and other forms of political engagement (such as interest-group activity).

Consumer sovereignty, on the other hand, suggests that our choices as consumers are our primary means of exerting influence over the market, ultimately with social ramifications. By choosing which products we purchase we affect the choices on offer and determine what succeeds and fails in the marketplace. For example, by refusing to buy aerosol cans that contain CFCs we are able to prevent greenhouse climate changes by putting pressure on companies to produce an alternative that will sell.

By positioning citizens as consumers we may see a reduction of society's democratic character and potential. As Graham Murdock expresses it: 'Whilst the exercise of citizenship presupposes collective action in pursuit of equality and fraternity as well as of individual liberty, the ideology of consumerism encourages people to seek private solutions to public problems by purchasing a commodity. It urges them to buy their way out of trouble rather than pressing for social change and improved social provision' (Murdock, 1992: 19). But Murdock's scenario does not allow for the possibility that 'buying our way out of trouble' can in fact result in social change, and not always for the worse. Consumption can become a 'patriotic duty', as it did in the US after September 11, 2001 – the Governor of California for one visited Disneyland to plead for tourists in the name of economic recovery.

However, the theoretical divide between citizen and consumer is somewhat problematic. First, a central component of citizenship is that we have a means of learning how to behave and act as citizens. Our cultural consumption, and in particular our media consumption, teach us about our society and how to act in it. The activity of consumption therefore plays an important role in the formation and promotion of civic virtue in today's society (see Hartley, 1999).

Second, a sphere of activity has developed around consumerism in order to protect consumer rights and to represent consumers within the political process. The consumer protection movement plays a significant part in democratic forums, providing a collective strategy to ensure that entitlements are met and calling on government and legal intervention where necessary (Braithwaite and Drahos, 2000; Goggin, 2001).

See also: **Deregulation, Privatisation, Regulation**

CONTENT ANALYSIS

A social-science method of investigating mass-mediated texts with a view to making wider claims about the content of various media channels. It is based on the concept of frequency, and involves investigating the frequency of presence or absence of predetermined categories. Concerned with the collection and interrogation of statistical information, it aspires to objectivity. Recent practitioners, however, have acknowledged the subjective element inherent in the process, especially when creating dimensions for research (see Hansen *et al.*, 1998: 95). What remains central to content analysis is that the method is undertaken systematically, is able to be replicated in other contexts and may rely on a proprietary computer program such as NU*Dist.

Casey *et al.* (2002: 41) argue that one of the advantages of content analysis 'is that it requires adherence to systematic rules and procedures'. This includes precise definitions of research objectives, objects of study and terms utilised in the project. In addition, the size of sample must be significant for the desired outcome of the research. How to classify and code the results of analysis is often left to the researchers themselves, but is usually defined by the scale and objectives of the research.

It is important to begin content analysis with a clear account of what is being looked for within what type of medium. The sample size of research will often be determined by research objectives (and budget). Undertaking preliminary or diagnostic research may involve a small 'pilot' sample, whereas tracing a trend in content may involve a larger sample, taken over a number of years, with full statistical safeguards.

One of the problems inherent in content analysis is that the classification of content is necessarily open to challenge. This is why

Casey *et al.* (2002: 42) note that content analysis 'tends more often to be used as a starting point or in conjunction with other methodologies than as a method standing alone'. Content analysis is reassuringly quantitative, but it is best carried out in conjunction with careful textual analysis and audience research to show how the findings about frequency of occurrence connect with the form in which such content is actually experienced by readers and viewers.

See also: **Methodology, Text/textual analysis**

Further reading: Berger (2000); Hansen *et al.* (1998); Riffe *et al.* (1998)

CONTENT INDUSTRIES

Also known as the 'copyright industries'. Businesses based upon the value of intellectual property, trading in intangible, creative and information-based products. The content industries include both content originators (production companies, creative artists and authors, software and games designers) and distributors or deliverers (e.g. broadcasters, publishers, Internet service providers, telcos). The content industries include, for instance: advertising, book publishing, cinema, computer games, corporate communication, magazines, music, newspapers, online publishers, performance, radio, software, TV and video, theme parks, web design.

See also: **Creative industries**

CONVERGENCE

The integration of telephony, computing and media (broadcasting) technologies, and thence the integration of the businesses, markets and the social interactions associated with them. Responding to a television programme (broadcasting) via an online (telecommunications) website that measures viewer responses and votes (computing) is a basic form of convergence. Being able to do all of this via a single device is a further possible result of convergence.

The adaptability of digital information has enabled a particular type of industry restructuring. Service industries, including broadcasting and telecommunications, have traditionally operated in domestic markets with industries centred on standardised services delivered to mass markets. These structures have been assumed in policy-making arenas in the past. As convergence is linking these traditionally separate industries through digital networks, traditional industry structures are no longer as relevant. Industries and markets are integrating, as well as technologies, thus print, screen and website can now be seen as platforms for the same content-provider.

Some of the possible consequences of these changes involve networks supporting a range of services, new competition between previously distinct businesses, service innovation with a focus on **customisation** and flexibility, the potential for niche markets and a greater scope for international trade in services and goods.

Convergence is causing a number of countries to revisit their communications policies. As the same content can now be received across once separately regulated media – television, radio and the Internet – governments are considering the extent to which **regulation** will need to be re-thought on order to deal with these changes. For instance, the UK has brought together its formerly separate regulatory bodies for telecommunications, television and radio under one umbrella agency, Ofcom.

Changes brought about by convergence mean that the traditional one-to-many information distribution structures will no longer be preserved, victims of technological constraints. To continue to receive information from singular, 'closed' or inaccessible sources without entering into participatory dialogue and production will be the result of industrial, political or cultural forces rather than technical constraints.

CONVERSATION ANALYSIS

The search for patterned regularities in the details of conversational behaviour. The approach has its roots in a particular branch of sociology known as ethnomethodology, which concerned essentially with identifying the fundamental categories and forms of reasoning used by members of society to make sense of their everyday social world. As such, it was part of a continuing reaction in the human and social sciences against the ill-considered and over-optimistic use of quantitative and statistical methods.

True to its sociological origins, conversation analysis is interested in verbal interaction primarily as instances of the situated social order. Practitioners of this approach study conversation as a rich source of observable material on how members of society achieve orderliness in their everyday interactions with each other. They view conversations as jointly constructed, practical accomplishments, and seek to display from the close analysis of transcribed talk the methods adopted by participants to achieve this orderliness – the conversational structures within which participants function and the interpretative work which they undertake. In line with this project, conversation analysis has provided detailed accounts of how the taking of turns is managed in conversation and how turns are linked together in coherent ways. Some types of utterance are, predictably, related to each other in pairs such as *summons* + *answer, question* + *answer* or *greeting* + *greeting*, and related pairs such as these provide strong linking formats as part of the sequential organisation of talk.

See also: **Pragmatics**

Further reading: Atkinson and Heritage (1984); Levinson (1983)

COPYRIGHT

Copyright is a form of **intellectual property** and is concerned with the legal status of information. Ownership of creative or informational content allows facts, ideas and artistic or literary works to be traded. Information is now a recognised asset in itself rather than an instrument through which we manage assets (Branscomb, 1994). Copyright restricts others from copying or reproducing a product or information, for example, music, a book, etc., but also less obvious properties such as a star's name or the design of a form, without the consent of the person or agency that claims copyright. As a result, copyright provides a means for entitlements to be realised and assists in allowing information to be valued economically and thence traded.

The 'information age' has brought about new issues in copyright. Not only is information now recognised as a valuable asset, but also its availability and the means by which we access and order it are undergoing immense change.

The creator of a piece of software may spend significant time and effort to produce a useful application. That software could potentially be freely shared with millions around the world. Or the producer of it could claim copyright (i.e. license usage), restricting the ability of others to reproduce the information without paying a fee or incurring legal penalty. There are several issues here:

- Digital information can be reproduced without losing quality in the process: that is, digital information is easier than analogue to pirate.

- The benefit of copyright is that it allows the creator of a sought-after information asset to reap a reward for its exploitation. If software or any other creative or inventive information were to be distributed without such reward opportunities, then many would be discouraged from creating it in the first place.
- Protecting and restricting the flow of information also presents significant problems. To some extent, information is a public resource. If people cannot gain access to it then their own ability to innovate and produce, or to discuss and debate, will be limited. Business opportunities will be diminished and a 'democratic deficit' will ensue. The 'information commons', where the collective exchange of ideas takes place, can be potentially confined by legalistic protections that deny access to information, especially when copyright is aggressively pursued by big corporations against private individuals or public educational institutions.

The free software 'open source' movement, integral to the development of the **Internet**, was founded on the principle that innovation required collaboration and access to information. If legal or technological measures had been put in place to ensure that code or software could not be used without permission from the creator/owner, then the development of the Internet would have been substantially slower. It also may have developed an entirely different character as a result.

Potential profits are often the central motive behind legalistic controls on information. As Boyle (1996) and others have pointed out, large companies have taken advantage of laws intended to assist independent creators to gain a market advantage, with the implication that their 'ownership' becomes so expansive that it restricts the ability of others to create. In fact the information economy is subject to the same monopolistic tendencies as the industrial one. At the same time, however, the 'copyright industries' or the **content industries** that are becoming so important to the world economy cannot exist without copyright.

See also: **Author/ship, Convergence, Digital/analogue distribution, Intellectual property**

CREATIVE INDUSTRIES

The creative industries are those that take traditional creative talents in design, performance, production and writing, and combine these with media production and distribution techniques (for scale) and new interactive technologies (for customisation) in order to create and distribute creative content throughout the service sector of the new economy. The mode of production is 'Hollywood' not 'Detroit' – project-based and innovative, rather than industrial and standardised. It is characterised by networks and partnerships. Consumers have given way to users – interactive partners in further development of the creative product.

The creative industries provide content products for the new knowledge economy. It is here that the major social and consumer impact of new interactive media technologies is felt, since people are much more interested in content than in technologies as such. The appeal lies in the story, sight, song or speech, not in the carrier mechanism. This is increasingly true where the potential for distribution of creative content via the Internet and other new interactive communication forms is being realised. In addition, audiences increasingly expect high-tech content, interactivity and customisation in traditional arts, media and entertainment industries.

In this context, creative content is not confined to leisure and entertainment products, but extends to commercial enterprises in general. As the new interactive media technologies evolve from **b2b** to b2c applications, creative content will be the central requirement, whether the application is for a bank, an educational institution or an entertainment provider, or whether the user is in **'sit up'** or **'sit back'** mode.

Previously distinct industries have rapidly integrated. Advances in technology and increases in network performance have created a fertile environment for the incubation and growth of new sectors and the opportunity for existing disciplines to find new commercial applications. For instance, animation and creative writing both found new application in the development of computer games, which themselves have evolved from one-person to interactive games, with multiple players, via the Internet.

The stimulation of the 'intangible' sector relies more than ever on creativity, flair and risk-taking imagination – on creative enterprises feeding constantly updated new content into technologically advanced knowledge-based industries. But content providers no longer need to be located in metropolitan centres or one of the many 'silicon (v)alleys' in order to play a global role. Music, animation, design, publishing, interactive media, e-commerce and entertainment are all cottage industries on the creative or supply side, relying on small/medium enterprises (SMEs) and freelance creative talent working via short-lived projects. The need in this context is for interdisciplinary clusters, flexible and highly porous teams, creative enterprises rather than large-scale vertically integrated industries.

The creative industries are a significant sector of the global economy. The UK government has identified the following cluster as the creative industries:

- Advertising
- Architecture
- Arts and antiques markets
- Crafts
- Design
- Designer fashion
- Film
- Interactive leisure software
- Music
- Performing arts
- Publishing
- Software
- Television and radio

In the UK these creative industries generated revenues of around £112.5 billion and employed some 1.3 million people in 2001. Exports contributed around £10.3 billion to the balance of trade, and the industries accounted for over 5 per cent of GDP. In 1997–8, output grew by 16 per cent, compared to under 6 per cent for the economy as a whole (Culture, Media and Sport, 2001).

In addition, the following sectors were recognised for their 'close economic relationships' with the creative industries:

- Heritage
- Hospitality
- Museums and galleries
- Sport
- Tourism

It may be argued that the 'creative industries' extend and dissolve ever further into the services sector, and that this entire sector is faced with the challenge of using creative inputs to support core business. Furthermore, entire industries have emerged to support the creative sector, including impresarios, agents, management companies, publicists, events and exhibition managers, and knowledge and cultural entrepreneurs (see Leadbeater and Oakley, 1999).

CULTURAL CAPITAL

The theory of cultural capital argues that, like economic wealth, access to and possession of cultural and symbolic power work to produce and reinforce social distinctions. The term was first employed by Bourdieu (1984). The theory outlines how education, taste and systematic patterns of consumption of cultural goods are not only socially stratified, but are also productive sources of power in their own right. Evaluations based on taste distinctions have turned out to have economic and status consequences – pecking orders were established by how much cultural as well as economic capital a class or individual could command.

Fiske (1987) attempts to overcome the dystopian nature of Bourdieu's thesis by introducing the term popular cultural capital. He argues that this form of capital 'is an accumulation of meanings and pleasures that serves the interests of the subordinate' (1987: 18). With popular cultural capital, individuals are able to form subjectivities based on an opposition to dominant values, or as he states, find 'power in being different' (1987: 19). For Fiske, television and its traditional genres are symbolic of this process.

This populist tone is absent in the work of Bourdieu and subsequent studies that have followed his approach (see for example Bennett et al., 1999). In these approaches, the stance of the authors themselves may de-legitimate the culture of those under analysis because of their own investment in cultural capital. For example, Bennett et al. comment with surprise that '[i]t may carry just as much kudos at a dinner party to show that you know the current line-up of the Spice Girls as to know the name of Philip Glass' latest composition' (1987: 200).

With theories of **class** currently undergoing reconsideration, the notion of cultural capital may too need re-examining. As the above example demonstrates, knowledge workers may share prejudices against or ignorance of popular culture, and so serve to reproduce cultural capital along very traditional lines. But simply inverting established taste hierarchies, or assigning positive evaluations to popular or kitsch culture in order to oppose existing cultural capital, is naive. A major re-assessment of the way cultural capital is necessary, because the scale, global reach and economic importance of popular culture are now so great that it is a determining force both economically and culturally in its own right.

See also: **Class**

Further reading: Bourdieu (1984)

CULTURAL CITIZENSHIP

Publicly acknowledged rights and obligations associated with cultural identity. Citizenship theory is concerned with how we conceive the rights and obligations implicated in membership of a political community, as well as the identity that it confers on us. It focuses upon the necessity of such a membership either in the legal sense, to make society more governable, or as something to be desired for the purposes of inclusion, nationality or equality. Cultural citizenship concerns movement from the latter towards the former, a tendency that has become increasingly prominent since World War II.

Citizenship theory has experienced a revival in political theory over the last decade in relation to unresolved questions surrounding **identity politics** and group rights. As Kymlicka and Norman write: 'it is a natural evolution in political discourse because the concept of citizenship seems to integrate the demands of justice and community membership – the central concepts of political philosophy in the 1970s and 1980s respectively' (1994: 352). Furthermore, globalisation has brought into question the nation-state's claim to be the sole provider of citizenship rights, a result of the increasingly global nature of economics, human rights (treaties) and the movement of people across borders for work, exile or refuge. Whether citizenship remains a concept that should be pursued and reconceptualised as a result of the changing political landscape or whether we are experiencing a 'breakdown in citizenship' is a key theoretical problem of our time.

T. H. Marshall (1965) set out three categories of citizenship rights, which have remained the conceptual pillars around which much citizenship theory is built. For Marshall these rights have been accumulated over the course of history:

- *civil* rights from the seventeenth and eighteenth centuries (primarily legal rights);
- *political* rights from the nineteenth century (whereby rights were institutionalised through the parliamentary system);
- *social* rights which developed in the twentieth century (education, health and pensions brought about through the emergence of the welfare state);

and, a recent addition to understandings of citizenship rights,

- *cultural* citizenship.

The social movements of the twentieth century brought increasing demands for rights based on identity and group cultures into the political arena: feminism, gay rights, Indigenous rights and the black civil rights movement in the US, to name a few. Marshall's notion of a unified and homogenous citizenry, dedicated to a single cultural and political project was contested. The political community consisted of fragmented, competing and culturally diverse groups. Citizenship had to be conceived within the realities of contemporary democracies: namely that 'the security provided by the authorities cannot just be enjoyed; it must itself be secured, and sometimes against the authorities themselves' (Walzer, 1989: 217). Where democracy consisted of a changing cultural landscape under a continual process of negotiation and dispute, citizenship could no longer be seen as the possession of a common culture and heritage.

'Differentiated citizenship', as Young (1990) named it, entailed certain groups being recognised not simply as individual citizens, but as possessing rights as a result of their status within a group. Although as individuals, members of minority groups may possess the same rights as others, they may have less political power. Only by recognising such groups is it possible to actively pursue a diverse and equal society. Claims for Indigenous land rights, quota systems to encourage more women in political or executive positions or the institution of **multiculturalism** as a government strategy, are concessions to the need for cultural rights.

However, cultural citizenship has not survived without criticism. Some maintain that cultural groups are in a constant state of change owing to political, economic and social forces (Kukathas, 1995). Although people may gather together collectively to influence political structures, it is their rights as individuals that must ultimately be protected. And protection of the group may be at the expense of those that choose to differentiate themselves from the group. Furthermore, with the complex, shifting terrain of culture and identity, the potential terrain of citizenship theory is becoming potentially limitless.

See also: **Multiculturalism**

Further reading: Hartley (1999); Miller (1998)

CULTURAL POPULISM

The ascription of democratising tendencies to cultural practices and pursuits, including that of acting as audience or reader of popular entertainments. The term was made familiar by Jim McGuigan (1992), who criticised cultural studies, in the person of John Fiske especially, for finding resistive political potential in the act of pleasurable media consumption. McGuigan and others disliked the textual turn in cultural studies, since it had diverted attention from the economic side of popular culture, and from what they could recognise as bona fide 'political activism' in cultural critique.

The idea gained ground, especially in media sociology and political economy, that taking the pleasure and textuality of popular culture seriously was misguided or even pernicious, because in the end what people did with the media they enjoyed was subordinate to the power of the corporations who distributed those media (see Ferguson and Golding, 1997). People needed not to consume texts pleasurably if resistively, but to be warned off altogether, presumably to give them time to organise protests (this position was adopted by the Glasgow Media Group, for instance). Analysts who were interested in the text/reader relationship were berated for populism because they were said to be following rather than criticising popular tastes. Thus, opponents of cultural populism thought analysts should take a 'normative' position outside of popular culture in order to offer a corrective diagnosis of its downside (Douglas Kellner, 2001: 144–145). The idea that ordinary punters might not need such protection was rarely aired.

There was very little *debate* about cultural populism, largely because it is an accusatory term, a charge, and therefore used only by its opponents, rather than a term researchers identified with: you won't get a research grant for proposing to study it. In fact cultural populism was by no means merely 'bad theory'. It was an early, if not always coherent, recognition of a fundamental shift away from the high modern obsession with production, and a timely prod of the analytical agenda towards consumption. This shift has become ever more important as the broadcast era gives way to the interactive era, since the old assumptions that production is determining, causal and also the locale of power and profit, are ever more plainly at odds with the facts, especially in the cultural economy. Producers (from farmers to film-makers) are mere satellites of those who really rule the economic roost, namely distributors. And consumers no longer passively absorb standardised products (if they ever did) – they are *users*, and have a direct influence on the further customisation of what they select to interact with.

Cultural 'populists' recognised that ordinary pleasures, such as watching television, contained clear elements of civic education – a public good (Hartley, 1999: 43–44). Furthermore, audiences and consumers are increasingly able to use previously exclusive technologies such as video-cameras as little more than pens – instruments of any form of communication they choose, from doodling and self-expression to art and even political intervention (see for example **culture jamming**).

CULTURAL STUDIES

The study of:

- the nexus between *consciousness* and *power* – culture as politics;
- *identity*-formation in modernity – culture as *ordinary* life;
- *mediated* popular entertainment culture – culture as text;
- the expansion of *difference* – culture as plural.

Cultural studies developed in the UK out of Marxism, structuralism and feminism in the intellectual sphere, and from literary, sociological and anthropological studies in the disciplinary domain. It took culture to be the sphere in which class, gender, race and other inequalities were made meaningful or conscious, and lived through either by resistance (subcultures) or some sort of 'negotiated' accommodation (audiences). Culture understood in this way was the terrain on which **hegemony** was fought for and established.

Clearly this approach to culture differed markedly from that of the traditional literary and art critics for whom culture was the sphere of aesthetics and moral or creative values. Cultural studies sought to account for cultural differences and practices not by reference to intrinsic or eternal values (how good?), but by reference to the overall map of social relations (in whose interests?). The 'subject' of cultural studies was no longer 'the human condition' but 'power'. The shape of cultural studies has been directly influenced by its own struggle to decolonise the concept inherited from literary and art criticism, and to make criticism itself more self-reflexive.

Cultural studies has developed a body of work which attempts to recover and place the cultures of hitherto neglected groups. Initially this entailed attention to the historical development and forms of working-class culture and analysis of contemporary forms of popular culture and media.

Partly in response to the intellectual and political upheavals of the 1960s (which saw rapid developments internationally in structuralism, semiotics, Marxism and feminism), cultural studies entered a period of intensive theoretical work. The aim was to understand how culture (the social production of sense and consciousness) should be specified in itself and in relation to economics (production) and politics (social relations).

This required the elaboration of new theoretical models, and the reworking of certain central organising concepts (for example, class, ideology, hegemony, language, subjectivity). Meanwhile, attention at the empirical level was focused on ethnographic and textual studies of those cultural practices and forms that seemed to show how people exploit the available cultural discourses to resist or rework the authority of dominant ideology.

Thereafter, a series of intellectual and political encounters progressively remodelled the shape and direction of cultural studies. Serious dialogues were conducted with feminists (attention to subcultures ignored women), sociologists (problems of method and generalisability), psychoanalytical theorists (identity and subjectivity), anthropologists (ethnographic method), post-colonial and 'subaltern' writers (multiculturalism, the Anglo-American bias of cultural studies), Foucauldians (debates about power), policy-makers (the ability of cultural studies to engage in public policy formation) and cultural activists (culture jamming).

Throughout its short history, cultural studies has been characterised by attention to the politics of both methods of study and academic disciplines. It makes explicit what other academic disciplines often leave implicit – that the production of knowledge is itself a 'ruse to power'.

Further reading: Carey (1989); Grossberg *et al.* (1992); Hall *et al.* (1980); Turner (1990)

CULTURE

The production and circulation of sense, meaning and consciousness. The sphere of meaning, which unifies the spheres of production (economics) and social relations (politics). In other words, culture is the sphere of reproduction not of goods but of life.

If you are planning to use the term 'culture' as an analytical concept, or if you encounter its use, it is unlikely that you will ever be able to fix on just one definition that will do for all such occasions. However, it will often be possible to use or read the word clearly and uncontroversially: Welsh culture, youth culture, a cultured person, Victorian culture, working-class culture, intellectual culture; or even a cultured pearl, bacterial culture, agriculture, cultivation of the soil. The trouble arises when you notice that even in these examples the term culture seems to mean half-a-dozen different things. What on earth do all these things share that can be encompassed by the single term?

The answer is that there *is* no necessary connection. The term *culture* is multi-discursive; it can be mobilised in a number of different discourses. This means you cannot import a fixed definition into any and every context and expect it to make sense. What you have to do is identify the discursive context itself. It may be the discourse of nationalism, fashion, anthropology, literary criticism, viti-culture, Marxism, feminism, cultural studies or even common sense. In each case, culture's meaning will be determined relationally, or negatively, by its differentiation from others in that discourse, and not positively, by reference to any intrinsic, self-evident or fixed properties.

Culture as a concept is historical: its established senses and uses result from its usage within various discourses. It stems, originally, from a purely agricultural root: culture as cultivation of the soil, of plants, culture as tillage. By extension, it encompasses the culture of creatures from oysters to bacteria. Cultivation such as this implies not just growth but also deliberate tending of 'natural' stock to transform it into a desired 'cultivar' – a strain with selected, refined or improved characteristics.

Applying all this to people, it is clear that the term offers a fertile metaphor for the cultivation of minds – the deliberate husbandry of 'natural' capacities to produce perfect rulers. It is not without significance that this usage of the term roughly coincided with the establishment of the first stage of the modern market economy – early agrarian capitalism in the seventeenth and eighteenth centuries. The production of a strain of men who are not 'naturally' (by divine right of succession) fitted to rule but who are nevertheless powerful is made sense of, by those men themselves and for the benefit of others, by the systematic dissemination of the metaphor of culture.

However, the early hegemony of the aristocratic land-owning capitalists was subjected by the nineteenth century to the altogether more disruptive development of urban, industrial and commercial capital. No sooner was culture established as a term that referred freely to rulers without echoes of rhizomes than economic and political changes began to challenge the naturalised right of the cultured to rule. Entrepreneurial and imperial capitalism appeared to be no respecter of culture. Instead, the term was denounced by Marx (culture which means works of wonder for the rich also means rags and corruption for the poor), and apparently ignored by the capitalist and middle classes alike. It was left to the intelligentsia, especially its liberal-conservative, moralist-humanist literary element, to take up the concept. Here, during the mid-nineteenth century, it began to be honed into a quite precise notion, one which is still influential today.

Culture was established, especially by Matthew Arnold and his followers, as the pursuit not of material but of spiritual perfection via the knowledge and practice of 'great' literature, 'fine' art and 'serious' music. Since the goal was perfection, not just understanding, and spiritual, not material, culture was seen as the training of 'discrimination' and 'appreciation' based on 'responsiveness' to 'the best that has been thought and said in the world'. The cultural critics strove then to prescribe and establish a canon of what exactly could be counted as the 'best'. But such critics also tended to see themselves as an embattled community struggling against the encroachments of material civilisation and scientific technology to preserve the 'sweetness and light' of culture and disseminate it to the benighted denizens of mass society. In such a climate it is not surprising to find that the 'treasures' of culture are assumed to belong to a pre-industrial past and a non-industrial consciousness. Modern proponents of this concept of culture-as-embattled perfection have been influential in offering an ideology to highly placed elites in government, administrative, intellectual and even broadcasting circles within which their *sectional* interests can be represented as *general* interests.

Culture has not yet recovered from this history. The concept itself has undergone a period of decolonisation. It is argued by those who object to the elitist notion of culture that it dispossesses most people, leaving a 'cultured' few and an 'uncultured' majority. Further, there seems to be an uncanny degree of fit between this division of culture and other social divisions – for instance, those of class, gender and race. It seems that the cultural critics' discourse of 'excellence' works not so much to preserve timeless and universal treasures but, much more immediately albeit less obviously, to translate class and other kinds of social primacy into cultural capital. The struggle to dismantle the supremacy of elite, high English culture was championed first by Hoggart (1957) and Williams (1958). Their initiative has been taken up in the form of **cultural studies**, in which the concept of culture has undergone a radical transformation, moving towards the formulation offered at the beginning of this entry. Since the late 1960s the notion of culture has been reworked largely in terms of Marxist, feminist and multiculturalist approaches. Although the issues have by no means been clarified, let alone resolved, they can be stated. Culture is now seen as a determining, not just a determined, part of social activity, and therefore culture is both a significant sphere for the reproduction of social power inequalities and a major component of the expanding world economy.

See also: **Class, Difference, Discourse, Hegemony, Ideology, Language, Nature, Popular/popular culture, Signification, Structuralism, Subjectivity**

Further reading: Turner (1990); Williams (1981)

CULTURE AS SERVICE INDUSTRY *see* creative industries

CULTURE JAMMING

A billboard with an image of the American flag looms over a building in Times Square, New York. A closer look reveals that although the stripes may be conventional, the stars are in fact corporate logos: IBM, Nike, Windows, Playboy, McDonald's among them. Alongside the flag are the words 'declare independence from corporate rule' and a web address (*www.adbusters.org*). The implied message is that corporations now rule America (that is, America(tm)), constitute its national identity and claim its public space. Subsequently Adbusters received a call from Disney's Miramax Corporation asking them to take down the billboard or replace it as they were planning to film in Times Square. Instead, Adbusters called for public input into how the flag could be changed in response to Disney's request (one suggestion was Mickey Mouse head silhouettes instead of stars).

Named 'culture jamming' by San Francisco band Negativland in 1984, but also known as 'guerrilla art' or 'citizens' art', this is true high- and low-tech interactive media. One strategy to 'unswhoosh' the Nike advertising campaign was to change the slogan 'Just Do It' to 'Just Stop It'. A separate attempt to jam Nike saw MIT graduate student Jonah Paretti try to take advantage of Nike's offer to personalise shoes by having the company stitch the word 'sweatshop' onto his order of a pair of Nike shoes. Although Nike refused, the e-mail correspondence between Paretti and Nike over the incident was sent to millions of people around the world. Other jams have included changing the Apple logo to a skull and transforming the word Shell to read $hell (with the 'hell' emphasised). Internet hackers redirect visitors to subversive sites. Every year people in the US, Canada, Australia, Japan and Europe participate in 'Buy Nothing Day' in order to highlight their country's overconsumption compared with the third world. In an inversion of shop-lifting, zine makers surreptitiously place their zines between other publications in bookshops in the hope that someone will read what otherwise is unacceptable to the publishing industry.

As these examples highlight, culture jamming is about doing rather than theorising the media. Or, as Naomi Klein puts it, culture jamming is 'writing theory on the streets' (Klein, 2000: 284). Adbusters' founder, Kalle Lasn, writes that 'communication professors tell their students everything that's wrong with the global media monopoly, but never a word how to fix it' (Lasn, 2000: 116). Texts on culture jamming are generally 'how to' guides that celebrate the public's right to utilise public space in order to intervene with corporate messages. They openly assert the audience's engagement with texts, refusing to accept that any media is a one-way communication device, adding a whole new dimension to media theory's 'active audience'.

See also: **Anti-globalisation**

Further reading: Branwyn (1997); Hazen and Winokur (1997); rtmark.com

CULTURE WARS

The name given to debates about the contemporary condition and prospects of Enlightenment concepts of art, truth and reason. The debates circulated within and between academic, intellectual and journalistic domains in the 1980s and 1990s, in the US and other countries such as Australia and the UK. They were sometimes conducted as coded forms of conflict about other things entirely, for instance, influence over the curriculum for training journalists or access to research funds and to policy-makers, or even circulation boosters in opinion media. Sometimes the culture wars seemed little more than 'generation-gap' squabbling between old high modernists and not-so-old postmodernists (McKenzie Wark, 1994; Mark Davis, 1997; Catharine Lumby, 1997). The weekend newspaper version cast the debate as a joust; hard to take seriously but fun to do, hurling well-argued abuse at political opponents in the name not of self-interest but of large philosophical concepts.

The theatrics masked real issues: reality, truth and reason were said to be undermined by those who introduced 'relativism' into the study of human activity. The latter included postmodernists, advocates of political correctness, theorists, deconstructionists (i.e. followers of continental rather than empirical philosophy), feminists, post-colonial critics and anyone doing media or cultural studies. What was at stake was a shift

from	to
modern	postmodern
universal	relative
reason	emotion (or else 'irrealism')
production	consumption
imperial	post-colonial
urban	suburban
government	identity
decision-maker	celebrity
public life	private life
men	women
information (or else art)	entertainment
words	pictures
literature	media

and so on. These oppositions were often taken to be versions of politics, with traditional leftists seeking to hold to the modernist line, and therefore to the terms in the left-hand column against what they saw as the politically disabling allure of at least some of the terms in the right. But such a stance was itself cast as increasingly conservative, as the radical changes, implications and potential of the phenomena identified in the right-hand column became more insistent in both intellectual and public life. It became necessary to reform what 'counted' as 'left-' or 'right-' wing stances, and to treat with scepticism any presumption that a given opposition *entails* a given political position. Intellectually, that process of reform took the form of the 'culture wars'.

The culture wars had a journalistic aspect, by which established canons and hierarchies of taste and style were used as punch-bags for similar arguments. Journalists and critics joined the fray to defend such things as the Western literary canon, clarity and plainness of writing, reason and science as the royal road to truth, etc.; apparently they needed defence against relativism, theory and 'irrealism' (respectively). Despite its heroic appearance much of this stuff was in itself pure inconsequential entertainment. It was partisan controversialism done to provoke readers (sales). But in the meantime, it continued to be the case that Western notions of art, truth and reason could no longer be seen as self-evidently virtuous. For as well as progress, Enlightenment culture had produced grotesque negatives – apartheid as a 'science'; the Holocaust as an application of 'reason'; the American Way of freedom experienced as its opposite by people 'othered' via gender, class, race, ethnicity or colonial subjection. The culture wars were a public attempt to think through how such opposites did and should *interact*. The wise observer watched the interaction, and did not seek to choose between the opposites.

CUSTOMISATION

Customisation is a response to increasingly fragmented niche markets, whereby businesses are replacing old strategies organised around *mass* consumption habits with services aimed at more selective, or *personalised*, buying choices. For instance, where cultural choices such as broadcast media consumption were once limited to only a few channels directed at large audiences, recent trends in multi-channelling mean that programming can be directed at smaller, more specific audiences.

In the media industries, customisation is said to be a result of **convergence**. Instead of buying the paper that everyone else reads, online news service subscribers can now customise what they receive into a 'Daily Me' version of events. This can be seen as an empowering development. It assumes that greater diversity of products and media will be on offer, including new content for once marginalised or excluded groups. However, as Cass Sunstein (2001) argues, customisation can also confine or limit society's democratic potential. People can avoid what they don't already like. As a result, *exposure* to the unfamiliar – cultures, ideas and information – is likely to be reduced. This has caused some to regret the passing of standardised mass communication, which forced readers and viewers to see what they didn't choose or desire to see, in news bulletins, etc. However, customisation may simply be a formal recognition of what people do anyway, since no-one reads the whole of a newspaper or watches everything broadcast on TV, so 'avoidance' is structural whether at the supply or at the consumption end of the communication chain.

See also: **Convergence, Consumer sovereignty**

CYBERDEMOCRACY

Self-governing virtual communities. Cyberdemocracy is a concept that sees the **Internet** as a technology that has a transformative social influence: participation extends democracy (rule by those involved) either within its own social space or in society at large.

Cyberdemocracy is an optimistic concept that surfaced out of the early days of the Internet. It is related to earlier conceptions of 'electronic democracy'. In 1970 Robert Paul Wollf asserted that 'the obstacles to direct democracy are merely technical' and proposed that electronic voting machines be set up in every home, attached to the television set (Wollf, 1970: 34). Cyberdemocracy relies largely on the principles of access and the free exchange of information. The accessible and participatory nature of the Internet was seen to make it an ideal democratic space wherein people could communicate freely and participate in forums built for collective decision-making. Nicholas Negroponte wrote in 1995 that 'the access, the mobility, and the ability to effect change are what will make the future so different to the present', and that digital information would be an 'empowering' force beyond people's expectations (1995: 231). Cyberdemocracy propelled the adoption of Internet technologies and promoted an ethos of free information exchange that seems likely to continue to characterise at least a proportion of Internet activity.

According to Mark Poster, asking what *impact* the Internet might have upon society, culture and politics is to ask the wrong question. The Internet is more like Germany (a social space that turns people into Germans) than it is like a hammer (a tool that has an *impact* on nails, but doesn't turn people into hammers) (Poster, 2000: 403). Looking at the Internet as a tool, to determine what its effects on democracy are, sees it merely as creating an impact upon the existing social surface. For Poster, this denies the possibility that the Internet brings *new social spaces* within which identities and communities can exist; turning people into 'Netizens', in effect.

Alternatively, when viewed as a **public sphere**, the Internet is a forum within which human interaction occurs and where power relations are configured. Cyberdemocracy, for Poster, is potentially 'something other than democracy in any shape that we can conceive given our embeddedness in the present'.

One of the questions of cyberdemocracy is whether it is a given result of technological development or whether it requires a commitment to developing particular types of forums and networks that are inclusive and constructed with democratic principles in mind (Calabrese and Borchert, 1996). Many writers point out that the majority of online forums more accurately resemble either anarchy or dictatorship than democracy (see for example Smith and Kollock, 1999). Attempts to construct cyberdemocracy include the civic networking movement, which sought to establish infrastructure and applications designed to connect people via digital cities (Tsagarousianou *et al.*, 1998).

The success of such projects is largely dependent on whether enough citizens have access to the technology and skills on order to participate within the democratic process they seek to instigate. Here cyberdemocracy lags behind rather than differs from political democracy, which requires literate citizens and, over several centuries, has instituted the infrastructure (universal elementary education) to produce them.

As Calbrese and Borchert have pointed out, instances of cyberdemocracy have existed and will continue to exist. Whether they are random, institutionalised or commonplace is perhaps 'not what is most important about democracy' (Calabrese and Borchert, 1996: 264). From this angle, cyberdemocracy is not about asserting that cyberspace is inherently democratic, but that cyberdemocracy can exist wherever people choose to make it.

See also: **Accessing, Digital divide, Public sphere**

Further reading: Hague and Loader (1999); Sclove (1995)

CYBERNETICS

Cybernetics is a science of communication concerned primarily with the controlling of information within biological or man-made systems. Its primary focus is the adaptive or self-controlling abilities of systems – from how people perform logic to the possibilities for artificial intelligence or problem-solving (heuristic) computer programming. As such, it is an interdisciplinary pursuit ranging across mathematics, biology, psychology, logic and communications.

Central to the science of cybernetics is the principle of feedback, whereby the output is relayed back to modify the input. For example, automatic systems within a car may have sensing devices that change the temperature inside the car according to signals received from the environment. Cybernetics often focuses on intelligent, or human-like, behaviour as well as on technological and biological innovation.

See also: **Cyborg**

CYBORG

The image of the cyborg describes a fusion between human and machine, the organic and the technological. Cyborgs exist now in our everyday lives in such forms as artificial limbs, immunisation, pacemakers and Internet chat rooms. In all of these technologies the division between the body and the machine is difficult to locate. Culturally, the cyborg allows for the creation of strategic identities in a technologically mediated society.

The cyborg was first invoked in the cultural studies context by Donna Haraway in her 1984 essay *A Manifesto for Cyborgs*. The cyborg, for Haraway, is a concept through which a feminist dialogue can be opened up, but one capable of avoiding socialist-feminist appeals to an organic, or natural, state of femaleness. Any appeal to unity denies the fact that gender and class consciousness are forced upon us by historical experience. Haraway sees it as more useful to look for invention and hybridity in place of wholeness and essentialism, what she calls a 'feminist science'. In cyborg theory, technology is not seen as a threat but accepted as having merged with the natural to the point at which the boundaries are no longer fixed but are instead recognised as constructs and tools of domination that can be shifted and challenged. As the cyborg is a hybrid of organism and machine it is therefore 'the illegitimate offspring of militarism and patriarchal capitalism' (Haraway, 1984: 193), but one which is not faithful to its parent. The cyborg takes science and technology beyond a masculinist tradition of progress and breaks down the binaries of culture : nature, civilised : primitive, mind : body. It therefore provides a means to overcome an imposed 'natural' state of being that confines the individual to oppressive power relationships. The cyborg is transformative and **postmodern** as 'the certainty of what counts as nature – a source of insight and a promise of innocence – is undermined, probably fatally' (1984: 94). Although Haraway's vision of the cyborg is not restricted to cyberspace, it implies that expression in cyberspace – both through and within technology – will have ramifications for real-world politics.

See also: **Cyberdemocracy, Virtuality**

Further reading: Halberstam and Livingston (1995); Kirkup *et al.* (2000); Stone (2001)

DATACASTING

The word datacasting can mean simply the distribution, or streaming, of digital data. However, it is used more specifically to describe digital television services beyond traditional broadcasting. Broadcasting (analogue) is thought of as continuous, with a content of linear narratives, and distributed from one-to-many. Datacasting (digital) allows for interactive services (such as access to the Internet), data that you might request on-demand (such as weather reports or stock quotes) or pay-per-view subscription to giant audio-visual archives (e.g. TiVo).

All digital information consists of interchangeable and discrete bits of information, making datacasting and broadcasting technically indistinguishable. The word datacasting, when used to describe digital television services, is therefore referring to the industry and regulatory characteristics of datacasting services rather than the technical features. It is generally used to describe particularly innovative (as opposed to conventional) content that may require a degree of **interactivity**.

See also: **Broadcasting, Convergence, Interactivity**

DEIXIS

Words or expressions whose precise meaning always depends upon the particular context of their situation. *Deictic* items in effect point outwards (*deixis* is derived ultimately from the Greek, 'to show') from the text to the extra-linguistic context. They include words such as *this*, *that*, *here*, *there*, *us*, *you*, etc. Deictic items may be seen as falling into three major categories: *person deixis* such as 'I', 'you', 'he/she/it', 'we', 'they', 'me', 'mine', 'us', 'ours', 'them', 'theirs'; *temporal deixis* such as 'now', 'then', 'yesterday', 'today', 'tomorrow'; and *place deixis* such as 'here', 'there', 'away', 'this', 'that'.

Part of the interest of such apparently commonplace items is the way in which they shift their meaning from context to context by referring to different entities: thus 'I' refers to whoever is speaking at the moment of utterance. This can pose problems during early language development. Precisely because the referent is always shifting, children take time to identify the meaning of deictic terms and can mistakenly reverse their application, saying, for example, 'pick you up, Daddy' instead of 'pick me up, Daddy'.

Deixis is also interesting for the way in which it raises crucially important issues about language and meaning. Consideration of deictic terms helps to show how the meaning of many utterances does not reside purely in the words themselves, but depends also upon the context in which the words are uttered. For it is only by reference to context that we can recover the particular meaning of particular deictic expressions.

Further reading: Levinson (1983); Lyons (1977)

DEMOCRATAINMENT

In commercial democracies, public participation in public affairs is conducted increasingly through highly mediated entertainment media and commercial rather than public institutions. The term was coined by Hartley (1999), as an extension to already identified hybrids such as infotainment and **edutainment**.

DEREGULATION

Deregulation is intended to stimulate competition and efficiency through the removal of bureaucratic and legislative barriers. It is the reduction or rejection by government of existing policies that impose rules (in the form of **regulation**) on both private industry (e.g. media corporations) and public organisations (the BBC, for example). Deregulation was the political buzzword of the Reagan–Thatcher era in the 1980s, when wealthy New Right foundations commissioned economists to produce studies hostile to regulatory activity and 'targeted the media to be conquered, second only to direct political power itself' (Tunstall, 1986: 12). Since then it has developed into a much more general policy direction for governments of all persuasions.

In the US, deregulation of the communications industry was justified by technological convergence. As technological barriers between distinct industries began to dissolve, companies were encouraged to diversify their markets in order to increase efficiency and innovation. This in part required a relaxation of antitrust laws (regulation designed to prevent monopolies). It was assumed that competition, rather than regulation, was an appropriate means to overcome market bottlenecks.

Although competition can result in positive market outcomes, effectively introducing it can be problematic. Deregulation has been criticised for encouraging mergers and acquisitions throughout the communications industry, squeezing out smaller players and causing a reduction in diversity and choice. Competition through deregulation has also, in some instances, led to the abandonment of community obligations and public interest requirements for the benefit of industry (see Caporaso and Levine, 1992).

Recent thinking on effective policy-making seeks to overcome the intellectual stalemate of the pro-market (deregulation) vs pro-public (regulation) positions by looking to responsive policy processes that seek cooperation between government regulation, industry self-regulation and community mobilisation. Known as 'New Progressivism', or 'the Third Way', the intention of these approaches is to foster wealth creation and innovation through the provision of education, healthcare reform and urban regeneration (Giddens, 2000).

As Tunstall has argued, deregulation does not remove an industry from politics or political attention. To deregulate is to release an industry from bureaucratic control, making it subject to commercial interests and the attention of political lobbying. When there are fewer rules, the significance of the rules that remain becomes greater. But, 'the abolition of some rules also makes the surviving rules seem more ambiguous and more vulnerable to alteration or abolition' (Tunstall, 1986: 6).

See also: **Globalisation, Privatisation, Regulation**

Further reading: DeRosa (2001); Gayle and Goodrich (1990); Head (1991); Kellner (1990)

DIACHRONIC

To study something diachronically is to study it as a system changing over time. The term *diachronic* is particularly associated with the work of the Swiss linguist Ferdinand de Saussure, who set up a distinction in linguistic study between studying language as a system of meanings at one moment in time (*synchronic linguistics*) and studying changes in the system of meanings from one temporal point to another (*diachronic linguistics*). When he formulated this distinction (first made public in his 1911 lectures) the linguistics of his day was still concerned primarily with historical analysis. It was thus concerned with the origins of language and families of languages; with changes in pronunciation from one period to another; and with tracing changes in the meaning of individual words from their origin in a source language. Saussure regarded these endeavours as fundamentally flawed, because they were atomistic and neglected the inter-related components of the system by focusing on isolated elements. The proper historical study of language depended, for Saussure, on initially describing the overall shape of the language, synchronically, before proceeding to the description of its change over time. Synchronic study, in Saussure's view, was prior to diachronic study; and the latter became – in effect – the comparison of temporally discrete synchronic states.

In this sense, Saussure was not, as has sometimes been claimed, against the historical study of language. On the contrary, he was concerned to establish the historical study of language (*diachrony*) on a sounder footing. However, one effect of his *Course in General Linguistics* ([1916] 1974) was to re-orient the whole direction of linguistic research away from the study of historical change towards the current state of the language, so that historical linguistics has, until recently, suffered a long period of neglect.

See also: **Synchronic**

Further reading: Culler (1976); Saussure (1974)

DIALECT

A socially or regionally marked version of a language made up of distinctive patterns of sentence construction, vocabulary and pronunciation. The use of one dialect rather than another depends basically upon the social class and regional origins of the speaker. Examples of dialect differences in English cover a wide range of phenomena and include matters such as: the use of multiple negation ('I hadn't got nothing to fall back on'), which is common in some English dialects but not in others; variation in vocabulary (the same object – a sports shoe, for instance, may be designated differently, as *plimsoll, dap, sandy pump*, etc., in different dialects in different parts of the UK); and distinctive patterns of pronunciation (such as using a glottal stop instead of 'it/' in words such as *bitter, Luton, letter, bottle, butter,* which is common in parts of London).

The latter kind of variation, purely in terms of sound, is also known as accent. Accent, however, refers *only* to pronunciation, and is thus not as inclusive a term as dialect, which embraces a wider range of linguistic variation. Indeed, in the UK it is possible to find the standard dialect being spoken in a range of regional accents.

Everyone speaks a dialect, whether it be a non-standard regional dialect or the standard dialect. The standard UK dialect itself evolved out of a particular regional dialect of the south-east English Midlands and gained pre-eminence not because of any intrinsic linguistic superiority, but simply because it was the dialect spoken in that part of the country that was particularly influential in the emergence of the modern UK nation-state. It was the dialect spoken at the universities of Oxford and Cambridge, and by important sections of the mercantile class. Thus, its growing adoption from the fifteenth century onwards as the preferred dialect in education, in certain key professions such as the law, and indeed for written communication in general, is more a question of historical contingency than any special linguistic qualities.

Its adoption as a standard dialect, particularly for written communication, leads to nominative pressure on other less socially prestigious dialects. This in turn gives rise to the mistaken view that the norms of the standard are inherently more correct than those of other dialects – a judgement which is unconsciously based on social factors rather than a linguistic consideration. From a linguistic viewpoint all dialects are equal in their ability to communicate the intentions of their users, even although a particular dialect can become identified with a particular communicative role.

See also: **Code, Diglossia, Pidgin**

Further reading: Hughes and Trudgill (1979); Montgomery (1986)

DIALOGIC

A property of all signification, that of being structured as dialogue. The term was coined by Volosinov in order to stress the continuous, interactive, generative process of language, as opposed to the Saussurian emphasis on its abstract, structural form. Volosinov (1973) argues that all language is expressive of social relations, and hence that every individual utterance is structured as dialogue. That is, the way an utterance is organised by a speaker/writer is oriented towards an anticipated response in the hearer/reader.

Furthermore, once the utterance is received by its addressee, it results in meaning and understanding only through a dialogic interaction with what Volosinov calls 'inner speech' – a kind of internal dialogue that not only renders signs into sense, but simultaneously takes the process further by generating a response that is capable of being uttered as the next 'moment' of the dialogue.

Volosinov argues that this feature of signification is not tied to speech alone, but characterises all utterances. Even monologues or soliloquies (speech without an addressee) are internally structured as dialogue. The same goes for utterances whose addressees are neither present nor known to the addresser – for example, books and media output. This book is dialogic in that each word, sentence, entry, and the book as a whole, is oriented towards a supposed addressee, and thus takes account of anticipated responses in the way it is selected, organised and sequenced.

See also: **Author/ship, Multi-accentuality**

DIASPORA

The original Diaspora was worldwide Jewry. The term has lost its capital letter and been generalised in cultural theory to refer to any migrant or cosmopolitan 'community' and experience (see Clifford, 1997). Diasporic communities are groups of people that are distanced from their homeland – as political migrants, economic migrants in search of work or refugees escaping war. The experience of exile may be accompanied by a sense of belonging to the former homeland and a continued allegiance to that remembered culture within a host country. For some communities, such as the Iranian community in Los Angeles or the Vietnamese in Melbourne, the homeland is a denied concept owing to its occupation by a regime of which they are not part (Cunningham, 2000). Diasporas are therefore heterogeneous cultures, spatially separated from their place of origin yet living between places in their identity and cultural life. The psychological and cultural experience of diaspora can be one of hybridity, exile, nostalgia, selective adaptation or cultural invention.

The term is useful for moving beyond conceptions of ethnicity that depict unitary notions of culture contained within national borders. Diasporas present a complex picture of ethnic identity, whereby groups participate in activities that maintain aspects of their homeland within the host country while at the same time participate in the lifestyle and culture of their new home. The experience of diaspora is one of group memory, a desire to preserve and carry the languages, tastes, dress and rituals of home within a new temporary or permanent space. It is therefore a notion of ethnicity that involves the movement of people, and cultures. It is not only a 'looking back' to the past, but the making of new communities and the transformation of traditions, neighbourhoods and cultures.

Only some migrant groups attract the term. There is said to be a Chinese diaspora, throughout the world, but not a British one: Brits are called 'expats'. There is a Vietnamese diaspora, but not a Serbian one among ethnic Serb communities throughout the Balkans and elsewhere. It seems that 'diaspora' applies to migrants whose dispersal has occurred under some sort of duress, whether military-political or economic. There is no *American* diaspora, for instance.

See also: **Ethnic/ethnicity**

Further reading: Cohen (1997); Cunningham (2000); Mirzoeff (2000); Naficy (1993); Sreberny (2000)

DIEGESIS

A term used traditionally to describe the total world of a **narrative**. Aristotle used it to describe how literature was a process of *telling* a story that did not involve *showing* it. The ideal was to tell a story so artfully that the art was not noticed by the audience; everything would appear to be diegetic, or inside the story, not dialogic, or a component of the story-telling. Film theorist Christian Metz developed this definition in his **semiotic** analysis of cinema in which he understood diegesis as 'the signified of the narrative' (Stam *et al.*, 1992: 38).

Diegesis recognises that codes and conventions give a film **text** its meaning, and that these codes and conventions are shared by filmmakers and their audiences. For example, if a character in a film turns on a radio and music is heard on the soundtrack, we understand that the music is part of the character's world in the narrative – the music is diegetic. In contrast, if music is introduced in the film without prompting by the narrative or by the characters (e.g. the score that accompanies action), this is understood as a non-diegetic technique. Non-diegetic conventions also include voice-overs, credit sequences, editing, camera work and those rare occasions when characters address the camera directly.

Diegesis is understood to be central to realist representations, and like **realism** itself, there have been many sophisticated challenges to traditional conventions. Baz Luhrmann's *Romeo and Juliet* is a film that employs a series of non-diegetic conventions to re-interpret a well-known narrative. The film uses a contemporary soundtrack, an urban setting and radical camera movement, yet retains Shakespearean verse. In this instance, playing with diegetic conventions forms part of the pleasure of the text, allowing an old narrative to be retold in a contemporary format. This example demonstrates how the concept of diegesis provides a means of discussing the formal conventions of a text without having to resort to the hierarchical values of **aesthetics**.

See also: **Aesthetics, Realism**

DIFFERENCE

A concept drawn from linguistic philosophy, specifically the writings of Ferdinand de Saussure and Jacques Derrida, which has become a focus for attempts to understand the fundamental capacity of language and writing to mean. For Saussure, difference is that attribute of the language system (**langue**) which allows its elements to be distinguished from one another and so to signify. At its simplest, the system of difference operates at the phonemic level, allowing a very restricted number of differentiated sounds (forty-four in English) in various combinations to signify a potentially infinite range of meanings.

Working to this exemplary model, it is possible to claim that difference is the foundation of meaning.

For Derrida, however, this is only the start of the problem, a start signalled by spelling difference 'incorrectly' – '*différance*'. Derrida criticises what he calls the *metaphysics of presence* as a recurring theme throughout Western philosophy. This is the ideal (metaphysical) situation in which speech (but not writing) is supposed to yield up to the speaker a pure, transparent correspondence between *sound* and *sense*, i.e. between language and consciousness. In short, meaning (thought) is *self-present* in speaking (language).

Derrida disagrees. For him, the traditional distinction between speech and writing, privileging speech as somehow original or pure, cannot be sustained. Writing, because of its distance (in space and time) from its source, and because of its capacity for dissimulation, is a traditional problem for Western philosophy – an impediment to the desire or craving for language to act as the obedient vehicle for thought. For Derrida, writing is not an impure '*supplement*' but is its *precondition*. The very characteristics of writing that led Saussure (and the phenomenologist Edmund Husserl) to set it apart from speech are those that Derrida finds it impossible to leave out. However, it is not his aim to replace speech as the model of sense-making with writing; his quarry is the *opposition* speech/writing in linguistic philosophy, and the 'metaphysical' tradition which seeks to arbitrate between the two terms in that opposition.

The notion of *différance* is one that Derrida would certainly refuse to call a concept, key or otherwise – his aim is not to settle or to define meanings but to *unsettle* them. It encompasses the post-Saussurian idea of differing, adds to it the Derridean idea of deferring (postponement of what could be present to another time – an 'absent presence' of meaning), and represents these paradoxical ideas (differing suggests non-identity; deferring suggests sameness albeit postponed, perhaps endlessly) in a word whose startling 'misspelling' can be discerned only through writing (since *différance* is pronounced orally the *same* way as the word from which it differs, *difference*).

Derrida's work was especially influential in the 1970s and early 1980s when the Saussurian terminology of signification was becoming well known. After Derrida, it wasn't possible to claim that signifiers referred to signifieds (an absent presence); on the contrary, signifiers refer only to themselves, and meaning is generated by a differential play of signifiers in an endless, self-referential chain, beyond which it is not possible to go for verification. That is to say, there is no 'experience' or 'reality' beyond signification which can act as a test or warrant of its veracity, for all experience and reality is already a representation in signification. Representation, far from being a duplicitous, textual, tainted 'expression' of otherwise pure thought, is all we have got – perception itself is already a representation, and pure consciousness cannot be 'expressed' since it is the differentiating activity of signification that constitutes consciousness. Finally, it is no longer possible to claim with confidence that individual subjects 'have' an identity (self-presence, self-knowledge), since identity is a product of difference – of the endless play of signifiers in the (absent) system of language.

Derrida co-wrote the script for postmodernism (subtitled 'the textualist's revenge') by positing the world as a text. His philosophy of doubt and radical scepticism led to the 'deconstructionist' movement, especially influential in the US (see **structuralism**).

Interestingly, there is a 'politics of signification' attached to the very notion of difference. Some would argue that Derridean post-structuralism ends up in an idealist, solipsistic, anti-materialist cul-de-sac, where the materialist contention that social existence determines consciousness is short-circuited, giving a new lease of life to an Alice in Wonderland version of critical practice which allows the world to mean whatever the critic decides (this accusation may apply to some examples of literary deconstruction). On the other hand, some have argued that Derridean doubt, scepticism and self-reflexivity are not *radical* philosophical positions at all, because these qualities have been central planks of Western philosophy since Aristotle and Plato. If so, this makes Derridean practice paradoxically a conservative force in intellectual culture, despite its unsettling implications. Certainly it is rationalist at heart, by no means an emotional or 'romantic' devotion to textual excess.

See also: **Author/ship, Binary opposition, Culture, Discourse, Individualism, Postmodern, Subjectivity**

Further reading: Lawson (1985); Norris (1982)

DIGITAL/ANALOGUE DISTRIBUTION

The word '**analogue**' is used to describe that which is 'analogous to the original'. Digital technology converts analogue (continuous) information into a binary language. This language consists of discrete 'bits' (short for 'binary digits') of information in the form of 1s (an 'on' state) and 0s (an 'off' state). How a strand of 1s and 0s is arranged (whether it is 01 or 10, 001, etc.) will determine how that information is decoded or reconstituted into the appearance of the original. As Nicholas Negroponte explains: 'the world is a very analogue place. From a microscopic point of view, it is not digital at all but continuous. Nothing goes suddenly on or off, turns from black to white, or changes from one state to another without going through a transition' (Negroponte, 1995: 15).

In terms of *distribution*, analogue signals are transmitted in a continuous wave whereas digital information is distributed as a code to be converted by the receiving equipment. As analogue technology is analogous to the original and digital technology is a conversion of the original into binary language, analogue technology is arguably more true to the original and should therefore offer a better quality sound or image. However, as digital bits are either 'on' or 'off', you will be able to receive digital content well or not at all, and digital information can be replicated infinitely without loss of quality. Analogue technology, on the other hand, can suffer from interference, where the wave of impulses are interrupted by competing signals: hence snow or unclear images on the set. It also suffers degradation through generations of copying.

There are economic implications to these technological differences. One is that digital distribution allows for interactivity (see **datacasting**) and therefore creates new marketing opportunities for media and content industries. Another is that digital distribution puts perfect rather than degraded copies at the disposal of 'pirates'. As analogue copies were never as good as the original, consumers were still likely to pay for quality goods (such as CDs produced by the record company). Digital piracy produces copies of a standard that cannot be differentiated from industry-produced goods, resulting in new **copyright** concerns.

See also: **Analogue**

Further reading: Negroponte (1995); Tassel (2001)

DIGITAL DIVIDE

The digital divide is the stratification of people according to access to interactive computer-based technologies – on one side, groups and individuals possessing the ability to participate within the network society, and on the other, those who are absent or excluded from it. It is the gap between the information-rich and the information-poor.

It was estimated that in 2001, 429 million people around the world were online, the equivalent of 6 per cent of the world's population. Of these 429 million people, 41 per cent lived in North America. In contrast, only 4 per cent of the world's online population lived in South America, 27 per cent in Europe, the Middle East and Africa combined and, despite the large population of the area, only 20 per cent of the online population logged on from the Asia Pacific (although this will soon change as China boots up) (Benton Foundation, 2001).

The communications technologies interconnect people into a network of ideas, information, e-commerce and virtual communities. Those who are excluded are not able to participate to the same degree in the **network society** or be placed in a position of advantage within its economy.

The evidence suggests that the distribution of **connectivity** is tied to the allocation of resources and education. For instance, in the US nearly 65 per cent of college graduates have home Internet access, whereas only 11.7 per cent of households headed by persons with less than a high school education are online (Rohde and Shapiro, 2000). Thus, the digital divide also includes, or follows, differential levels of literacy and education.

As Castells (1996: 34) writes: the 'speed of technological diffusion is selective, both socially and functionally'. The digital divide is the result of strategic flows of information that are not bound by nation-state territories. The digital divide is just as likely to be experienced between two neighbourhoods within the same city as between age groups or between language groups. It can even separate different individuals in the same family or household.

As with other areas of development theory and practice, strategies for overcoming the digital divide can be contentious (see Wilkins, 2000). It is widely accepted that inequitable access to information and communications technology (ICT) must be overcome. But there are always political questions about how to do this. For instance, is information dissemination (on issues such as the prevention of the spread of HIV/AIDS) the ultimate goal in a given area, or should development programmes be looking at ways to empower communities to develop their own strategies through ICT use? If so, who within that community should be responsible for the allocation of resources and the creation of useful programmes? Furthermore, is it acceptable to assert the importance of online communication in areas that are in urgent need of basic resources such as food and water?

The digital divide is important to public policy because an 'underclass' of the digitally poor is not only likely to prove electorally recalcitrant when it comes to supporting 'new economy' initiatives, they are also unavailable as consumers for the burgeoning businesses of e-commerce and new interactive media entertainment. Further, the more that information and electronic interactivity move to centre stage, the more that the digital divide will disenfranchise those not connected, contributing to what has been termed the 'democratic deficit' in modernising societies.

Further reading: Joseph (2001); Katz (1988); Norris (2001); Wyatt *et al.* (2000)

DIGLOSSIA

The presence within a speech community of two related, but contrasting, linguistic varieties – one of which is high status, the other low status – which are used in complementary contexts. Thus the high variety will most likely be used for news broadcasts, religious services, newspaper editorials and traditional poetry, whereas the low variety will be used for everyday conversation, sports commentary, soap opera and other informal contexts. Clear examples of diglossia are to be found in the Arabic-speaking world. In most, if not all, Arab countries two varieties of Arabic exist side by side – Colloquial Arabic learnt informally at home as the first language, and Classical Arabic acquired by explicit instruction at school. The grammar, pronunciation and some of the vocabulary of the two forms of Arabic are different. The language of the Qur'ān – the sacred text of Islam – is in Classical Arabic; and partly for this reason the high variety is fairly uniform throughout the Arabic-speaking world, despite strong regional variations in the local variety of Colloquial Arabic. Indeed, the availability throughout the Arab world of Classical Arabic helps to guarantee a degree of mutual intelligibility when speakers of quite divergent forms of Colloquial Arabic meet. Other diglossic situations may be found in Greece (between Classical Greek and Demotic Greek) and in Switzerland (between High German and Swiss German). While English-speaking communities do not seem to display such strong internal division into two contrasting varieties, it is still possible to recognise a cline or scale of competing varieties which are accorded differing degrees of prestige.

See also: **Code, Dialect**

Further reading: Ferguson (1972)

DISCOURSE

A term now quite widely used in a number of different disciplines and schools of thought, often with different purposes. Most uncontroversially, it is used in linguistics to refer to verbal utterances of greater magnitude than the sentence. *Discourse analysis* is concerned not only with complex utterances by one speaker, but more frequently with the turn-taking interaction between two or more, and with the linguistic rules and conventions that are taken to be in play and governing such discourses in their given context.

However, the concept of discourse has also developed, separately, out of post-structuralism and semiotics. Here it really represents an attempt to fix, within one term, some of the theoretical ground gained in the early days of the structuralist enterprise. To grasp its significance you have to remember that in this early period structuralism/semiotics was above all an oppositional intellectual force, whose proponents were attempting to criticise and transform the inherited habits of thought and analysis about the question of where meaning comes from. Traditionally, and even now most 'obviously', meaning was ascribed to objects 'out there' in the world, and to the inner essences and feelings of individuals. Structuralism took issue with these ideas, insisting that meaning is an effect of signification, and that signification is a property not of the world out there nor of individual people, but of language. It follows that both the world out there and individual consciousness are themselves comprehensible only as *products*, not *sources*, of language/signification. But the problem with this conclusion is that it is too free-floating and abstract; it gives the impression that – not only in principle but also in practice – the world and the word can mean whatever we like.

Life isn't so simple. The abstract concept of 'language' proved inadequate to account for the historical, political and cultural 'fixing' of certain meanings, and their constant reproduction and circulation via established kinds of speech, forms of representation, and in particular institutional settings. This is the point at which the concept of discourse began to supplant the now imprecise notion of 'language'. Unlike 'language', the term *discourse* itself is both a noun and a verb. Thus it is easier to retain the sense of discourse as an *act*, where the noun 'language' often seems to refer to a thing. In its established usages, discourse referred both to the interactive process and the end result of thought and communication. Discourse is the social process of making and reproducing sense(s).

Once taken up by structuralism, largely through the writings of Michel Foucault (see **power**), the concept of discourse proved useful to represent both a very general theoretical notion and numbers of specific discourses.

The general theoretical notion is that while meaning can be generated only from the langue or abstract system of language, and while we can apprehend the world only through language systems, the fact remains that the resources of language-in-general are and always have been subject to the historical developments and conflicts of social relations in general. In short, although langue may be abstract, meaning never is. Discourses are the product of social, historical and institutional formations, and meanings are produced by these institutionalised discourses. It follows that the potentially infinite senses any language system is capable of producing are always limited and fixed by the structure of social relations which prevails in a given time and place, and which is itself represented through various discourses.

Thus individuals don't simply learn languages as abstract skills. On the contrary, everyone is predated by established discourses in which various subjectivities are represented already – for instance, those of class, gender, nation, ethnicity, age, family and individuality. We establish and experience our own individuality by 'inhabiting' numbers of such discursive subjectivities (some of which confirm each other; others, however, coexist far from peacefully). The theory of discourse proposes that individuality itself is the site, as it were, on which socially produced and historically established discourses are reproduced and regulated.

Once the general theoretical notion of discourse has been achieved, attention turns to *specific discourses* in which socially established sense is encountered and contested. These range from media discourses such as television and news, to institutionalised discourses such as medicine, literature and science. Discourses are structured and inter-related; some are more prestigious, legitimated and hence 'more obvious' than others, while there are discourses that have an uphill struggle to win any recognition at all. Thus discourses are power relations. It follows that much of the social sense-making we are subjected to – in the media, at school, in conversation – is the working through of an ideological struggle between discourses: a good contemporary example is that between the discourses of (legitimated, naturalised) patriarchy and (emergent, marginalised) feminism. Textual analysis can be employed to follow the moves in this struggle, by showing how particular texts take up elements of different discourses and articulate them (that is, 'knit them together').

However, although discourses may be traced in texts, and although texts may be the means by which discursive knowledges are circulated, established or suppressed, discourses are not themselves textual.

Further reading: for discourse analysis in linguistics see Coulthard and Montgomery (1981); for the concept of discourse in post-structuralism see Mills (1997) and Sturrock (1979), introduction and chapter on Foucault.

DIVERSITY

Recognition of difference in politics, culture and heritage. Early discussions of diversity in the media context concentrated on diversity of ownership of media corporations, in order to ensure plurality of published opinion. The idea, backed up by media ownership laws in many countries, was that multiple viewpoints were preferable to a limited selection. More recently the idea of diversity has been extended to entire cultures: the rise of **multiculturalism**, and post-colonial and diasporic theory has led to calls for diversity as a fundamental goal of human endeavour, as well as public policy.

The exact outcomes of media diversity policies can be difficult to identify. One area of activism in the name of diversity has been the attempt to disrupt existing hegemonic structures by enabling minority groups to be represented or to participate in the production of media content. For instance, diversity is a chief concern of studies that investigate industry practices in the casting of performers from culturally diverse backgrounds. Diversity is also often used as a justification for public service and community broadcasting. In both of these instances the goal is to address the lack of representation of particular groups in commercial media.

See also: **Diaspora, Ethnic/ethnicity, Hegemony, Public sphere, Regulation**

DIY CULTURE

The form taken by youth activism and media citizenship in and after the 1990s. Associated with raves and free dance parties, **culture jamming**, eco-protests such as anti-road-building campaigns and DIY media such as *Squall*, a magazine produced by and for squatters

(McKay, 1998). By extension DIY culture referred to new possibilities for self-determination down to the individual level, emancipated from territorial and ethnic boundaries; a kind of voluntarist citizenship based on cultural affiliation rather than obligations to a state or territory (Hartley, 1999).

Interactive media changed the by-now traditional relation of mass media, where one centralised (corporate or state) institution communicated *to* many anonymous individuals. But the conceptualisation of that relation had itself evolved. Mass society theory posited a passive mass that responded behaviourally to stimuli. Marxist analysis wanted an active, struggling mass, but one that was still oppressed, repressed or otherwise overpowered or 'overdetermined' by the hegemony of state and commercial institutions. A variant of that position was Michel de Certeau's notion of 'poaching', suggesting that individuals and citizens took or appropriated their own meanings from within the given structures of power and influence, much as pedestrians make their own way, their own patterns, meanings and uses, out of the streets of a city whose structure and direction they cannot alter (see de Certeau, 1984).

Meanwhile ethnographies of audiences for media began to develop a notion of community with internal relations of mutuality, solidarity and action for their various subjects, whether these were studied in terms of their social class (Morley, 1980), gender relations (Morley, 1986; Gray, 1992), ethnicity (Gillespie, 1995) or sexual orientation (Doty, 1995). With interactive media, customisation and feedback, the concept of the user displaced that of the audience. Instead of culture determining or even dictating identity, via institutions and obligations people had to live with whether they liked it or not, DIY culture described a more interactive relation between centralised institutions and individual people or groups.

Hartley (1999) extended the concept of DIY culture into this context on the basis of the evolving history of citizenship. Classic citizenship theory, based on the work of T. H. Marshall in the 1940s, recognised three historical stages to citizenship:

- civic freedoms (individual rights)
- political freedoms (voting rights)
- social freedoms (welfare and employment rights)

Following analytical trends of the time, Hartley suggested adding two further historical stages to citizenship:

- cultural citizenship (paradoxically corresponding with the era of mass media such as television) involved the winning of cultural freedoms (identity rights);
- DIY citizenship (to date) DIY rights allowed for the freedom to choose affiliations.

Phase 5 was DIY culture. Instead of accepting their role as passive media audiences or consumers, people could form or join taste constituencies or communities of affiliation and produce their own culture.

See also: **Cultural citizenship, Culture jamming, Democratainment**

DOT.COM CRASH

In May 2000, the world witnessed a major crash in Internet stock prices (see **nasdaq**). The biggest casualties were the 'dot.coms': e-businesses trading on web addresses. Despite the popular mythologising of Internet entrepreneurs as inexperienced graduates, blame cannot be cast completely on the dot.com workers themselves. There was substantial intellectual capital in many of the failed businesses. As Mills (2001) writes: 'the share prices collapsed simply because they had been bid up to irrational and unsustainable levels'. Venture capitalists in particular had leapt to provide start-up dot.coms with sometimes astoundingly large sums of money, placing unreasonable expectations on new firms in a new industry to get it right first time. Investors expected to reap fast returns, unfazed by the fact that few dot.coms could claim to be making a profit. In other words, the new, weightless economy was too lightly entered into.

At the same time, the Federal Reserve was creating an excess of money in order to cope with the expected devastation of Y2K. In the subsequent anticlimax, excess money was poured into the dot.com sector by Wall Street brokers. When the Federal Reserve decided that monetary tightening was needed, the dot.coms were the major casualties. Commentators in the pages of business journals competed to devise the slickest epitaph for the once hip industry. The 'dot.com crash', became the 'dot.bomb', the 'dot.dumb' and the 'tech wreck'. The abbreviation 'b2c', as in business-to-consumer, became the Silicon Valley's term for 'back to Cleveland' (Fischer, 2001).

Afterwards, it was repeatedly stated that 'the crash was a good thing' (Gimein and Diba, 2001). The **new economy** did not die and history remained on its side. The expansion of railways in the 1850s, and of cars in the 1920s, were both followed by horrific stock market collapses in the US, but neither railways nor automobiles went away. Similarly, the technological innovations developed during the rapid expansion of the Internet will lead to a sustainable industry in the long term, despite the crash.

DUMBING DOWN

A term used by cultural elites as an intellectual 'KEEP OUT' sign. It is used when a concept, event or issue has been made available to a wider audience by being presented differently or more simply. The film *Forrest Gump* was a particularly popular target for the dumbing-downers who saw the film as a populist, mainstream rendition of American history.

Critics and intellectuals have a way of making their position legitimate by using exclusive language. By declaring that using mainstream culture to convey complex ideas is dumbing down, some seek to maintain the division between the intellectuals and everybody else. It is a refusal to acknowledge that learning, the production and communication of important ideas, and creative expression can occur in popular texts.

If *Forrest Gump* – a white, simple-minded, male – can walk through events such as the civil rights movement of the 1960s or the Vietnam War and remain unscathed, innocent and unreflective, then criticism of the film's rendition of American history is warranted. However, accusations of dumbing down do little to make this point clear. Rather, it implies that American history is better restricted to the audiences of history books and documentaries.

E-COMMERCE

Since the 1980s at least, businesses in most industries have been utilising some form of electronic technology in their commercial transactions. Widespread activities such as electronic funds transfer, automated banking facilities, tele-shopping and credit card transactions, can be included in the larger field of e-commerce, totalling trillions of dollars worth of financial activity. Economists often acknowledge the breadth of the e-commerce realm, yet focus on the area of e-commerce concerned with value-generating activity that occurs over the Internet or other networks that use non-proprietary protocols such as Intranets.

Non-proprietary systems are easy to access and are inexpensive compared to the dedicated communications systems of earlier forms of e-commerce. Where the latter relied on pre-existing commercial relationships and processes, e-commerce that takes place over the Internet uses standard coding and the World Wide Web interface. Consumer and business efficiency, in terms of cost, distance and time, and potential scale, is therefore the key attribute of Internet e-commerce. The OECD in 1999 predicted that this new commercial arena would 'radically alter economic activities and the social environment through its influence on day-to-day, routine business dynamics' (Wyckoff, 1999).

Since the **dot.com crash** of May 2000, e-commerce enthusiasts have toned down such predictions. E-commerce initiatives continue successfully to expand a range of business interests, but e-commerce is now seen as an additional means of business distribution that complements, rather than eliminates, other distribution avenues (such as physical shop-front presence). Established retailers with significant resources, brand recognition and real-world presence have successfully expanded their business through e-commerce. Profiting from new, Internet-only business initiatives has proved less successful. The chain-store Toys'Я'Us were able to maintain their electronic presence beyond a debilitating Christmas season while their Web-only competitor eToys folded.

Computer goods, entertainment, travel and discount brokerage sales account for more than 80 per cent of the online retail market. The majority of e-commerce activity, however, occurs between businesses (see **b2b**) rather than directly with the consumer. Business-to-business transactions that require speed and efficiency and the ability to overcome distance are more easily translated into the electronic realm than are retail sales.

See also: **Globalisation, Internet, Network society**

EDUTAINMENT

On the model of 'infotainment', 'edutainment' is a hybrid term which describes the use of media entertainment techniques in educational services. The term had pejorative connotations as part of the 'dumbing down' debate, suggesting that the substance of education was being sacrificed for the sake of ratings. But several truths were lost in that rhetoric.

- First, education itself has always been communicative as well as content-rich: the very term 'education' means 'drawing out' in Latin, referring to the Socratic method of teaching by drawing truth out through dialogue (not shovelling truth in via examinable 'facts').

- Second, throughout the mass-broadcasting era, entertainment has had an educative function. Films, popular newspapers and magazines mastered the technique of conveying information that people weren't previously interested in – often straightforwardly educative information about the state of the world, wonders of nature, the human condition, the costs and benefits of progress, etc. They used appealing visual and verbal techniques, circulation-boosting games and competitions, and attractive personalities, to win viewers, readers and listeners, and to persuade them to attend to things they didn't like.

- Third, education is itself a mass medium, and has been so at primary level since the nineteenth century. With the advent of lifelong learning, even tertiary education aspired not merely to mass coverage of the population, but to universal coverage. It became impossible not to use these techniques, even where they had been resisted previously.

- Fourth, once the challenge of universal education was accepted, the 'law' of **aberrant decoding** kicked in. Educators could not safely assume any shared code, or prior knowledge, among students. Like the universal entertainment media, they delivered texts of high **redundancy** (predictable information), with strong plot lines and characterisation, using charismatic presenters, in order to gather the diverse population within the fold, so as to teach them.

Naturally, the media could do this best when they took a good educator and made them into good television. In the sphere of cultural criticism, it all began with John Berger's *Ways of Seeing* (Berger, 1972), although Berger's series was in part a 'reply' to Lord Kenneth Clark's earlier and widely lauded series *Civilisation*. British TV has maintained an excellent record of edutainment: David Attenborough on all things living, Robert Hughes on art (an Australian living in the US, Hughes made several series for British TV), John Romer on archaeology, Howard Goodall's *Big Bang* on music, Patrick Moore on astronomy, Delia Smith on cooking. Americans cover their own history well – the

Civil War series created an entire genre of similarly presented narratives. Australia has a thriving export industry in nature and wildlife documentaries. This form of serious, interesting, entertaining information became the staple of entire channels such as Discovery or the History Channel.

Soon the media/education interface became very fuzzy. Traditional institutions used media and interactive technologies (video, online and interactive delivery) and entertaining 'software' (charismatic lectures) to service the learning needs of more students than could ever squeeze into their library. Open and business-related learning were both commercially catered and state supported. Publishers converted their backlists into virtual universities, entrepreneurs standardised learning services for profit. In short, 'education' merged with 'entertainment' in the name of the democratisation and universalisation of knowledge, via the recasting of education from its 'modern' status as national-state institution to its 'postmodern' status as customised learning services for sovereign and borderless consumers.

EFFECTS

The media effects tradition was the only game in town during the early decades of media research, especially in the US. Based on social psychology and aspiring to scientific status, the effects model sought to show *causal* links between media content and individual behaviour. It investigated the effects of sexual and violent content in popular film and television, comics or popular music on adolescents, women and other, supposedly vulnerable, groups.

The effects tradition arises from early communications studies, in which communication was understood as a linear process. Mass media were thought to stick messages into people much as a hypodermic needle squirts drugs into a body. Thus, producers of media **texts** were thought to inject representations and images into viewers (who had no choice but to accept them), and these 'stimuli' were expected directly to influence individuals' behaviour, opinions, attitudes or mind-set.

Research using this model was in two stages. First, researchers literally counted images and representations on TV that were considered worrying – 'violent acts' for instance – using **content analysis**. This established the existence of a problem. Second, sample 'subjects' were 'exposed' to the 'stimuli' – they were asked to watch a video tape – and their 'behaviour' was recorded, either directly using galvanometers and the like, or inductively via diary reports and questionnaires. The 'effect' of 'violence' on 'individuals' could then be measured. The researchers then attempted to link their results to social trends.

The problem with a methodology such as this is that it substituted the experimental situation for reality, and regarded audiences as isolated individuals, ignoring factors such as context and personal ideologies that viewers negotiate when watching media texts. The fact that energetic adolescent boys seemed more uppity when they had just seen a TV action show was said to demonstrate that television *causes* violence. Such a conclusion would have been much more convincing had researchers shown that the same 'stimuli' had the same 'effect' on a 'controlled' group of people who were not noted for their propensity for aggression – ministers of religion, for instance. But such work was never carried out. There was a good deal of wish-fulfilment in 'effects' research.

Challenges to the assumptions of the effects model began in the 1970s, with researchers such as Umberto Eco (1972) and Stuart Hall (1973) setting out to investigate whether single texts offered a variety of readings to differing audiences. Media studies recognised the impossibility of carrying out such a task on individuals and instead chose to instigate projects looking at individuals as members of nominated groups defined by, for instance, class, race and gender. Writers such as Hall, Fiske (1987), Ang (1985) and Morley (1980) all claimed that watching media texts was a process of negotiation between the text, a given audience and what ideologies, beliefs and values those groups bought to the process. From this research it was argued that audiences could no longer be thought of as passive recipients of information, rather that they were readers, who accepted, rejected, subverted and negotiated all media texts.

Gauntlett (1998: 121) provides a useful summary of the problems of the effects model. He suggests for instance that the tradition tackles the problem backwards, with researchers often looking at media images and tying these into recent deviancies, rather than approaching this research in reverse order. Pertinently he asks why the 'basic question of *why* the media should induce people to imitate its content has never been tackled' (1998: 127). The difficulty of knowing individuals, as opposed to the relative ease in a methodology that relies on counting, may provide some insight.

Government regulatory bodies, interest groups and sociologists all seemed to be exempt from the effects they saw in others among the population. What was it that made these groups invulnerable? The effects model is yet another of the dangerous categorisations that plague both the media and its audience, because the underlying agenda is always to suggest that if the media can be changed, the audience will become more civilised (like the researchers and their sponsors).

See also: **Audiences, Content analysis, Discourse, Violence**

Further reading: Gauntlett (1998)

ENTERTAINMENT

A regime of universally intelligible mainstream output from the leisure and content industries. Entertainment seems a common-sense term, but as deployed in contemporary media it comprises a complex condensation of individual gratifications, textual forms and industrial organisation.

Entertainment's production costs are high, so like other cultural or creative industries it is driven towards audience maximisation and the reduction of unit costs. The 'ideology' of such a regime is that these commercial imperatives merely supply the demands of the consumer: the form of entertainment reflects what is wanted. While strenuous efforts are indeed made to keep entertainment products both novel and appealing, it is also the case that such products are organised around an industrial mode of production, typically 'mass' communication of standardised content to a consumer who has little input into it. Hence entertainment is not so much an escape from the everyday cares of capitalism, but a highly advanced expression of them.

ETHNIC/ETHNICITY

Of peoples from other cultures. From 'ethnic' cuisine and crafts to subordinated national groups living in nation-states, the word 'ethnic' is a category for everything that fits outside of the dominant group or culture, especially when the latter is white, Western, mainstream culture. If you go into your supermarket you may find lentils on the 'ethnic' shelves. But in its darkest manifestation, ethnic has become a euphemism for genocide – 'ethnic cleansing'.

Although ethnicity as a concept has been used to disavow and overcome racist discourses, its use within the social sciences has often been used interchangeably and problematically with concepts of **race**. Ethnicity is conventionally understood to mean common, or shared, characteristics attributed to common descent. As the term ethnicity encompasses cultural qualities and attitudes, a seemingly natural correlation is often assumed between genetic lineage and cultural identity. By explaining cultural identity through biological makeup in this way, the concept of ethnicity can lead to reductionist conclusions and cultural essentialism: 'they are like that because it is in their blood' (Gillespie, 1995: 8).

As with the term 'race', one's ethnicity can be construed as something predetermined and inescapable. When this is coupled with ideas of otherness, subordination, marginality and foreignness, ethnicity can imply that a person's culture and status are fixed and unavoidable, and that this is what confirms them in that status. Ethnicity is often employed in conceptions of the **nation** to consolidate national identity as something typical of a particular geographic territory. However, the national identity invoked by the term ethnicity is generally not one's own but that of other countries/cultures.

Stuart Hall's work was influential in developing new understandings of ethnicity as something that everyone is part of. For Hall, ethnicity 'acknowledges the place of history, language and culture in the construction of subjectivity and identity, as well as the fact that all discourse is placed, positioned and situated, and all knowledge is contextual' (Hall, 1988: 29). Ethnicity is crucial to identity formation, yet it is not something predetermined or complete. Ethnicity, for Hall, is a 'project', something that we continually shape and through which we position ourselves.

See also: **Diaspora, Multiculturalism, Nation, Race**

ETHNOGRAPHY

A method of research that evolved out of the field of anthropology. It studies a group 'from the inside'. In anthropology this technique has been used as a means of understanding non-Western people's rites, culture and means of survival. In communications research, ethnography is concerned with understanding media audiences. During (1993: 20) argues that the approach has been adapted within cultural studies as a means of moving beyond theoretical discourses.

Within communications research, it is possible to identify three types of audience research (During, 1993: 21). *Quantitative research* involves undertaking large-scale surveys with a view to tracing a particular trend or pattern amongst participants (see Bourdieu, 1984;

Bennett *et al.*, 1999). The second type, *qualitative research*, utilises in-depth or focus interviews to identify similar patterns (see Morley, 1980; Morrison, 1998). Both of these methods resemble aspects of marketing research and are used within the media industry for tracking TV ratings. The final type of research is *ethnography*, which relies on **participant observation** (see Hobson, 1982). Arising directly from anthropological approaches, it involves the researcher immersing themselves with a nominated group in an attempt to gain insight into their choices and behaviour (for example, their viewing choices and practices).

Critics of ethnographic research question whether it is possible to gain an objective view of a culture simply by observing it. In particular, individuals involved in participant observation may be influenced by the observer's presence, thereby affecting the outcomes of the research. Can participants act or speak 'naturally' in the presence of a researcher? Do the participants subconsciously perform the role they believe the researcher wants to see or hear? The immersion of a researcher within a nominated group cannot guarantee unlimited access to the lived reality of that group, only a 'partial truth' (Clifford, 1986).

There are also concerns over the role of the researcher in ethnography. Whilst the necessary data collection associated with this method is acknowledged in ethnographic accounts, little mention is made of the actual process of writing. As Clifford (1986: 2) argues, ethnography often 'reflects the persistence of an ideology claiming transparency of representation and immediacy of experience'. This suggests the importance of recognising the researcher's own subjectivity and what it is that they bring to the research. The researcher, much like the group under analysis, will also be subject to ideologies and discourses that impact on the conclusions drawn. The researcher, like the objects of study in ethnography, should be understood as part of the text that may limit the findings of the project.

A development within ethnographic audience research that sought to avoid the issue of objectivity was the study of fan cultures undertaken by researchers who saw themselves as part of the same collective (see Jenkins, 1992; Brooker, 2002). Here, the researcher makes no claims to objectivity, offering instead an insight from within a particular group. This subjective approach provides two texts – the role and the assumptions of the researcher and the findings of the inquiry. This approach overturns the need to speak on behalf of, and instead offers the possibility of a 'two-way transmission of information' (During, 1993: 22).

See also: **Audiences, Effects, Methodology, Objectivity, Participant observation**

Further reading: Clifford (1986); Gillespie (1995); Moores (1994)

EX-NOMINATION

'Un-naming'. Things that are so obvious that they do not need to be named; they are naturalised. The term was coined by Barthes (1973). In relation to class, he showed that the bourgeoisie in France at the time was the 'class that does not want to be named'. Although there were political parties in the National Assembly that supported capitalism, none came straight out with it and called themselves 'The Capitalist Party'. This was another example of **ideology** at work. The process worked towards naturalising existing arrangements of power. Whilst the examples he used may not be as relevant today, the issues brought forward by the concept can readily be applied to other aspects of contemporary culture.

The idea of **gender** is certainly one area in which ex-nomination still seems relevant. As many have argued, men are rarely nominated or named in many discourses. An example of this is the ITV drama *The Bill* in which, following police nomenclature, the women have the title WPC (Woman Police Constable) while their male colleagues are simply PCs (not MPCs). In politics, when women enter parliament, it somehow seems only natural for journalists to report their role as wife/ mother as well as politician, and comment on their appearance. Male politicians who are fathers are rarely asked about balancing work and childcare.

Ex-nomination is normal in discussions of **race** and sexuality. Richard Dyer (1997) as a white male notes how other people are raced – 'but we are just people' (1997: 1) – highlighting the naturalising process that comes with ex-nomination. It is rare to hear news about a crime announcing that 'police have arrested five white youths' although it is not uncommon for people of colour, be they Asian, black or Aboriginal, to be nominated in such reports. It is also rare to hear people referred to as heterosexual. Indeed, heterosexuality is the 'sexuality that does not want to be named': the study of sexuality is usually concerned with the 'sexual other', 'defined in relation to normative heterosexuality' (Richardson, 1996: 1).

As these examples demonstrate, ex-nomination works to mask discursive practices and to normalise certain categories in contrast to others. The ideological implications of this process are that certain privileged positions in culture are able to present themselves as beyond **discourse** and outside of the act of naming.

See also: **Identity politics, Representation**

Further reading: Fiske (1989b)

FOREGROUNDING

A communicative element may be said to be foregrounded when it is made the focus of attention for its own sake. The term derives from the work of the Russian and Czech Formalists during the 1920s who developed the concept as part of a theory which argued that literature was a specialised and distinctive mode of communication. Literature (and poetry in particular) was different from everyday communication because of the systematic foregrounding of selected linguistic components. These stood out against the background of everyday communicative norms in one of two ways – either by rule-breaking or by rule-making. Thus, one kind of foregrounding consists of manipulating the normal rules of linguistic communication by bending or breaking them, as in the following poem by e. e. cummings:

> Me up at does
> out of the floor
> quietly Stare
> a poisoned mouse
> still who alive
> is asking What
> have i done that
> You wouldn't have

Among other things, the first four lines scramble the more usual ordering of elements in an English clause, which in normal prose writing would be likely to read 'a poisoned mouse does quietly stare up at me out of the floor'. This is one of several ways (including, for example, the adoption of unusual patterns of punctuation) in which the poem breaks the normal rules of English.

Another kind of foregrounding involves the superimposition of extra rules or patterns beyond those required to ensure intelligibility.

The use of rhyme, alliteration and metrical rhythm amounts to just such patternings at the level of sound in poetry.

Foregrounding may also be achieved through additional syntactic patterning as in the following short poem by Shelley:

> One word is too often profaned
> For me to profane it;
> One feeling too falsely disdained
> For thee to disdain it;
> One hope is too like despair
> For prudence to smother;
> And pity from thee more dear
> Than that from another.

The first four lines of the poem are built up from a simple syntactic pattern of the following type:

> One $-X-$ (is) too $-Y-$ $-Z-$ed
> For $-M-$ to $-Z-$ it;

where X = noun, Y = adverb, Z = verb stem and M = pronoun. The pattern is so strong at the beginning of the poem that the second pair of lines exactly parallels the syntax of the first pair. The rhetorical force of the last two lines, however, derives – in part at least – from the way in which it breaks from the pattern established so strongly at beginning. In both these ways, therefore – by rule-making and rule-breaking – elements of the language are foregrounded.

According to the Formalists this foregrounding was more than language calling attention to itself. 'Making strange' the language in this way was in fact part of making everyday experiences unfamiliar. By manipulating the rules of the language, literature extends its communicative possibilities, frees itself from its automatic ways of rendering the world and achieves special rhetorical effects.

However, a crucial shortcoming of the Formalist account is the way in which it neglected to notice some of the identical processes at work in non-literary texts. Parallel structures of syntax, for instance, may be found quite commonly in political speeches, advertising and other kinds of persuasive discourse. Thus, when Neil Kinnock (a UK Labour politician) produces the following sentences in the course of a speech, he is adopting precisely the kind of repetitive syntactic patterning identified by the Formalists as peculiar to poetry:

We are ruled by a Government
whose rhetoric is resolution but whose reality is industrial ruin,
whose rhetoric is efficiency but whose reality is collapse.
Their rhetoric is morality,
their reality is unemployment, which splits or scatters families.

Similar kinds of syntactic patterning may also be found in advertising:

PERFUMERY
THE PERFUME YOU WEAR SAYS A LOT ABOUT YOU
The range we have says something about us.
Nothing triggers memories as strongly as scent.
Just a hint of a familiar fragrance brings back that Time.
That Place.
That Person.
Names are forgettable
Even photos fade,
But perfume lingers.

Here again, as with the poem and the speech, we can find in the first
two lines of the advert a parallel syntactic structure:

The –X– –Y– –Z– says –N– about –Y

where X = noun, Y = pronoun, Z = verb and N = quantifying
expression. We also have quite marked sound patterning with an
identical initial sound used in the words 'familiar', 'fragrance',
'forgettable', 'photos', 'fade' and 'place', 'person', 'perfume'. In light
of evidence such as this, it would seem that the attempt of the
Formalists to identify poetry (or even 'literariness') with foregrounded
features of language is impossible to sustain. Instead, what counts as
poetry seems to be as much a matter of social judgements as textual
properties. However, this does not mean that the notion of
foregrounding is thereby only of historical interest. It is noticeable,
for instance, that the kind of extract singled out above from a political
speech is precisely that part of the speech most likely to elicit applause
in the context of its initial delivery, and the part most likely to be
excerpted for subsequent news broadcasts. Foregrounded uses of
language, therefore, seem to be strongly associated outside literature
with rhetoric – with acts of verbal persuasion – and the notion of
foregrounding retains its interest as part of this broader study.

See also: **Code, Metaphor, Text/textual analysis**

Further reading: Atkinson (1984); Bennett (1979); Leech (1966)

FRANKFURT SCHOOL

The principal members of the Frankfurt School encompassed philosophy, sociology, literary criticism, economics, psychology and political science in their expertise. Max Horkheimer, Theodore W. Adorno, Walter Benjamin, Erich Fromm, Leo Lowenthal, Herbert Marcuse, Franz Neumann and Friedrich Pollock are considered to be the major contributors, with Jürgen Habermas identified as the School's leading second-generation thinker.

The Institute of Social Research was established in Frankfurt in 1923. The historical importance of this time set the scene for the theoretical direction that the Institute (labelled the Frankfurt School in the 1960s) would take. Lenin was to die a year after the group's formation, signifying the advent of Stalinism in Russia and what was to become a centralist and tyrannical turn in the Russian Revolution. The Social Democratic Party in Germany, whilst maintaining Marxist rhetoric, pitted itself against more revolutionary socialist groups. By 1930, the deterministic Marxist belief that socialism was an inevitable progression from capitalism appeared less certain as fascism swept through Germany, Italy and Spain. As Held writes, the rise of Hitler signified 'the end of an era and, for all those committed to the struggle against capitalism, a desperate irony' (Held, 1980: 19).

'Critical theory', the umbrella title for the Frankfurt School's contribution to cultural studies, emerged out of the theoretical tradition of Marxism and the critical philosophy of Kant. Although critical theory does not present a singular theory or worldview, the school was united in its position that fascism was the result of a crisis in capitalism. This departure from Marxism lay in the belief that capitalism had developed strategies for avoiding crisis and the possibility of demise through proletariat revolution. The working class, which was to serve as the agents of revolution for Marx, was seen by the critical theorists to be caught up in what they saw as capitalism's tendency towards conformity. Technology, mass production techniques, the commodification of artwork and new class configurations were limiting the opportunities for a disruption of the existing social order. The culture industries – or 'distraction factories' as Kracauer called them – were central to the massification of ideas and the resulting cultural uniformity that left little room for productive political action.

The process of investigation for the Frankfurt School theorists had to be radically different from traditional philosophical idealism. If idealism had failed, as they believed, to unify separate disciplines through rational order, then the task of philosophy must be 'a process of continuous interpretation'. Interpretation for Adorno involved constructing historical truths out of the text of the social world (Pensky, 1997). Like a multidimensional puzzle, everyday articles, modern art and music, streets, films and dress that appeared to be randomly positioned could simultaneously be seen to make up a clear picture. Their encoded messages, Adorno believed, could be misleading and superficial if read apathetically. In order to see the true picture – and to bring about the dissolution of the puzzle itself – the viewer must necessarily take a step back, engage in continual critique, shattering accepted conceptual systems. This was the task of the critical theorist, intended to release conceptual thought from the repressive confines of scientific reason and to point out the gaps and exits on the pathway to a seemingly unavoidable capitalist type of 'progress'.

Adorno called this approach negative dialectics. Negative dialectics is a means of confronting ideologies as they manifest in social relations. This requires recognising that we only grasp the meaning of objects by attaching our own conceptual label to them: our history, knowledge, thoughts and assumptions. 'Identity thinking' is therefore bringing our generalised conceptions to act as a classifying scheme to new experiences in order to comprehend what would otherwise be unmediated intuition. If we are able to acknowledge the insufficiency of this comprehension, then we are able to view the value of the object as part of a historical process. Only through such 'immanent' criticism can we know its limitations, contradictions and place within the world. Therefore, rather than seeing society as simply an object (as it is understood through a scientific approach), it is a subject-object: it is the object as well as the subject of knowledge. In order to understand society, we must know its processes, and by doing so we can disclose its contradictions. Although the Frankfurt School theorists differed widely in their approaches, their legacy has become that of the power of critique: 'with criticising ideology and thus helping to create awareness of the possibility of a break with the existing structure of domination' (Held, 1980: 357).

Perhaps the most significant contribution of the Frankfurt School was its lasting transformation of the political out of the limited subjects of the state and economy and into new areas of ownership, culture and everyday life (although literary critics sought to do this also). In doing so, the critical theorists presented a unique analysis of culture and the ways in which ideologies penetrate everyday activities and concerns. However, in breaking away from established philosophical schools, and yet offering no clear direction or means to overcome the domination they identified, the Frankfurt School has attracted a great deal of hostility. Marxists have criticised the School for failing to ground their assessment within a practical economic analysis, and for sacrificing materialist science for metaphysics. More recently within cultural studies, the Frankfurt School has been accused of presenting an unsatisfactory notion of domination within the cultural industries. In portraying mass culture as a means to a type of 'thought control', Adorno and Horkheimer in particular overestimate the deliberate, conspiratorial use of technology to shape attitudes. This approach ignores the fact that culture is created out a complex interplay of a range of influences and institutions and that audiences are capable of engaging with and selecting culture rather than being merely passive recipients.

See also: **Public sphere**

Further reading: Bronner and Kellner (1989); Wiggershaus (1994)

GAMES (COMPUTER/VIDEO)

Games – beginning in the 1970s as 'video' games, progressing to become known as 'computer' games and now just as 'games' as they displace analogue pastimes – are the newest 'mass medium' of technological-recreational fantasy entertainment. They are played using TV/computer screens and software and may be located residentially or in retail arcades. Of Japanese and Korean origin (Nintendo, Sega, Sony), they represent the first mass medium not invented in the West. Games began with a one person vs one machine (software) format, but are now fully interactive, with multiple players linked over the Internet. Famous at the outset for 'manga'-style graphics, straightforward martial-arts violence and the promotion of reflexive skills, games have proliferated in type, diversified their user-base (they are now used by girls and 'wrinklies' as well as adolescent boys) and become as sophisticated as movies in the graphics and spatial architecture department. Indeed, the movie and games industries are converging with movie versions of games such as *Tomb Raider* or *Dungeons and Dragons*, and games versions of movies.

The earliest home video game is thought to have been *Pong*, launched by Atari in 1972. An electronic table-tennis game, its rudimentary design was superseded at the beginning of the following decade by more graphically sophisticated arcade games such as *Space Invaders* and *Pac-man*.

It is surprising to note the lack of critical inquiry into this medium. What work has been done, however, suggests that, like other media before them, computer games reveal the ways in which society deals with the introduction of new technologies. Research began in the early 1980s with psychological studies, undertaken (as one would expect) to investigate the effects of game playing on children (see, for instance, Cooper and Mackie, 1986). While not all studies revealed the same response, popular public discourse at the time replayed the media effects tradition, suggesting links between game playing and violence among boys, attention disorders and anti-social behaviour. Here was a continuation of the very same rhetoric that had greeted the popular press in the early days of the nineteenth-century, Hollywood, comics and television in the 1950s, 'video-nasties' in the 1970s and the Internet in the 1990s. In other words, games continue to provide evidence that new popular media are greeted with anxiety by control cultures.

Other researchers have investigated the relationship between games and gender. Some chose to examine the representation of women in games (for example, Provenzo, 1991). Others were more concerned with the gender-specific nature of the games industry (see Cassell and Jenkins, 1998). The concern here was that game playing appeared to be a masculine activity: games were developed by males for males. Girls and women were ostracised by technological development and computers, giving their male counterparts an unfair advantage in later life (Cassell and Jenkins, 1998a: 14). Here again, the anxiety about access and skills acquisition related to technology rather than to games themselves. And the gender divide in games is no longer so starkly one-sided: women and girls now both design and play them.

Media studies has used analytical tools designed for previous forms of media to analyse new forms – much like the application of film theory to television in its early years. The same is true of games. Using narrative analysis Skirrow (1990) has argued that games share elements that are common to most literature and film narratives. But as Darley (2000: 160) argues, gaming is about puzzle-solving leading to further spectacle, rather than to narrative closure of the traditional kind. Narrative analysis may not be appropriate to games; certainly when game formats have been made into feature films, they are routinely criticised for lack of narrative development and sensibility. Critical judgements aside, games are structured around action/space rather than narrative/time, and around use not story-telling.

Some comparisons between games and other media have proven more useful. Fuller and Jenkins (1995) argue that the narratives and game playing of games are analogous to the emergence of early science fiction writing in the late nineteenth century. Both create imaginary spaces for intellectual exploration. Jenkins (2000) continues to explore this idea by arguing that the experimentation and innovation provided by games are beginning to reveal themselves in cinema. For Jenkins, the multidirectional plotting of *Run Lola Run* and the reality/fantasy binaries of *The Matrix* demonstrate the influence of new games media on older forms of entertainment.

Darley (2000: 25) notes that while games were a progression from science fiction and Tolkienesque fantasy genres, they are also the descendants of pinball. Research into video games as *games* and the role of 'gameplaying' is a recent development (see Banks, 1998). Here, the emphasis is on the activity involved in video games rather than simply the content or aesthetics. Continuing research in this area aims to suggest new ways of understanding the interactivity between individuals and technology.

Further reading: Darley (2000); Jenkins (2000)

GATEKEEPER

A term that refers to key personnel involved in the decision-making processes of news production. Originally, the role was understood as being situated between news gatherers (journalists) and the public: *editors* kept the gate – opening or closing it for each story as they decided which information was newsworthy. Recent adaptation of the term has seen it applied to *managers* of the media, as well as news wire services and *owners* of media channels.

The importance of gatekeeper theory rests on an understanding of the conditions under which these personnel make their decisions. While practitioners understand their role as a professional one, analysts argue that gatekeepers are influenced by a range of practices, and these in turn influence their decisions. They include personal ideologies and values, as well as organisational and structural procedures. While the term is usually applied to media involved in the production of news, it is possible to consider its relevance elsewhere. Film-studio executives, television programme-buyers and radio play-list decision-makers could also be understood to be fulfilling the role traditionally set out by gatekeeper theory.

New media technologies such as digital broadcasting, pay-per-view and the Internet are seen as challenging the gatekeeping role. But this may prove to be a utopian assumption. Certainly with the Internet, search engines can be understood as digital gatekeepers. Performing the role of deciding what information is relevant to your query, search engines may not be bound by personal ideologies, yet they are a product of the structural and organisational procedures of the provider who supplies them. They may also be subject to legislation that requires them to filter information, thereby causing them to perform a gatekeeping role on behalf of the state.

Further, it is clear that there is economic value in gatekeeping: people *want* information checked, evaluated and edited for them by professionals. Despite the huge amount of freely available information on the Internet, many of the most popular websites are those that edit, organise and manage information on behalf of consumers; indeed, they belong to brand-name media titles such as major newspapers and TV stations.

See also: **Bias, News values**

Further reading: Berkowitz (1997)

GENDER

A categorisation that separates men and women on the basis of assumed behaviours, values, attitudes and beliefs. Gender has come to be contrasted with sex, which refers to biological differences. Gender assumptions are based on ideology. Sexual differences are based on genitalia (biology). While sexual differences may be natural/scientific, gender differences are cultural.

As with any cultural constructs, gender *roles* must be learned, not least through the media. Early feminist approaches sought to question media representations of women, and 'sex-role stereotyping', using the tools of content analysis, semiotics and structuralism. More recent work has reconsidered this aim by asking whether it is possible for the terms 'man' or 'woman' to denote a common identity. The idea here is that claiming a gender as a means to deconstruct it inadvertently supports its construction and use in representation. The thing objected to is perpetuated by the very form of the objection.

This strand of thinking has invited attacks from those who argue that gender is not a matter of discourse or representation so much as a lived experience. But experience should not be attributed to distinct genders. Perceived behavioural differences and the reality of gender experience themselves result from discourses and ideology and the culture that supports them.

See also: **Discourse, Identity Politics, Ideology, Representation**

Further reading: Butler (1990)

GENRE

Genre can be understood as the categorisation of media **texts** according to shared characteristics. Arising from film studies (and before that literary and art criticism), the term can also be applied to fiction, popular music and television as well as media not usually thought of in generic terms, such as magazines or even news reporting.

Steve Neale (1981: 6) argues that genres can be understood as 'systems of orientations, expectations and conventions that circulate between industry, text and subject'. Accordingly genre analysis will concentrate either on the producers, the directors or the audiences of these texts. It is argued that for the producers, or more broadly speaking the industry that produces generic texts, genre stands as a means of creating an identifiable product for sale. This is evident in analysis of Hollywood where it has been argued that 'creativity' is forsaken in favour of formula, the latter being a term used to denigrate the specificities of film genres. The same hierarchy can be seen to exist in other media – in fiction between 'creative' literature (non-generic) and generic forms such as romance or thrillers, or in television between the 'single play' (non-generic) and 'formula' formats such as soap operas or game shows.

The relationship between creators of media texts and genre has remained largely within the tradition of film theory. Directors such as John Ford, for example, are praised for their subtle manipulation of genre (see McBride and Wilmington, 1975) and for utilising the conventions of genre to remit their personal vision of culture and society.

Praise such as this is rarely awarded to the audience in the study of genres, as audiences were understood to use genre simply as means of making choices of what to view, read or listen to, and as a means of interpreting these texts. Early research went as far as suggesting that for audiences, genres 'demarcate appropriate thought, feeling and behaviour and provide frames, codes and signs for constructing a shared social reality' (Ryan and Kellner, 1988: 77).

In film theory, genres are recognisable largely for recurring iconography, repetition of **codes** and conventions, as well as familiar plot lines. Iconography refers to those elements which make up the visual aspects of a text – for instance, in Westerns a certain style of clothing and familiar setting for the action such as a desert or a mid-Western American town – with horses – is expected. Codes and conventions can best be explained as the technical elements that contribute to generic meaning. They include the song and dance numbers in a musical, or the darkened point of view shots and menacing soundtrack in a horror film. While these features can readily be uncovered in genre analysis, they are also subject to variation – an extremely important feature of the generic text – and one that is most revealing in the narrative.

Neale argues that 'each new genre film tends to extend [its] repertoire, either by adding a new element or by transgressing one of the old ones' (1990: 56), as is apparent in the film *Scream*. Although classified as a horror film, *Scream* was by no means typical of the conventions, as its use of comedy at the expense of the rule of genre demonstrated. Films such as these confirm that genres can be progressive, dynamic and subject to re-invention; but then fall back into formula (see *Scream 3*).

See also: **Mode of address, Narrative**

Further reading: Grant (1995)

GLOBALISATION

The components of globalisation are nothing new. Traffic across borders has been vigorously pursued for centuries. Cultural exchange and interdependence have occurred throughout history through colonisation, trade and exploration. The acceleration of industry via technological innovation describes the industrial age as much as the information age. And the notion of a citizenry of multiple allegiances subject to more than one sovereign power has long been the case in some countries, especially former colonies.

The word 'globalisation' is better used to describe a recent *intensification* of networks, alliances and interconnections in economics, cultures and politics and the particular form that they now take rather than the occurrences themselves.

The economic phenomenon of globalisation has seen the deployment of business and capital across borders at an unprecedented pace since the 1980s. It entails changes in the systems and structures of trade. Examples include:

- communication systems through which business is conducted;
- work practices and the skills required to direct capital effectively;
- new legal and institutional regimes required to control, order and manipulate markets.

In the process, globalisation has seen international trade and capital uprooted from national economies. **E-commerce** allows for the trading of goods in international electronic space, stimulating the creation of new services and faster flows of capital, capable of transcending direct government strategies of control and intervention. With new technology foreign currency markets can transact billion-dollar transfers across the world in a split second (see **nasdaq**). Not only is the extension of the economy into areas beyond nation-state governance causing concern over the ability of nation-states to act, but the pace and magnitude at which capital is mobilised have left banks incapable of influencing exchange rates in ways in which they are expected to (Sassen, 1999).

The map of globalisation is one where separate national economies are becoming part of a new decentred economy. Nation-states now do not have national economic strategies so much as 'strategies operating in a global economic system' (Castells, 1999: 48). Fears that countries will lose their autonomy – that globalisation will bring about the dissolution of nation-states – have emerged as a result, reinforced by the formation of trade blocks, a single currency for Europe and the development of international law.

However, nation-state power is essential for globalisation processes in many respects. States are complicit in globalisation as it is their consent that advances the global economy in order to improve their own economic standing. Furthermore, the dominant countries have played an important role in the provision of legal and policy frameworks essential to the operations of multinational corporations.

Globalisation is not simply an economic occurrence. Its cultural dimension includes global entertainment, fast food, fashion and tourism. Cultural globalisation is often understood as a form of Americanisation (see Nordenstreng and Schiller, 1993). However, such an approach denies the diversity of ways in which products are received, engaged with and transformed through cultural use. Such strategies and uses are far from uniform. 'Global' culture can exist alongside local and traditional communities, identities and tastes, encouraging a multiplicity of cultures and providing possibilities for new cultures to emerge.

Meanwhile, no-one can afford not to play. Countries such as China, which has a strongly centralised and nationalistic political culture, and a strong fear of both internal chaos and external interference, nevertheless greeted its belated acceptance into the WTO in December 2001 as a major milestone of national development. China's own size, dynamism and specificity will inevitably have 'feedback' effects on the globalised economy further down the track – influencing as much as it is influenced. The same is true for India.

Further reading: Calabrese (1999); Featherstone (1990); Lechner and Boli (2000)

HEGEMONY

A concept developed by Gramsci in the 1930s and taken up in cultural studies, where it refers principally to the ability in certain historical periods of the dominant classes to exercise social and cultural leadership, and by these means – rather than by direct coercion of subordinate classes – to maintain their power over the economic, political and cultural direction of the nation.

The crucial aspect of the notion of hegemony is not that it operates by forcing people against their will or better judgement to concede power to the already-powerful, but that it works by winning consent to ways of making sense of the world that do in fact make sense. They also happen to fit with the interests of the hegemonic alliance of classes, or *power bloc*. Hence our active participation in understanding ourselves, our social relations and the world at large results in complicity in our own subordination (see **power**).

The idea of winning consent extends the concept of hegemony beyond the analysis of class as such. In cultural analysis, the concept is used to show how everyday meanings, representations and activities are organised and made sense of in such a way as to render the interests of a dominant 'bloc' into an apparently natural and unarguable general interest, with a claim on everyone. Thus studies which concentrate on the hegemonic aspect of culture will focus on those forms and institutions which are usually taken to be impartial or neutral; 'representative' of everyone without apparent reference to class, race or gender. Such institutions span both public and private spheres – including the state, the law, the education system, the media and the family. They are prolific producers of sense, knowledge and meanings. Aside from their ostensible function, their cultural importance lies in their role as organisers and producers of individual and social consciousness. Although they are relatively autonomous from one another, peopled by different personnel with different professional skills and ideologies, nevertheless these cultural agencies collectively form the site on which hegemony can be established and exercised.

It follows that hegemony operates in the realm of consciousness and representations; its success is most likely when the totality of social, cultural and individual experience is capable of being made sense of in terms that are defined, established and put into circulation by the power bloc. In short, hegemony naturalises what is historically a class ideology and renders it into common sense. The upshot is that power can be exercised not as force but as 'authority', and 'cultural' aspects of life are de-politicised.

See also: **Bardic function, Class, Culture, Ideology, Power**

ICT

Information and Communications Technology. An update of Information Technology (IT).

IDENTIFICATION

A process that involves claiming characteristics attributed to another in order to make sense of the self. This theory of identification has its roots in psychology and psychoanalysis, which aim to understand the notion of the individual. Identification in these paradigms refers to the process of socialisation.

In media studies, theories of identification often refer to representations and their cultural consequences. In identifying with characters, the audience is thought to forgo the constructed nature of representations, experiencing them as if they were real (Fiske, 1987: 169). This process of identification allows representations to be understood as part of nature, instead of being experienced as cultural constructions. The implications of this have been explored by theorists such as Mulvey (1990), who argues that cinema uses conventions that invite identification with male characters while objectifying females. Mulvey's argument suggests a subordinate position for women is created via the conventions of the media. But such notions, organised around a psychoanalytical (and therefore transhistorical) concept of 'the' male gaze, have proven disabling and confining, giving very little scope for challenging and changing the process and terms of identification with media images.

See also: **Image, Mode of address, Representation, Subjectivity**

IDENTITY POLITICS

Social action organised around cultural rather than civic or political subjectivities. Identity politics aims to provide a form of political participation for those who are excluded from the traditional means of representation. Examples of this could include the feminist movement, gay and lesbian activism, ethno-nationalisms, as well as movements based on disability, youth and the environment.

Although identity politics is sometimes said to have arisen from the political upheavals of the 1960s, it is possible to recognise the suffragette movement of the 1900s as an early form of identity politics (see Parkins, 1997). In attempting to gain women's access to the right to vote, the suffragettes stand as an example of the grouping together of people with a shared identity for the purposes of political activism. Anti-colonial struggles throughout the twentieth century in the British, French and other European empires were also important in the development of identity politics. The civil rights movement in the 1960s and the rise of feminism brought such issues to the heart of contemporary public life, and to the top of the political agenda in Lyndon B. Johnson's Vietnam-era America. They called attention to the way that the traditional political sphere had failed so many, even its own supposed beneficiaries. At this point, attention was called to how 'education, language, lifestyle and representation were imbued with social consequences' (Shattuc, 1997: 2). The shift from public to private politics was succinctly captured in one of feminism's most famous slogans – 'the personal is political'.

The concept of identity is now often viewed as relying on shared characteristics that are cultural rather than natural/biological. As a result, political alliances based on an essentialist identity – one fixed in nature (origins and 'blood' or genes) rather than made in culture – is often viewed with alarm within radical circles (see Grossberg, 1996). Spivak's notion of 'strategic essentialism' (see Landry and Maclean, 1996) tries to get round the problem. It suggests forgoing the notion of the socially constructed and reclaiming a fixed identity in debates over cultural politics and policies. For while we may agree that, for instance, sexuality is a culturally constructed signifier, the rights and privileges awarded to heterosexual and homosexual individuals are markedly different. Here, 'strategic essentialism' supports the notion of a group of individuals coming together under the identity of 'gay' to participate in debates over equality, access and vilification. Similar arguments may be made about ethnic identity (see Gray, 2000) and ethno-nationalism, including Indigenous politics. Here, 'identity' means more than 'living as and being accepted by others in that culture'; it means having authenticated bloodlines showing a certain ethnic descent, consequential upon which may be various entitlements and rights, from land to welfare, policed, some have suggested, by DNA testing. Such a development in other domains of identity politics – for example in relation to the sometimes posited 'gay gene' – would be highly controversial.

Examples such as this illustrate that identity politics is by no means self-evidently radical or progressive, despite the fact that it is usually associated with marginal groups and with bringing disparate individuals together in the name of social, political and cultural equality. Another recent development in identity politics that demonstrates its reactionary potential is the rise of the men's movement (see Biddulph, 1994). Doubtless there are issues to do with masculine identity that need airing, but 'marginal' would not be the way to describe them. Some of the rhetoric of the men's movement is explicitly designed to undermine feminist positions; here 'identity' is presented as embattled when challenged *from* a marginal position.

IDEOLOGICAL STATE APPARATUSES

The material or institutional form taken by ideology in specified historical circumstances in class societies. Known in the trade as ISAs, and distinguished from RSAs or *repressive state apparatuses*, the two terms were coined by the French Marxist philosopher Louis Althusser (1971).

- *RSAs* are the complex of coercive or regulatory forces available to and directly under the control of the state. They include the penal system, the police, the army, the legislature and government administration. These are distinguished by their legitimated authority to command (whether we like it or not).
- *ISAs*, on the other hand, are various social institutions that arise within civil society (the sphere of the private, as opposed to the state). They too perform regulatory functions, and reproduce ideology 'on behalf of' the state. They include education, the family, religion, the legal system, the party-political system, culture and communication. They are characterised by consent rather than coercion and by their relative autonomy from the dominant economic class or its representatives in the state.

The function of ISAs is to reproduce our submission to the relations of production – to discipline us into the kind of subjectivity most conducive to the maintenance and continuity of the existing relations of production. They do so by representing class interests as both natural and neutral. They translate class into other terms. For instance, education is neutral because all are equal in front of the examination. But only certain ideologies pass exams. The legal system is neutral because all are equal in front of the law. But only certain acts are criminalised, and only certain ideological subjects are convicted. The media are neutral because their representations of the social world are impartial. But only certain ideologies are represented as worthy of impartial treatment; others are not. The party-political *system* is neutral because within it all positions and opinions can be voiced: except for non-party, extra-parliamentary political voices.

Further reading: Althusser (1971)

IDEOLOGY

Knowledge and ideas characteristic of or in the interests of a class. By extension, ideology can refer to the ideas of groups other than classes – ranging from gender (male ideology) to jobs (occupational ideology). Ideology is seen as any knowledge that is posed as natural or generally applicable, particularly when its social origins are suppressed, ex-nominated (see **ex-nomination**) or deemed irrelevant. In cultural/communication studies, ideology is seen as the practice of reproducing social relations of inequality within the sphere of signification and discourse.

Ideology as a theoretical concept comes from Marxism. In classic Marxism, the forms, contents and purposes of knowledge, representations and consciousness are not understood as abstracted from the material and social activities of production and class antagonism. On the contrary, the activity of production gives rise directly to knowledge of nature, and this knowledge of nature is directed towards further and increasing production by bringing all its myriad aspects as closely into line with general natural 'laws' as possible.

It is Marx's contention that knowledge of society arises in the same way – directly from class antagonism. But whereas knowledge of nature may be (at least in principle) of benefit to all classes, knowledge of society is produced and reproduced in the interests of those who are for the time being in a position of social supremacy (the ruling class). Thus, for Marx, knowledge of society differs from knowledge of nature by representing *as* natural those social arrangements that are in fact historically contingent. This is the starting point for a theory of ideology. The fundamental premises on which the Marxist concept of ideology is based are expressed in two of Marx's most celebrated contentions:

> The mode of production of material life conditions the social, political and intellectual life process in general. It is not the consciousness of men that determines their being, but, on the contrary, their social being that determines their consciousness.

> The individuals composing the ruling class possess among other things consciousness, and therefore think. In so far therefore, as they rule as a class and determine the extent and compass of an epoch, it is self-evident that they do this in its whole range, hence among other things rule also as thinkers, as producers of ideas, and regulate the production and distribution of the ideas of their age: thus their ideas are the ruling ideas of the epoch.

(Marx, 1977: 176, 389)

If the ideas of the ruling class are the ruling ideas of an epoch, then 'bourgeois ideology', for instance, should not be understood simply as what individual members of that class think, but as the prevailing ways of making sense that are established throughout bourgeois society. These ways of making sense may be produced and distributed not by the ruling class directly, but by relatively autonomous and apparently fragmented groups, ranging from intellectuals and teachers to media professionals and hairdressers.

The contention that social being determines consciousness gives rise to the Marxist notion of *false consciousness*. In the case of the ruling class itself, false consciousness occurs when that class imagines that its position in society is determined by the laws of God or nature – as in the doctrine of the divine right of kings for feudal monarchs, or the doctrine of individualism and the conception of society as a social contract in bourgeois philosophy. False consciousness for subordinate classes occurs when they make sense of their social and individual circumstances in terms supplied by the prevailing ideology, rather than in terms of their own class interests in opposition to the dominant classes. In this context, ideology is seen as the production and distribution of ideas in the interests of the ruling classes.

Thus ideology is the means by which ruling economic classes generalise and extend their supremacy across the whole range of social activity, and naturalise it in the process, so that their rule is accepted as natural and inevitable; and therefore as legitimate and binding.

For Marx, not all knowledge of society is necessarily ideological. In particular, the science of historical materialism (Marxism) itself could not be seen as an ideology, given the notion of ideology as illusory knowledge. The understanding gained in the struggle to change both society and nature is partial and limited and can be mistaken but, for Marxists, the objective existence of natural and historical laws is not open to question; nor is the belief that materialist science provides the means to make those laws known.

The concept of ideology has proved very influential in the study of communication and culture. So much so, in fact, that it has become somewhat over-extended in use. In particular, ideology has been reduced to a mere reflection of the economic base in some popularised versions of Marxism. As a result, ideology is often confined to the superstructure, where it is defined in terms of 'bodies' of thought, beliefs, ideas, etc., which reduces it from a conceptualisation of social relations and practices to a set of empirical things.

Just as language is hard to analyse if you look at words rather than the laws which produce words, so the reduction of ideology to ideas does not explain their production or forms. The concept needed to be re-theorised, and this led to the idea of *ideology in general*. This notion is associated in particular with Althusser (1971), for whom ideology is the mechanism which turns individuals into subjects, but it is also implicit in Volosinov (1973). It implies that all knowledge, whether scientific or otherwise, is produced within language, and that language is never a transparent medium through which truth can be observed. Hence all language is seen as ideological, and truth as a product not as a motivator of language. It follows from this that no specific discourse (including Marxism itself) is exempt from ideology. Instead, there are at any one time numbers of contending ideological discourses in play within an overall social formation, and that what is at stake in the way they are produced, deployed, regulated, institutionalised and resisted is not only knowledge but also power.

However, at the level of specific ideologies, it is clear that ideology is not a unitary medium that we inhabit like fishes in the medium of the sea. Even within what is often called a *dominant ideology* there are contending and conflicting positions – as between, say, different educational philosophies and policies. And ideology is always encountered in institutional forms and local circumstances which ensure that there is never a complete fit between dominant class interests and dominant ideology. Further, however naturalised and successful dominant ideologies might seem, they are always in contention with resistance to them from 'below', either in the form of coherent alternatives (feminism, Marxism) or as practical accommodations/rejections (see **subcultures**).

The concept of ideology has become central in the study of the media in particular and communication in general. It is useful in insisting that not only is there no 'natural' meaning inherent in an event or object, but also that the meanings into which events and objects are constructed are always socially oriented – aligned with class, gender, race or other interests. Further, ideology is not a set of things but an active practice, either working on the changing circumstances of social activity to reproduce familiar and regulated senses or struggling to resist established and naturalised sense thus to transform the means of sense-making into new, alternative or oppositional forms, which will generate meanings aligned to different social interests.

Further reading: Cormack (1992); Hall (1982); Hawkes (1996); Larrain (1979); Turner (1990)

IMAGE

The objectification of self-knowledge for communicative purposes. At an individual level, one's 'image' is made up of the cues by means of which others make sense of the **performance** of the self. These include visual attributes (one's looks and clothes) and intentionally communicative acts (speech, interaction with others), but also behavioural characteristics that project an image beyond the control of the self (a 'tearaway', 'self-confident' image, etc.).

At a cultural level, image is the alienation of personal attributes for semiotic purposes. The 'image' of various groups in the media, especially those taken to be vulnerable or open to victimisation, has been much studied. This is because it is widely feared that such alienated images of the self are projected back into real selves by the media, with material effects on behaviour and self-esteem.

The media images of women, ethnic minorities and various groups organised around marginal tastes, lifestyles, subcultures or regions have all been studied, often by an investigator who represents the group thus portrayed. Examples include 'images' of: women as projected by Hollywood and fashion; black, Aboriginal or migrant people projected in the news; gays and lesbians in popular culture; regions such as Northern Ireland or Palestine (for which 'calm footage' is all too rare). Such images are thought to have cultural and political, not just individual, consequences. Some analyses are sophisticated, for instance Annette Kuhn's *The Power of the Image* (1990), based on cinema theory and feminism. Others are more demotic, hotly contested within popular media themselves, including those by advocate organisations and activists, for a sample of which, see any issue of *Adbusters*.

Commercial organisations themselves have entered into image politics. For instance, Anita Roddick, founder of the Body Shop, purveyor of beauty and cleansing products, maintains a high-profile politico-advertising campaign against 'impossible' images of women (i.e. supermodels). Olivier Toscani, inspiration and photographer for Benetton, has made a career and a brand name out of subverting stereotypical images with Benetton advertisements.

The term 'image' has figured prominently in Western philosophy, ever since Plato proposed that humans do not perceive truth directly, but only in an indirect, distorted 'image'. Humans cannot see themselves as they are, Plato argued. Knowledge is perceived in distorted, indirect form, as if it were projected, like the shadows of dancers grotesquely capering on the wall of a cave in the light of the campfire. Such 'shadow-in-the-cave' images of a reality that is located elsewhere and beyond experience are all that humans can hope for, thought Plato. Thence, a conviction took hold of Western thinking that 'images' were opposed to reality, coterminous with illusion.

The natural pessimism of intellectuals was force-fed with a strong diet of self-loathing during the Christian era, when 'image' tended to be associated with the 'graven' or 'corporeal' – that is, with the trumpery and seductions of the flesh, attended by the temptations that contemplative monastic writers had to conquer. Thinking about 'images' became focused on the visual, the fleshly and the seductive, and on expressions of loathing for all that (and for women, who unwittingly but literally embodied it). Images drove the poor monks mad by luring then away from contemplation of the divine. Hence, and curiously, Western tradition has insisted that the most corporeal and self-evident *things* are 'illusory', while transcendent, metaphysical, irrecoverable phantasms are regarded as real.

Contemporary media and communication studies, to say nothing of politics, have inherited some of this confusion, regarding 'image' as unreal, illusory, seductive, feminised. Anything that devotes time to producing and maintaining its image in a professional way is automatically suspect – the very language is inherited from misogynist loathing of flesh – an image is 'tarted up', etc.

Less fatally, 'image' is now firmly locked into the *visual* register: people worry about looks, not sounds, for instance, and rarely get hot under the collar about the 'portrayal' of this or that group in music. The concept of image has become a staple of art history and cinema studies. This is a worry for film and television studies, for the fixation with images as largely visual phenomena neglects the complex interplay between sight, sound and sequence that screen media exploit. As a result, otherwise astute analyses appear to have been undertaken by people who are not clinically but culturally deaf.

Despite the pejorative attitude of the philosophical and metaphysical tradition, an image *industry* is now well established, from PR and marketing specialists, **spin** doctors and pollsters, to fashion advisers and stylists. No-one lasts long in public life, whether they are politicians, entertainers, athletes or even philosophers and bishops, without paying attention to their 'image'.

IMPARTIALITY

The doctrine of not taking sides in the reporting of public affairs in the broadcast (but not newspaper) media. Impartiality is the practical and pragmatic exercise of an accommodation between broadcasters and parliamentary political parties (especially the two governmental parties). It is a strategy whereby reporters are supposed to take account of: (1) a full *range* of views and opinions; (2) the relative *weight* of opinion (this means that established or orthodox views get priority over challenges to them); and (3) *changes* that occur in the range and weight of opinion over time.

Traditionally, impartiality had to be exercised *within* programmes. That is, if you quote a Tory viewpoint you must quote also a Labour viewpoint during the same programme. Since the advent of Channel 4, the notion of impartiality *between* programmes has gained acceptance. Here the idea is that, if the subject demands it, you may give just one position in a single programme, knowing that others will give the opposing view at another time. This development occurred largely as a result of pressure from broadcasters themselves. Some wanted to establish 'positioned journalism' with its own point of view, while others objected to having to stop a good story in its tracks while 'the two sides' slugged it out.

Impartiality is often distinguished from two other concepts, namely *balance* and *neutrality*. It is intended to overcome their shortcomings. Balance is the allocation of equal time to opposing viewpoints, where what is said is less important than the time given in which to say it. Neutrality is the indiscriminate accessing of any and every viewpoint without any principle of selection. This is deemed unsatisfactory because parliamentary politicians do not take kindly to airtime being given to groups or parties dedicated to the overthrow of parliamentary politics. Thus communist, nationalist and socialist parties operating outside the parliamentary framework are routinely denied access without broadcasters having to admit that they are failing to be impartial – they are merely not neutral. As a result, the doctrine of impartiality can be seen as a major prop to the parliamentary (two-party) *system*. It is, in the UK at least, a statutory requirement laid on broadcasters by Parliament.

IMPLICATURE (CONVERSATIONAL)

The kind of meaning conveyed implicitly rather than explicitly through an utterance. The term is important in **pragmatics** and derives from the work of the philosopher H. P. Grice (1975) who in a quite radical way contrasted the logic of philosophy with that of everyday conversation. In particular, he pointed out how utterances in everyday conversation often mean much more than they actually say. In order to explain how this can be, he proposed that conversation proceeds on the basis of a fundamental principle – the *cooperative principle*. This can be summed up using four basic maxims, or ground rules, which conversationalists tacitly follow:

- the *maxim of quality* states that speakers should be truthful and should not say things which they believe to be false or for which they lack sufficient evidence;
- the *maxim of quantity* requires that speakers should be as informative as is required for the purposes of the conversation and should say neither too little nor too much;
- the *maxim of relevance* states that what speakers say should fit in with and relate to the purposes of the conversation at that point;
- the *maxim of manner* requires that speakers should avoid obscurity, prolixity and ambiguity.

It is on the assumption that these maxims still hold some way, even when they appear to have been 'flouted', that we make sense of conversation. What happens briefly is this: when a maxim has apparently been flouted by an utterance we try to derive some meaning from it that will leave the maxim and the cooperative principle in place. This inferred, non-manifest meaning is the 'implicature'. Thus, B's reply in the following exchange does not seem literally to meet the terms of A's question:

A: Where's Bill?
B: There's a yellow VW outside Sue's house.

In this sense it apparently flouts at least the maxims of quantity and relevance and thereby fails to conform to the cooperative principle. In practice, however, we assume B to be cooperative at some deeper level and look for some proposition that would link B's actual reply with some manifestly relevant and cooperative reply to the question. In this case B effectively conveys that 'if Bill has a yellow VW, then he may be in Sue's house'.

The notion of conversational implicature provides an important way of going beyond highly literal and strictly logical approaches to meaning: it is a way of emphasising how the meaning of an utterance lies not just in the words we use but in the deductions and inferences that may be made on the basis of them. But the idea is not without its difficulties. There is considerable debate about exactly how many maxims you need to define adequately the cooperative principle. Some commentators have proposed as many as eight or more. Others have suggested that they can all be reduced to the one maxim – 'be relevant'. Nor is it certain how strong the cooperative principle is in itself. Some speech genres – such as adversarial cross-examination in the courtroom, the combative political interview on television or the full-blown marital quarrel – would seem to exhibit serious, systematic and fundamental departures from such a principle. And yet, for the theory of implicature to work, it is not a principle that can be applied variably.

See also: **Pragmatics, Semantics**

Further reading: Grice (1975); Leech (1983); Levinson (1983)

INDEPENDENCE

A concept of scale and opposition, with no intrinsic features. Independent film and video production, for instance, includes an incommensurable array of different personnel and practices, each defined contingently as independent against a specific mainstream. Thus, Hollywood directors working outside the major studios are independent – e.g., David Lynch. Countries outside the major film production centres (Los Angeles and Bombay) compete in the international film market as independents – thus the multi-million-dollar-grossing Australian film *Crocodile Dundee*, second only to *Top Gun* in its release year (1986) in both US and world markets, is an independent film.

Types of independence differ. They are organised around different mobilising discourses: community, avant-garde, agitprop (i.e. *agitation and propaganda*), art, connoisseurship, free enterprise, etc. In each case the mobilising discourse produces specific sets of practices. In one country's overall cultural production, independence often signals a production or practice that works more or less self-consciously against the grain of mainstream entertainment. Such independence may imply:

- different, alternative or oppositional processes of production (for instance, working against traditional divisions and hierarchies of labour);
- different aesthetics (experimentation at the level of image, narration and structure, promoting attention to meaning-construction, rather than to 'show-and-tell' plots with 'tennis-match dialogue');
- a self-reflexive concern with the practitioner's role as well as with subject matter or financial returns;
- different relations with audiences (getting away from 'bums on seats' towards active engagement with audiences as spectators or as participants);
- serving a defined audience 'constituency' rather than the 'mass' (e.g., women, workers, a region or community, people involved in political, social or environmental action).

In addition, *independent* has been used to describe sources of funding. The term is a euphemism for 'capitalist' or 'commercial' in the British broadcasting scene, where the main commercial channels in both television and radio (ITV and ILR) and their regulatory bodies (the ITC and Radio Authority) are dubbed independent – presumably because of state ownership. At the same time the 'independent film sector' uses the term to help secure public funds from bodies such as the Arts Council, the British Film Institute and local councils for low-budget, non-commercial production. Hence the same term has been found useful at the opposite extremes of the film world.

INDIVIDUAL

A synonym for a person. The word is derived from a medieval conceptualisation of the nature of God – three persons but *indivisible*. People were 'individual' because they had indivisible souls. By extension it is an adjective for that which cannot be divided further – a term of contrast to collectivities or generalities of various kinds: an individual tree as opposed to a wood. When used as a noun and applied to people, 'individual' is used in a way that the *OED* has dismissed as 'now chiefly a colloquial vulgarism, or a term of disparagement'. But, of course, it is in just this sense that the term *individual* is most familiar nowadays: a seemingly scientific non-gendered word used to describe a person.

INDIVIDUALISM

The mainspring of bourgeois/capitalist philosophy; the doctrine that individuals are the starting point and source of human action. That is, each person 'owns' his or her capacities (especially their capacity to labour) and is not in debt to society (or to a feudal overlord) for these capacities. Hence individuals are free to sell their labour power for whatever can be had for it, and are not obliged to consider anyone else in the process. This 'freedom' of the individual, then, is what underlies the operation of the 'free' market economy. The only inhibitors of individual freedom in this model are *competition* (where what can be had for labour power is limited by the value it can command in a competitive market) and *contract* (where each individual's social relations take the form of *commodity exchanges*: for example, labour for wages with mutually binding conditions).

Individualism is rarely discussed in studies of communication, but its assumptions are implicit in a great variety of theorising on the subject. The most common occurrence is for the notion of the free individual, who is essentially complete and taken to be the source of action and meaning, to form the 'unit' of study. According to this notion, communication takes place when individuals *exchange* messages (the contract model), or audiences are made up of aggregates of individuals (abstracted from discursive, economic and political relations except in so far as these can be rendered as variables *within* an individual), or social forces are understood as *deriving from* individual actions.

The alternative perspective to individualism certainly does not deny the existence or action of individual people. However, it does maintain that their existence and action are the *product* and not the *source* of social relations and signifying systems. As a result, the concept of *individualism* has been displaced in, for instance, structuralist, semiotic, Marxist and feminist writings by the concept of **subjectivity**.

Further reading: Macpherson (1962)

INFORMATION SOCIETY/INFORMATION ECONOMY

Until recently, theorists described society as post-industrial, distinctive for its service-based, rather than manufacturing-based, economy (Bell, 1980). Service-based economies have not been eroded, and yet it is said that we have entered a new paradigm, one that is built upon the wide-reaching term *information*.

What is it that alerts us to the fact that we are living in an information society? The use, storage and distribution of information have been pivotal to social structures throughout history (Carey and Quirk, 1989). If all societies are reliant upon information as the determinant of power, can we claim that *this* era is the information society and that previous centuries were not?

Some argue that it is the proliferation of information-based *markets* that define the information age. They observe the rapid increase in the *amount* of information-based products. Coyle (1998: ix) sees proof of the advent of an information society in the fact that a single musical greeting card contains more computer power than could be found on the entire planet in the year 1945. We now have computers for processing information, mobile telephones for communicating, fax machines for transmitting documentation, computer games for entertainment. Even familiar items are now information-rich where once they were materials-rich: the value in cars used to be in the steel; now up to 70 per cent of the value of a new Toyota is in the informatics.

Businesses strive to identify the consumer through market research figures. Scientific frontiers are being pushed through the decoding of biological information, such as the human genome project, the pursuit of cloning (information replication). Out of this we are witnessing and challenging new ethical issues involving the use of information – in the media, medicine and surveillance technology. Legal battles over the use and distribution of information, entitlement and authorship are becoming more pressing and increasingly controversial. With these factors combined, it appears that now more than ever, markets and culture are being accelerated and dispersed through information technologies.

The possession of *information capital* is surpassing labour as the means to wealth creation. In this respect, the information society is not just a reliance on information; it is the magnitude of its use and its centrality to the processes of the market and everyday life. Machinery, industry and wage-labour pre-dated the industrial age, but were exploited in the nineteenth century to the point at which they came to transform the way that people lived and viewed their lives. So it is now with information.

The information society has been heralded by some as representing a new-found freedom. An information society contains an informed population, capable of self-expression and political and cultural participation through new technologies (see Leadbeater, 1997). For others, 'Technology is technology; it is a means for communication and transportation over space, and nothing more' (Carey and Quirk, 1989: 140). But the information age has also brought with it a new set of anxieties. The ability to use information technologies in surveillance is seen by some as a means to social control and power, and an end to privacy. Foucault's reading of Bentham's panopticon, a prison in which the inmates can be observed from a central point, but cannot know when they are being observed, is invoked as a symbol of the ability of new technologies to curb our behaviour (Foucault, 1977; Robins and Webster, 1988). Even if we are not being watched and recorded, and our purchases and activities collated, we assume that this might be the case and behave accordingly. The information society is not free, in these predictions, but controlled through a myriad of decentralised networks.

After describing the features of the information society, Manuel Castells decided that the term was too vague 'as knowledge and information are essential to all societies'. What is new 'is a new set of information technologies' (Castells, 2000: 414). As information is at the source of all life, the technologies that enable us to use information are capable of transforming society at every level. But whether or not the information society stems from a coherent set of facts or from theoretical construction is perhaps not entirely relevant. The idea has become part of our cultural reality as well as government policies. It is an information society because we choose to think of it in that way (Boyle, 1996).

See also: **Knowledge economy, Network society, New economy**

INFOTAINMENT

A term used to describe the blending of factual reportage with the conventions usually associated with fictional entertainment. In every-day usage, infotainment refers to particular types of television programming. Examples of this would include 'tabloid' current affairs programmes, as well as instructional or **lifestyle** formats such as cooking, gardening and home improvement shows. Here, the term comes to represent the means by which television is able to impart information in an entertaining way.

In critical discourse, the concept is often used to lament the loss of 'traditional' news values. Those who criticise infotainment often have a preference for modernist forms of communication, privileging reason over emotion, public over private, and information over entertainment. But the entertainment characteristics that inform contemporary journalism were to be found in its earliest incarnations. Sex, scandal, disaster and celebrity have been intrinsic to modern journalism since the Enlightenment (Hartley, 1996), so the shift to infotainment should not necessarily be considered a recent event.

Broadcast news on television cannot avoid the need to entertain and appeal to viewers. Capturing audiences is as much a priority for factual programming as it is for fictional/entertainment genres, so it is hardly surprising that over time news has borrowed characteristics from non-news formats. Narrative, spectacle, personality presenters, non-diegetic soundtrack and personalised address are all now central to the broadcasting of news in entertaining ways. The term infotainment then could be said to recognise the porous nature of television and its genres rather than a decline in the absolute values associated with journalism.

At the heart of criticisms levelled at the move to infotainment is the perceived damage to civil society, where citizens' rights to rational (political) discourse have been replaced by an influx of private (trivial) affairs. To agree with this is to ignore the major movements that have been able to gain visibility as a result. The environment, and issues regarding youth, sexuality and ethnicity are all contemporary political issues that have arisen outside of the traditional public sphere. Infotainment, with its evocation of style, celebrity, gossip and informality, provides a new space within which new paradigms of politics can be discussed, represented and made meaningful.

Infotainment is also necessary in a medium where **aberrant decoding** is the norm, because viewers have to be encouraged to attend to things they do not like or know about when their commitment to watching anything at all may not be high. In this context, infotainment may not be **dumbing down** people who would otherwise be reading *The Financial Times*, but taking information to places it would not otherwise reach, and thus may be seen as both educational and tactful.

See also: **News values**

Further reading: Langer (1998)

INFRASTRUCTURE

The physical platforms upon which systems, facilities and networks are run. Infrastructure is essential to the information communications technologies as it enables **connectivity** and provides services via **applications**. Roads, footpaths and buildings are infrastructure. In telecommunications, the required infrastructure is the telephone line or cable, or the satellite through which information is distributed. **Privatisation** has brought with it issues of access to infrastructure, whereby private companies are capable of controlling the use of infrastructure previously considered a public resource available to all.

INNOVATION

New economy R&D. The first step in the creation of new tools, products or creative works is an idea. Within traditional manufacturing industries, ideas circulate at a low rate, inhibited by routine, tradition and existing methods of reproduction using well-known patterns. Production, in the industrial economy, is produced by the technology at hand. In innovative fields (media, software development, biotechnology, music production, for example) ideas circulate between people rapidly. In this scenario, science and discovery create the new technologies, pushing products to new levels. The discussion of ideas, contributions from others, the eventual development of an idea into something new, is central to the success of these industries.

Landry and Bianchini (1994) distinguish creativity from innovation. They identify creativity as the process through which new ideas are produced, whereas innovation is the process through which they are implemented. Therefore, creativity is a pre-condition for innovation, but innovation – the evaluation and assessment of the creative idea – is what will make the difference in product development. For innovation to occur, it may entail stepping outside of routine or structure, and it can therefore be the result of dissent or a product of experimentation.

Often it is simply the ability to use old ideas as the raw materials for something new.

In the knowledge-driven economy, where companies rely on information to improve their products and create new ones, innovation becomes the central component for wealth-creation. Once the idea has been hit upon, it will then be necessary to locate the required resources, possibly a team to work on the development and knowledge of factors that might inhibit the production of the work. Entrepreneurs bring the idea to fruition. Innovation therefore requires a range of appropriate conditions, skills and knowledge in order to occur. Fostering the right conditions for innovation has become a chief concern within the science, business and arts industries of the knowledge economy.

See also: **Information society/information economy, Knowledge economy, New media policies**

Further reading: Acs and Audretsch (1990); Caves (2000); Landry and Bianchini (1994); Leadbeater (1997); Leadbeater and Oakley (1999, 2001); Rogers (1995)

INTANGIBLES

Assets such as knowledge, competence, intellectual property, know-how, the people in a company, its R&D, brands, reputation, customer relations, etc. Intangibles are much more important to the new knowledge economy than tangible assets such as plant, land, etc. (see Leadbeater, 1997: 44–45). Any business that exploits knowledge, culture or 'copyright' products or services is trading in intangibles. Culture is an intangible in economic terms.

INTELLECTUAL PROPERTY

Ownership of intangible information. Intellectual property casts information as being subject to entitlements. It is a legal framework that enables information to be *owned*, and hence allows the owner to constrict its use or determine who uses it. **Copyright** is one example of intellectual property, whereby duplication of books, music, artworks, etc. can incur penalty if performed without the creator's, or copyright owner's, permission.

Although intellectual property is a legal concept, its boundaries are far from clear. The tension between fair use of information within the public domain and private ownership – and the ability to be recompensed for a creation – is one that is constantly being negotiated in law and regulation.

The difficulties and contradictions of intellectual property are examined by James Boyle in his discussion of the law case *Moore* v *The Regents of the University of California 1990*. John Moore was a patient at the University of California Medical Centre in 1976 where he was being treated for hairy-cell leukaemia. During his treatment, Moore's doctors discovered a potential commercial value within his genetic makeup. Tests were conducted on Moore, taking samples of every conceivable bodily fluid, without Moore being informed of the doctor's commercial interest. Moore's spleen was also removed and a portion of it sent to the research unit. In 1981, the doctors patented Moore's cell-line, claiming intellectual property. Apart from the ethical considerations of Moore not being fully informed of the reasons for the extensive medical tests, the key issues in the case centred on whether Moore actually owned his own genetic information and the cells that contained that information. The court found that Moore did not own either. 'Thus', writes Boyle, 'though Johnny Carson has an enforceable interest in the phrase "Here's Johnny" (a phrase uttered by *someone else*), Moore does not have one in his own DNA' (Boyle, 1996: 23).

Boyle details the court's reasons for these findings. Most important among these was the court finding that Moore could not copyright his genetic material as this would hinder research. In this case, it is the public realm, the importance of the free exchange of information, that is being upheld. However, what about the commercial intentions of intellectual property in this instance? According to Boyle, the market for products related to this research was estimated at $US3 billion in 1990. Intellectual property was claimed by the doctors in order to gain accreditation for the discovery, but also to reap the financial returns for the information. As this case demonstrates, intellectual property allows ideas and information to enter the marketplace (see **biotechnology**).

A related issue is the extent to which anxiety over the capacity for piracy inherent within digital media has led to the development of encryption technologies and a rise in contractual agreements in order to ensure that intellectual property is protected. Where it was once assumed that the digital technology would allow for greater freedom in the exchange of information and services, there is the very real possibility that our rights in digital arenas will in fact be more tightly constrained than our rights in the analogue world. For instance, although paperback books can be borrowed or swapped without monetary exchange (this can come under the definition of 'fair use' or 'acceptable use' laws), certain e-books may only be accessible upon payment or once an agreement has been entered into.

Further reading: Drahos (1999)

INTERACTIVITY

Interactivity signifies the development of the relationship between person and computer, and with others via the computer. Our ability to have a two-way communicative process with technology means that we are not 'destined to become a race of baby-sitters for computers' (Bagrit, 1965: 1). Instead we are 'navigators', 'end users', 'surfers', in control of where the technology takes us. We can be constructive through our choices, and our own invention.

Marshall McLuhan wrote in 1964 that 'automation is not an extension of the mechanical principles of fragmentation and separation of operations. It is rather the invasion of the mechanical world by the instantaneous character of electricity' (ibid.:349). The 'instant inclusive embrace' of automated technology, meant that the consumer also became the producer, 'fusing' information and learning. The progression from the mechanical to the automated has brought with it new possibilities for participation, our ability to make choices: technology becomes a means to empowerment. In McLuhan's and Bagrit's early accounts, interactivity is an antidote to the factories of the industrial revolution in which people's work had to be adapted to accommodate machines. This imagery and language have reappeared in accounts of digital technology. By being able to direct, communicate and create through new interactive technologies, we are becoming 'rehumanised' (Pearce, 1997).

The excitement surrounding the emancipatory potential of interactive media has been curbed by more cautious theorists who remind us that the interactive uses of new technologies are not driven by democratic ideals on the whole, but by commercial imperatives, and that although these can coincide, they do not have to. As the development of the technology has been left largely to the market, citizen feedback is likely to entail online shopping, interactive game shows and discussion resembling talk-back radio (Calabrese and Borchert, 1996; Schultz, 1994).

See also: **Cyberdemocracy, Cybernetics, Cyborg**

INTERNATIONALISATION

Activities that occur between nation-states are *inter*national. Internationalisation suggests an increasing occurrence of such activities, but unlike **globalisation**, it does not imply that the nation-states are losing their control or their influence over flows of information and financial capital. Rather, the existence and autonomy of nation-states seem assured by the fact that international processes are only made possible by the complicity and consent of national governments.

Paul Hirst disputes that globalisation is taking place. For him, globalisation assumes that economic adjustments 'are not thought to be the subject of policy by public bodies or authorities, but are a consequence of "unorganised" or "spontaneous" market forces' (Hirst, 1996: 2). However, economic adjustments do not occur automatically but as the result of government policy, domestic expenditure and changes in political-economic power. 'The world-wide international economy has been determined in its structure and the distribution of power within it by the major nation states' (Hirst, 1996: 3).

Paul Krugman, in his book *Pop Internationalism*, also warns against overstating the advent of globalisation by pointing to historical international relations. Prior to World War I, Britain's overseas investments exceeded its domestic stock capital, 'a record no major country has ever come closer to matching since' (1977: 207). Krugman also points to the Statue of Liberty as an important reminder that migration was once welcomed and encouraged by nation-states that are now implementing oppressive policies in order to close their borders to refugees.

For David Held, Hirst's *Globalisation in Question* (1996) offered useful and important dismantling of the rhetoric of globalisation and its deployment in making the processes of neo-liberalism seem inevitable and indisputable. However, he asserts that the problems associated with globalisation, such as environmental and economic interdependency, cannot be solved at the level of the nation-states. Asserting that little has changed in international political structures does not offer new ways forward (Held, 2002). It also ignores the popular uptake of international and global traffic, which national governments certainly seem minded to manage as best they can, but which they clearly do not control.

See also: **Anti-globalisation, Globalisation, New economy**

INTERNET

In 1957 the USSR launched the first artificial satellite, Sputnik, into Earth's orbit, signifying the starting point in the use of technological progress as a means to Cold War supremacy. A year later, in response to Sputnik, US President Eisenhower established the National Aeronautics Space Administration (NASA) as well as the Defense Department's Advanced Projects Research Agency (DAPRA, later to become APRA).

It was DAPRA which in 1969 developed a nuclear war contingency plan in the form of a computer network designed to enable information to exist outside of a vulnerable, central location. 'Packet switching' technology, whereby messages are broken into 'packets' and supplemented by header information on the source and destination, meant that communication lines did not need to be dedicated to passing the information as was the case with circuit switching networks. DAPRA's decentralised communications network – the early Net, named APRANET – was developed within the exclusionary and highly classified confines of the US military with the assistance of a number of civilian scientific personnel.

The involvement of these researchers meant that the network quickly captured the attention of the wider computer science community who contributed a new culture of research-based information sharing, openness and peer review. The Request For Comments (RFC) system was established as early as 1969 (originally by post), as a series of freely available memos intended to provide a feedback loop for suggestions and research ideas that would assist the evolution of the network. This process of 'open access' to protocol specifications (the agreed-upon formats for distributing data) and collaboration in research for the development of the Internet's own design became an integral component in the theoretical characterisation of the Internet as a forum for democratic information distribution and innovation.

The system progressed rapidly. In 1969 four hosts were connected to the APRANET, and in 1970 the first host-to-host protocol was invented which allowed for the development of applications. International connection was established in 1973 with University College London and the first all-inclusive e-mail program was developed in 1975.

A new culture began to appear when, on 12 April of that year, Kevin MacKenzie e-mailed the MsgGroup (the first APRANET mailing list) suggesting that symbols be used to indicate the intended emotion of text messages – for example, :-) for indicating a smile. Although he was 'flamed' at the time, emoticons (or 'smilies') are now used widely to clarify the mood and intention of e-mail correspondence using the confines of the keyboard.

By the mid-1970s a number of state-funded computer networks had begun to appear. As these were intended for use by other research disciplines there was little need for the networks to be compatible. It was not until 1985 that the National Science Foundation network, NSFNET, made a commitment to the creation of an infrastructure to serve the entire academic community that the Internet began to take the form in which it exists today – a global and relatively seamless entity. Part of this process was the NSF's decision to make the Transmission Control Protocol/Internet Protocol (TCP/IP) mandatory.

The early history of the Internet is characterised by state funding, military interest and scientific research and, it has been argued, was constructed by a predominantly male workforce out of a particular ethos reflected in its architecture (Spender, 1995). A significant role was also played by individuals, such as Jon Postel, who established a team, the Internet Assigned Numbers Authority (IANA) to take responsibility for the assignment of Internet protocol parameters and, later, domain names. This was then transformed into the Internet Corporation of Assigned Names and Numbers (ICANN) with a board elected by Internet users worldwide. The voluntarist culture of the Internet's origins, often associated with community media ideals of access, diversity and democratic communication, was thus a construct of self-appointed, if publicly minded, individuals who played significant roles in the design of the architecture of the Net.

The Internet changed dramatically during the decade from the early 1980s to the early 1990s. Between 1981 and 1989, the number of computers linked to the Internet rose from 300 to 90,000. Growth was spurred on partly by consumer adoption of personal computers and also through cooperation and collaboration between university and private research bodies in the development of standardised commands and software development.

One such collaboration arose out of Bell Laboratories (run by the US telecommunications company AT&T), who explored the networking potential of Unix protocol. Students at Duke University in North Carolina subsequently developed a modified version of the Unix Protocol that enabled computers to network over a telephone line, leading to the creation of the USENET and bulletin board services (BBS). Bell continued to provide financial assistance to the USENET project, which expanded the user base by providing access to other communities and eventually to profit-making enterprises. When NSFNET, which linked five university-based super-computing centres, became the primary Internet 'backbone' (or primary national infrastructure), it developed an acceptable use policy that prohibited use of the backbone for activities not in support of research or education. The intended, and successful, outcome was the encouragement of commercial involvement at the local and regional level, away from the national hub, and the development of privately funded long-haul networks. When the APRANET was decommissioned in 1995, TCP/IP had marginalised most other network protocols and was on the way to becoming 'THE bearer service for the Global Information Infrastructure' (Leiner *et al.*, 2000).

In 1989 the Internet was transformed by a development by Tim Berners Lee and others at the European Laboratory for Particle Physics (CERN). Their new protocol was based on hypertext, which allowed for the embedding of links in text to other text and brought previously separate systems together. With this innovation came the World Wide Web in 1991.

This was followed closely by Marc Andreessen's Mosaic browser in 1992, which dispensed with the need for complex text interfaces and, along with innovations to increase bandwidth, opened the Net to new graphic possibilities. Increasing data traffic resulting in the need for upgrades was beginning to appear unsustainable by policy-makers and the NFSNET backbone was fully privatised in the mid-1990s. The telecommunications industry too began to experience massive deregulation and privatisation at this time. The line that distinguished the Internet as a publicly owned resource from a market-driven communication sphere was becoming increasingly blurred.

With the growth of commercial participation in the Internet, issues of competition and access have become central to concerns over the future of the Internet. An exhaustive lawsuit ensued when Microsoft's popular Windows '98 operating system was released with Microsoft's own browser integrated into the desktop, an action that was found in 2000 to contravene the US's Sherman Antitrust Act in attempting to monopolise the web browser market. The Microsoft antitrust case was an indication that the cooperative, open standards ethos that was integral to the development of the Internet had begun to change (Goggin, 2000).

Even less aggressive commercial strategies, such as coding, encryption and architecture development for the protection of privacy, certification and security, influence the availability of information on the web. 'Portals' – the points at which you begin to navigate yourself through the web (offering features such as search engines, databases, e-mail and news) have techniques to encourage, if not direct, users to where they want to go. AOL's **walled garden** strategy successfully directs their customers to remain within the AOL confines for 85 per cent of their Internet usage.

However, as the history of the Internet indicates, commercial involvement can stimulate innovation, access and diversity. Leiner *et al.* (2000) outline in their account of the evolution of the Internet how commercial vendors worked with researchers to develop interoperable standards. Further, BNN, AT&T and IBM – all private companies – were involved in the early phases in protocol and infrastructure innovation and construction. And although communication and innovation have been administered by decentralised techniques, hierarchies have always existed in terms of who has access to the knowledge, equipment – and hence the forums – of the Internet. The Internet has existed as a result of a fusion of the public and private sectors, volunteers and workers, regulation and dissent.

By 2020, it is estimated that Chinese will be the most common language on the Internet.

See also: **Cyberdemocracy, Digital/analogue distribution, Digital divide**

Further reading: Lessig (1999)

INTERPELLATION

A term from the writings of the French Marxist political philosopher Louis Althusser, referring to what he takes to be the process by which **ideology** 'hails' individuals as its subject. Sometimes translated as 'appellation'.

Individuals are said to be interpellated by the discursive, linguistic, symbolic order in which they live. Thus, for Althusserians, ideology is general and inescapable, as well as being a material product of ideological state apparatuses. Interpellation is the very mechanism by which people are subjected to ideology, and it is usually understood as a textual operation of 'audience positioning'.

Both the notion of interpellation and that of 'ideology in general' have been criticised since the early 1970s, when they were most influential, as being too essentialist and abstract. If interpellation is understood as 'hailing' (as in 'Oi! You!'), the question of what or who is calling must sooner or later arise. If the answer is 'ideology in general' we certainly avoid conspiracy theory, but this does not take us far in understanding specific ideological operations.

However, interpellation can be useful as a concept when applied to specific discourses, rather than to the operation of transhistorical general forces on abstract subjects.. For example, Laclau writes of a struggle between discourses in pre-war Germany, where the discourse of 'old Prussianism' interpellated a 'nationalist and authoritarian' subject, while 'in Nazi discourse ... the interpellated subject was a racial one' (1977: 116–142). In this kind of usage, interpellation has something in common with the concepts of **mode of address**, orientation and preferred reading, with the added conceptual advantage that it presumes the politics of **discourse**.

INTERTEXTUALITY

Best understood as the textual equivalent of cross-referencing, at a semiotic level intertextuality refers to the use of a given sign in other textual contexts. Postmodern theorists argue that intertextuality is representative of the contemporary period of humanity where meaning-making is possible only in relation to other texts. But the term is more useful as a means of understanding how the media make meaning. Certainly the concept is central to contemporary forms of media such as advertising and music video.

Intertextual properties of texts can include the following.

- *Generic characteristics*. Audiences attending a musical will bring with them an expectation and a shared knowledge of the conventions of the genre and will anticipate the inclusion of songs and dance numbers, and be able to predict when the next one will start.
- *Characters and the actors who play them*, especially in film. In the film *Batman* the character played by model Jerry Hall is given few lines to speak and comes over as rich, one-dimensional and not very bright. But viewers are also expected to know Jerry Hall as a model and from other texts such as tabloid magazines and the discourses they employ, for instance in discussing her relationship with Mick Jagger. Similarly, Arnold Schwarzenegger appears in films as a 'sign of himself', as well as a given character. The 'sign' of Schwarzenegger is that he is strong, professional and brave and will usually come away bloodied, broken, but undefeated. Where

Jerry Hall is a 'sign of herself' as a real person, Schwarzenegger's 'sign of himself' is a persona, built up in previous film roles.

- *Pastiche in advertising and music videos*, which often employ already-established visual styles and codes and will quote from or allude to each other. Madonna's video for *Material Girl* is often used as an illustration of how recycled images are appropriated to expand on the meaning available with the text. In this instance the costumes, the choreography and the outfitting of Madonna herself are a direct copy of a routine of Marilyn Monroe in *Gentleman Prefer Blondes*. Postmodern critics see this and similar moves in advertising as evidence of the insignificance of history and the installation of the pleasure of the spectacle. But it may be more useful to think of intertextuality as a means of understanding the fluid relationship among the media, the text and the audience.

See also: **Representation, Star/stardom**

Further reading: Fiske (1987); Taylor and Willis (1999)

KINESICS

The semiotics of movement, especially human movement and gesture. Movement, both of the body and by locomotion, is not merely functional but is also coded, meaningful and communicative. What is conveyed when you wave your arms about may differ considerably from the 'same' message uttered with arms folded. Walking is highly communicative, bringing posture, speed, direction, etc. to bear on meaning. It is further semioticised via such 'media' as the fashion catwalk. Dance is the aestheticisation of kinesic codes, and some versions of modern dance can be regarded as a mode of analysis thereof. Kinesics was introduced into psychological approaches to non-verbal and interpersonal communication by Birdwhistle (1970).

KNOWLEDGE

The foundation of the new economy. Knowledge, overlapping with information, culture and creativity, provides the know-how, ideas, intellectual property and creative works that have begun to supplant in significance the manufacturing or industrial economy across the developed world.

Traditionally understood, intellectual knowledge was 'contained' in one of the recognised disciplines or branches of formal scientific inquiry or their equivalent in the social sciences and humanities. Within such disciplinary specialisms, new knowledge could be tested against existing bodies, using established methodology and techniques of inquiry. This was explicit knowledge. Tacit knowledge or 'know-how' was of lower intellectual and social status, being regarded as technical, the province of artisans and mechanics, not scientists and intellectuals.

In the new economy, knowledge has become much more volatile, interdisciplinary and exposed to the workings of commerce, entrepreneurship and large-scale exploitation. Scientific, intellectual and tacit knowledge are much more interdependent; for instance in the IT area, where technical skills and intellectual innovation are inseparable.

Knowledge in the new economy has to be distinctive. It has to be easy to replicate, but hard to imitate (Leadbeater and Oakley, 2001: 19). Further, it has to be put into an entrepreneurial context, to mobilise capital resources and find a market. Such knowledge differs from the kind of 'public good' knowledge exemplified by the traditional sciences and disciplines. But it may still sustain public, even utopian, ambitions. Charles Leadbeater, for instance, argues that the new economy is about creating value, human and social as well as financial:

A modern society's goal should be to maximise the production and distribution of knowledge, to combine in a single ideal democratic and economic imperatives. Societies become more democratic as people become more literate, numerate and knowledgeable, capable of making informed choices and challenging authority, so allowing them to take charge of their lives. ... Political empowerment and economic opportunity stem from the same root: the spread of knowledge.

(Leadbeater, 1997: 222)

KNOWLEDGE ECONOMY

Charles Leadbeater uses chocolate cake recipes as a metaphor to describe the workings of the knowledge economy. A chocolate cake itself is what economists would describe as a rival good: If I eat it you will not be able to eat it. A chocolate cake recipe, on the other hand, is a non-rival good. Many people can use the recipe without it being depleted. In the knowledge economy it is the recipe that is valuable. It can be transferred to others and reproduced and copied by chocolate cake eaters around the world. The production of the cake is therefore not limited to one recipe owner, who would then have to spend significant time and resource producing many cakes. The cake belongs to many producers, with consumers becoming creators themselves in the baking process. As Leadbeater writes, 'knowledge can make a lasting impact on well-being: a recipe stays with you long after the cake has been eaten. The more an economy promotes the production and spread of knowledge, rather than just the exchange of goods and services, the better off we become' (Leadbeater, 1977: 33).

The knowledge economy is a significant new development in economic activity. The OECD estimated half of member countries' national output to be 'knowledge based' by the mid-1990s (Coyle, 1988). In a knowledge economy it is the use of information and ideas that power growth, not tangible assets (see **intangibles**). Giddens (2000) compares the market-to-book ratio (the difference between its material assets and saleable value) of Microsoft with General Motors. For Microsoft the market-to-book ratio is 13, whereas for General Motors it is only 1.6. Assets such as property and raw equipment can no longer be relied upon when assessing the value of a company as, in the knowledge economy, value lies in the expertise, ideas and innovative qualities of the workers.

For Manuel Castells (2000) the defining characteristic of the knowledge economy is not the *generation* but the *application* of knowledge in a way that feeds back to generate new knowledge – a virtuous cycle of knowledge creation. Information sharing in the knowledge economy is accumulative. Computer software is a code that can be distributed to many in order for them to create using the software information or structure. It is not used up or consumed, but reproduced, added to and utilised in the production of new innovations.

As a knowledge economy relies upon a knowledge base, developing strategies to foster an entrepreneurial, 'smart' society are becoming prevalent in policy arenas. Education is central to the cultivation of a knowledge economy, providing people with the skills to become creators and to use information shrewdly in business practice. Information and information technologies are also important in the development and distribution of knowledge, as are appropriate legal frameworks to ensure intellectual property protection.

See also: **Globalisation, Information society/information economy, Network society, New economy**

LANGUAGE

Speech – usually taken to refer to the whole body of words (vocabulary) and ways of combining them (grammar) that is used by a nation or people. However, the term has become associated with various specialised usages and problems in the study of communication.

The ordinary usage of the term tends to assume that language is:

- a specific language, such as Welsh, Nyungar or English;
- a nomenclature – an instrument for naming objects that exist out there in the world;
- an instrument for expressing thoughts that exist inside the head.

None of these usages has survived intact in the study of communication. First, language is studied as a *general capacity*, not as an aggregate of individual languages. Second, the relations between thoughts, words and external objects have been the focus of much theorising, the result of which is, at the very least, to bring into question any idea that words simply name objects or express thoughts. Both these ideas assume language to be a mere reflection of something else that is (it follows) not language – in this case, thoughts and objects. The objection to such an assumption is that it denies any active force for language, reducing it to a mere instrument, and that it fails to take into account the extent to which both thoughts and objects can be known only through their representation in some form of language.

Just as atomic physics started by isolating individual atoms but ended up by identifying much smaller particles and forces, so linguistics has identified language as comprising structures and rules operating between elements within words. The most basic is the phoneme, or unit of recognisably distinct sound that figures in a particular language. Different languages have different phonemes (there is no /j/ in Welsh, and no /ll/, /ch/ and, /rh/ in English). But all languages operate with a finite number of phonemes which can then be combined to form words. Language is thus no longer seen as a 'body of words', but rather as a generative structure or **langue** which is capable of producing signs. Beyond phonemic analysis, linguistics has developed around the study of semantics and syntax (rules of combination).

Linguistics has traditionally centred on speech. **Semiotics**, on the other hand, has taken over the Saussurian model of language and used it to analyse all kinds of signification other than speech – writing, architecture, television, cinema, food, fashion and furniture, for instance. There is no doubt that such sign systems do signify (that is, the way their elements can be selected and combined does serve to communicate meanings), but whether they do it *as* languages or *like* language remains a matter for debate.

Within communication and cultural studies there is widespread agreement that whether they are studied as languages or as language-like, signifying systems of all kinds share certain characteristics. These are:

- meaning is not a result of the intrinsic properties of individual signs or words, but of the systematic relations between the different elements;
- language is not an empirical thing but a social capacity;
- individuals are not the source of language but its product – language thinks itself out, as it were, in individuals.

Language always escapes the individual and even the social will. Some of the more important concepts and terms associated with the study of language are included under separate entries.

See also: **Code, Diachronic, Discourse, Language, functions of, Langue, Paradigm, Phonemic/phonetic, Semiotics, Sign, Signification, Structuralism, Synchronic, Syntagm**

Further reading: Culler (1976); Halliday (1978); Montgomery (1986)

LANGUAGE, FUNCTIONS OF

The purposes which language can be made to serve in different situations. Although we may regard language primarily as a means of making statements that are true or false (the *referential function*) or as an instrument for the communication of ideas (the *ideational function*), this is only part of the total picture. Thus, while the referential or ideational functions may be *seen* as prominent in news reporting, science writing, courtroom testimony and so on, several other functions have come to be identified as important in everyday language use. One well-known account of language function is supplied by Jakobson (1960), who identified the *phatic*, the *regulatory* (or 'conative', as he called it), the *emotive*, the *aesthetic* (or 'poetic' as he called it) and the *metalinguistic* functions as equally deserving of attention.

Many situations, for instance, involve a use of language for which issues of truth value are not at stake. Consider, for instance, situations such as telephoning a friend. If you ask 'How's things?' or 'How are you?', you are quite likely to be answered, 'Fine'. Subsequent conversation, of course, may well reveal that your interlocutor has one leg in plaster and can walk only with using crutches. And yet you would not thereby consider the initial response – 'Fine' – to be untruthful. This is because we commonly use language not just for articulating ideas but for making and sustaining contact, often using quite ritualised formulae which are almost devoid of content. This use is known as the **phatic** *function* of language. Conversations about the weather between relative strangers at bus stops in the UK are elaborate exercises in the phatic function.

Language is also used to affect the actions and dispositions of others by commands, requests, instructions and other more subtle acts of verbal persuasion. The language of air-traffic control, of advertising and of political campaigns relies heavily on this function, which is known as the *regulatory* or *conative function*.

In the case of the regulatory function the focus of the language is on the actions and dispositions of the addressee. In contrast to this, language may be used to express the feelings and dispositions of the speaker irrespective of whether an audience is present. This is known as the *emotive function* – language used (sometimes involuntarily) for the expression of feelings. Scratching the paintwork on the car is likely to lead to an outburst of the emotive function.

Language may also be used as a source of intrinsic pleasure. Young children learning their first language may derive great pleasure from playing with the sound properties of language, repeating and modulating sound sequences, sometimes without regard for their communicative potential, as in the following sequence between twins aged thirty-three months:

A: zacky sue
B: (laughing) zacky sue zacky sue (both laugh) ah
A: appy

B: olp olt olt
A: oppy oppy
B: appy appy (laughing).

(after Keenan, 1974: 171)

This kind of spontaneous linguistic play occurs amongst children whether on their own or in company right through the period of language development. Not only does it seem integral to the process of learning the first language, it seems not too fanciful to suggest that such activity may form the basis for later poetic uses of language. The general name for this kind of activity is the *aesthetic function*. More or less self-conscious playing with language operates in differing linguistic domains, involving not only sound-play as in rhyme and alliteration but also punning, ambiguity, grammatical rule-breaking and so on. Nor is it restricted to poetry proper. Advertising, for example, employs language as much in its aesthetic function as in its conative.

Another important, if sometimes overlooked, function is the use of language to explore and reflect upon itself, known as the *metalinguistic function*. A surprising amount of everyday discourse turns out to be *metalinguistic* – from the television interviewer's, 'Is what you're saying then Prime Minister ...?', to someone in an argument complaining, 'That doesn't make sense'. Grammar books and dictionaries, of course, rely heavily on the metalinguistic function, as does a book such as this, especially at those moments when it supplies definitions of terms.

The notion of function is important in the study of language, principally because it helps to emphasise the way in which language is much more than a tool for thinking with or a vehicle for conveying information. In this way, functional perspectives tend to stress a range of other pressures upon language, and other possibilities for its use, than the need to express some kind of 'propositional content' in a strict logical form that may be measured for its truth value. Thus, from a functional perspective, one can claim that language does a great deal more than define and express concepts. Indeed, the linguist Halliday has argued that when children are learning their first language they use it in the first instance much more to affect and interact with their social environment than to convey information. Halliday's account of language is generally functionalist in character, being predicated on the claim that many aspects of its organisation are ultimately derived from the functions or purposes that it serves.

The main drawback with the functional perspective is the difficulty of reaching rigorous definitions of the main language functions. Some accounts suggest three; others suggest as many as seven. A more recent approach known as **speech act** theory focuses more specifically on stipulating in detail a precise range of actions which discrete utterances are capable of performing.

See also: **Speech act**

Further reading: Halliday (1973); Jakobson (1960)

LANGUE

In Saussurian linguistics, the abstract system of signs and conventions underlying individual acts of speaking. The role of langue, therefore, may be seen as analogous to that of the musical score that underlies individual performances of a symphony or the rules of chess that make possible an unlimited variety of actual games. The symphony, for instance, exists independently of its individual performances – in which false notes may occur, distinctive choices of tempo may be adopted, and so on. Likewise, chess may be played with many different sequences of moves, on many sizes of board, with different kinds of pieces, and yet remain chess as long as the basic rules of the game are observed. In the same way, for English or Swahili or Gujarati, there is a common storehouse of basic, necessary conventions or rules which speakers of that language follow when framing their utterances. It is these conventions that constitute the langue for that language; and it is by following such shared conventions that intelligibility is guaranteed between speakers of that language. In this sense, langue is very much a social product shared between members of a social body as a whole and out of the control of any one individual.

As with so many important terms in modern linguistics, the notion of langue was developed initially in the work of the Swiss linguist Ferdinand de Saussure. For him, contrasting langue with **parole** was an important methodological step in isolating the object of linguistic enquiry by focusing on the institution (langue) rather than the event (parole). The distinction is similarly formulated in much modern linguistics, whether as competence versus performance in the work of Chomsky – or potential linguistic behaviour versus actual linguistic behaviour in the work of Halliday. In **structuralism** and in **semiotics** the notion of langue was extended to embrace other kinds of the sign than the purely linguistic one. Thus, patterns of kinship, the social organisation of furniture, food, and fashion have all been considered as examples *of* underlying systems.

See also: **Code, Parole, Syntagm**

Further reading: Culler (1976); Saussure (1974)

LIFESTYLE

As a term in cultural and media studies, lifestyle crops up in two contexts. The first relates to identity. Here, 'lifestyle' may be added to the list of identities covered in affinity politics, as another marker of difference: thus, 'class, race, ethnicity, sexual orientation, age, lifestyle, etc.'. This sort of lifestyle may relate to urban subcultures or to fanship, music, sport and the like. The second relates to the **content industries**. Here 'lifestyle' refers to a genre of TV programming and of general interest magazines devoted to non-news journalism about household matters (home improvement, gardening, pets), bodily enhancement (fitness, health, beauty) and consumerism (shopping, travel, fashion). This is the fastest growing sector of journalism, outperforming news journalism and establishing whole new market sectors, for instance the 'lad mags' which led the boom in lifestyle magazines aimed at both men and women and were such a feature of the 1990s. In the US (and on many international cable bundles) there is a TV channel called Lifestyle, which targets women viewers. 'Lifestyle' in both of these senses is a kind of 'middle-of-the-road' version of **DIY culture**.

LITERACY

The social institution of writing; by extension, the social institution of communication by any means other than speech. Literacy is not and never has been a personal attribute or ideologically inert 'skill' simply to be 'acquired' by individual persons. Nor is it a mere technology, although it does require a means of production both physical (a tool to write with and material on which to write) and social (a recognised notation or alphabet and a way of transmitting the knowledge required to manipulate it).

As a social institution literacy is subject to similar kinds of forces to do with its distribution and regulation as are other kinds of institution. Its early history is usually characterised by strict controls as to who had access (priesthoods and economic or administrative officials) and what it was used for (sacred and state business).

Modern societies are heavily committed to 'universal' literacy, and use it as an autonomous means of communication quite different from that of speech. This has led many observers to seek to account for the peculiarities of modern culture by reference to 'literate consciousness'. First among such critics was Marshall McLuhan (1962). More recently, literacy has become the focus of important debates about the ideological function of education since, it is argued, literacy is a vehicle for the dissemination of both values and practices (as well as skills) that may be effective in reproducing hegemonic order.

Without having to claim that writing 'caused' the forms of consciousness and through them the social organisation of twentieth-century society, it is still possible to study the extent to which literacy is more than just an innocent skill. It is ideologically and politically charged – it can be used as a means of social control or regulation, but also as a progressive weapon in the struggle for emancipation. Above all, however, a literate workforce is a pre-condition for industrialised production, and the reproduction of a literate workforce requires large-scale state intervention to disseminate the appropriate type, content and level of literacy for this purpose.

Literacy has come to be associated with alphabetic writing, and is commonly not applied to the decipherment of audio-visual media such as television. One reason for this is that throughout the broadcast era 'media literacy' was confined for most people to the ability to *read only*. You could watch television, but it was much harder to 'write' with it. Now new media technologies have brought down the prices of digital cameras to that of a good pen, and computer software enables new possibilities for editing and exhibition It is not too far-fetched to say that, as in the Renaissance period when written literacy began to proliferate, the gap between those who can read only and those who can both read and write is closing. Media literacy as a widely dispersed mode of two-way communication is at hand.

See also: **Orality**

LOCALISATION

Exploitation of the geographical niche. **Globalisation** has altered the movement of economic and cultural forces so that they are now less limited by geographic space and are more evasive of nation-state controls. It would seem that the geographic place in which industry and creative production are housed should be less relevant as the world becomes increasingly connected at a level beyond state jurisdiction. However, despite globalisation, regions and cities are still known for what they do well. Designer shoes are made in Italy, watches in Switzerland, films in Hollywood, audio equipment in Japan and Indigenous art in Australia.

The increased productivity made possible through industry **clusters** means that specialised local production is likely to prevail. In fact, as Porter has pointed out, globalisation can make locational advantage more important than it has been in the past as artificial barriers to trade and investment are strategically dismantled through international trade agreements. With new communication technologies, firms are less dependent on the physical features and resources of a place and can 'choose the best location for productivity and dynamism' (Porter, 1998: xii).

Krugman had a similar thing in mind when he stated that Los Angeles is no longer attached to the physical land that it occupies, but has 'cut loose from its geographical moorings' (Krugman, 1997: 209). Although it might be impossible (until after the earthquake ...), moving Los Angeles to a location 500 kilometres away would not necessarily impact upon the economic base of the city in the way it would have for cities of a century ago that were dependent on oil, water or climate resources. People go to LA because the film companies are there. Restaurants, retail and tourism, and new media from television to games and software designers, follow the film people. So LA still has a *local* economy, but one based on its 'position' as a world leader in creative industries, rather than its actual proximity to a coalfield. The next big city down the coast, San Diego, is not in the least like LA, because it has its own local (based on its geographical location) economy, based in part on a naval base and on its proximity to Mexico.

If the cities of today function as self-perpetuating networks, then local culture is also likely to be strengthened and to develop alongside global culture. In broadcasting, the public projects of mass information dissemination through government television and radio are no longer the primary source of information in a multi-channel, multimedia environment. A renewed interest in the local has emerged as the technological justifications for nationwide broadcasting are eroded. Digital television technologies will soon make local TV as cheap to gather and distribute as local radio.

In recognition of this, city councils and local and regional governments are looking increasingly to enhance and promote the lifestyle of their locality. With a dual agenda of social/neighbourhood regeneration and competitiveness within the global economy, these policy approaches have a specific focus on place rather than the nation as a whole. The mobilisation and coordination of funding bodies, arts, heritage and tourism agencies as well as private- and third-sector groups are central to this trend. By providing opportunities for creative workers, creating programmes for skills development and advancing cultural industries with a wide appeal, cities (and some towns) are attempting to stand out in the global landscape.

See also: **Cluster, New economy**

Further reading: Coyle (1998); Friedman (1990); Hall (2000); Hannerz (1990)

MASS COMMUNICATION

The practice and product of providing leisure entertainment and information to an unknown audience by means of corporately financed, industrially produced, state-regulated, high tech, privately consumed commodities in the modern print, screen, audio and broadcast media, usually understood as newspapers, magazines, cinema, television, radio and advertising; sometimes including book publishing (especially popular fiction) and music (the pop industry).

Caution should be exercised with respect to the term itself. The word 'mass' may encourage the unthinking replication of mass society theory, while the word 'communication' in this context masks the social and industrial nature of the media, promoting a tendency to think of them as interpersonal communication. Since mass communication is neither mass nor communication as normally understood, the term should be seen as something akin to a proper name.

Mass communication is not a concept that can be defined, but a common-sense category that is used to lump a number of different phenomena together in a non-analytic way. Attempts to define it, however, are plentiful, but they always fail. This is because they are forced to be too restrictive, in which case the definition does not do justice to all that we commonly think of as mass communication (it is hard to encompass the diversity of what constitutes print, cinema, radio and television within one definition). Or else they are forced to become too over-extended, in which case the definition ends up applying equally well to something that we don't think of as mass communication at all – for instance, education, religion or even speech itself.

Further reading: McQuail (1987)

MASS SOCIETY/MASS SOCIETY THEORY

An early twentieth-century model of the social organisation of industrial/capitalist societies which characterised them as comprising a vast workforce of atomised, isolated individuals without traditional bonds of locality or kinship, who were alienated from their labour by its repetitive, unskilled tendencies and by their subjection to the vagaries of the wage relationship (the *cash nexus*) and the fluctuations of the market. Such individuals were entirely at the mercy of

- totalitarian ideologies and propaganda;
- influence by the mass media (comprising, in this period, the press, cinema and radio).

Mass society theory was an understandable response to the economics and politics of the 1930s, and was neatly summed up in Charlie Chaplin's film *Modern Times* (1936). But it has hung on in a common-sense version which is associated largely with cultural and literary critics for whom industrialisation and modern society in general remain a regrettable aberration from values and habits which these writers fondly imagine used to prevail before the invention of machines, democracy and the like.

Mass society theory has been active in a wide range of media studies, where it tends to produce apocalyptic visions of what television and cinema are doing to the masses (but never, oddly enough, to the critic). Any time you speculate on what '**effect**' the media have on (other) people, especially if your thoughts turn to notions such as dependency, aggression, narcotisation, brutalisation and desensitisation, then you are thinking mass society theory. Don't! Go and watch television, and ask yourself why these things are able to afflict others if they aren't happening to you.

See also: **Audiences, Effects, Persuasion**

Further reading: Biddiss (1977); Carey, 1992; Swingewood (1977)

MEANING

The import of any signification; the product of culture. In the context of communication studies, meaning is the outcome of communication, and therefore is the object of study, not a given or self-evident quantum that exists prior to analysis. Hence meaning should not be assumed to reside *in* anything, be it text, utterance, programme, activity or behaviour, even though such acts and objects may be understood as meaningful.

Over the years the supposed *location* of meaning has drifted down the producer–commodity–consumer chain.

- In *pre-modern* (medieval) textual theories, meaning was divine, fixed in texts such as the Bible by God. Authorial intention was therefore unarguable: texts meant what their rather formidable '*producer*' said they did. All you had to do was work out what the Author 'meant'. Priests – 'authorities' – were on hand to do this for you.

- In *modern* times, textual theory located meaning in the *text*. Texts meant what they said. This was the heyday of modernist literary criticism, including the New Critics and Leavisites. You got at meaning yourself by using the technique of 'practical criticism' invented by I. A. Richards, which meant 'close critical reading' of the text, without reference to contextual features, including knowing who wrote it and when, or what other critics had said about it.

- In *postmodern* times, meaning was located in the *audience* or *reader*. Given the anonymous popular sovereignty of contemporary democracy, this was an egalitarian approach to meaning. It required large-scale sampling and ethnographic methods to get at what a text meant, because it meant what several million different people said it did.

It might be wise to hang on to all three of these links in the 'value chain' of meaning – they all have some influence over its production, circulation and reproduction.

Meaning has been proposed by Marshall Sahlins (1976) as a common 'third term' – added to material goods (economy) and social relations (politics) – to unify the anthropological study of culture. Meaning *in* economic and political arrangements thus becomes the proper subject of anthropology; and meaning becomes the product *of* culture.

Meaning is also the object of study in linguistics: see especially the entries for **pragmatics** and **semantics**.

MEDIA LAW

The media are shaped through legislation, **regulation** and the legal system. Government legislation specifies the laws that media institutions and individuals must comply with, while the legal system deals with how that law applies to a particular case. Legal systems vary according to the nation and municipality within which they exist. In general, however, media law (as common law) plays a significant role in establishing what actions are considered permissible within the media domain by setting precedents, whereby the outcome of particular cases may influence decisions in future cases.

As Armstrong points out, there is no sufficient word to describe the particular activities and occupations that media law is concerned with in particular. 'To publish' is often used in legal fields in the absence of a more encompassing term and is applied to areas such as television, film and advertising as well as print publishing. There is no designated body of media law, but rather 'most media law is the application of existing, wider categories of law to the special problems of the media' (Armstrong *et al.*, 1988: 6).

The field of media law includes the following areas.

- *Defamation* involves communication that injures someone's reputation. *Libel* refers to written defamatory statements and *slander* refers to spoken defamation.
- *Copyright* is a component of intellectual property law that exists to protect the rights of a creator of work to determine who reproduces, publishes or performs, adapts or broadcast a work.
- *Censorship* involves setting standards in relation to controversial or obscene material. It is a particularly problematic area in the US where it is often found to contravene, or be in conflict with, the First Amendment (constitutional law) right to free speech.
- *Broadcast law* is often reliant upon a combination of regulatory institutions and legal rules. The basis for broadcast law is to ensure that ordered and compliant use of limited broadcast spectrum prevails.
- *Antitrust*, or media ownership laws are intended to prevent monopoly control of media institutions and companies.

See also: **Copyright, Intellectual property**

MEDIASPHERE

The mediasphere is a term coined by Hartley (1996; see also Hartley and McKee, 2000) following Yuri Lotman's (1990) designation of the **semiosphere**. The semiosphere is the whole cultural universe of a given culture, including all its speech, communication and textual systems such as literature and myth. The mediasphere is a smaller 'sphere' within the semiosphere, and includes all the output of the mass media, both fictional and factual. The mediasphere, in turn, encloses the **public sphere**, and the 'public sphericules' that seem to have proliferated within it. The idea is that the public sphere is not separate from but enclosed within a wider sphere of cultural meaning, which is itself *mediated* as it is communicated back and forth from the cultural to the public domain.

MEDIUM/MEDIA

A medium (plural, media) is simply any material through which something else may be transmitted. Artists use 'medium' (a clear transparent liquid that 'transmits' pigments) in painting. A psychic medium is one who purports to transmit messages between the world of the living and that of the dead (see Sconce, 2000). Media of communication are therefore any means by which messages may be transmitted. Given the promiscuousness of human semiosis, just about anything can transmit a message, from a length of string with cans at either end to a wall.

By common usage, this broad meaning of the term has narrowed to focus on the 'mass' media (rather than on telecommunications). '*The* media' were the **content industries** devoted to reaching very large popular audiences and readerships in print (newspapers, magazines, popular publishing), screen (cinema, TV) and aural (recorded music, radio) media. During the twentieth century, these 'mass' media were characterised by their one-to-many centralised address, standardised content, high capital costs and technological innovation, and their tendency towards repertoire and genre. Despite their desire for ratings and reach, the 'mass' media had a take-it-or-leave-it attitude to audiences (i.e. audiences chose from among a repertoire of finished products; they didn't participate directly in content creation).

The media are still giant industries and still display tendencies towards monopoly and vertical integration, exemplified by organisations such as News Corp, which not only owns entire media industries in television, print and cinema, but also owns some of the sporting clubs and competitions whose matches draw viewers and readers to those media outlets.

Since the 1990s, with convergence among the content media, telecommunications and interactive computing, the situation has changed radically. New media, for instance computer games, are interactive between users and manufacturers, with a proportion of content actually coming from consumers, who are as much partners as clients of media content providers. In other words the one-to-many model of media has been superseded, and now 'content' has integrated with telecommunications and computer interactivity, allowing 'many-to-many' communication, including private individual to private individual.

The implications of this change for journalism, television and the 'mass' media are still being thought through, although the virtually limitless archiving capacity of the Internet, combined with the global scale of its potential reach, is already being exploited with sites for every specialist interest under the sun. Journalists are transforming into *editors* (manipulators of existing information) rather than *gatherers*. Television has evolved into various post-broadcast forms, including 'media' that use webcams to transmit private life into cyberspace, there to become public spectacle.

METAPHOR

A rhetorical term when one thing stands for another. Metaphors become embedded in languages to such an extent that some linguists, e.g. Roman Jakobson (1960), have argued that they are one of the fundamental mechanisms for meaning-creation (the other is **metonym**). Humans make sense of the world, of themselves and of their interactions by extending to unknown or new phenomena the characteristics of known ones, thus capturing new experience in terms of something already known. The embeddedness of metaphor is intriguing, since it is unclear how far metaphors of spatial organisation (e.g., up, down, higher, lower), for instance, condition people's thinking about each other's rank. Symbolic and social life is completely suffused with metaphor: there is really no such thing as 'plain English'. The choices made to produce almost any lexical string depend on embedded metaphor – indeed, 'lexical *string*' is a metaphor; 'depend' is a metaphor (Latin: '*hang from*'); 'em*bed*ded metaphor' is a metaphor.

Visual metaphors abound in cinema and TV, especially in the way that concrete visualisations stand for abstract ideas: there are both novel and clichéd ways to convey 'normality', 'threat', 'the city', 'prostitution', 'bad guy', etc. In television, visual metaphors are used to cue viewers as to the social standing of sitcom or soap opera characters or families – the style and decoration of fridges on the set, for instance. There was a vogue for *spice racks*, a visual metaphor that for a while was an almost infallible marker of the 'middle-class family' on British TV sitcoms.

METHODOLOGY

The study of, or explicit concern with, methods of investigation in research of any kind, or the body of methods used in any one branch. The methodological tool cupboard of communication, and cultural and media studies is capacious, because these are interdisciplinary fields. They have borrowed methods from sociology, anthropology and other social sciences with a history of serious concern for methodology, as well as from literary and textual analysis, in which formal method training has traditionally played a less prominent role. Methods are usually rule-bound modes of investigation, taking care to outline function and field of inquiry. Before a method is chosen it is important to establish what knowledge we are attempting to access and for what purpose. This is where methodology as the 'science' of method is useful, hovering behind such choices as a check not only on how well what is proposed fits in with established rules and procedures, but also on whether the right method for the job has been chosen.

Methods fall broadly into two categories – empirical and theoretical. Theoretical methodologies within communication and cultural studies include Marxism, psychoanalysis, semiotics, textual analysis, feminist and queer theory, as well as theoretical work done in contributory or neighbouring disciplines, from science to sociology. These types of methodologies are less interested in providing an individual method than they are concerned with the possibilities of understanding how we make sense of the world.

Empirical methods are concerned with studying actually existing recoverable artefacts. These may include quantitative data – the numbers and statistics that may result from content analysis, censuses and surveys. Or the data may be qualitative, e.g. that collected via participant observation or ethnographic methods. Both quantitative and qualitative data may be suitable for *generalisation*. But equally, individual texts are irreducibly empirical – you can prod them – so the practice of 'close textual reading', as done by cultural analysts since Richard Hoggart, is itself an empirical method. However, it is directed not towards generalisable but *particularistic* results. There are frequent squabbles between 'empiricists' and 'textualists', because although both are interested in an empirical object of study, the method chosen in each case is very different.

Quantitative, qualitative, ethnographic and 'textual' methods are all necessary in the overall methodology of cultural, communication and media studies. Hartley (1996) proposed that it is often more appropriate to employ what Paula Amad (1994) has called 'theory shopping' to chose the right method for a given inquiry. This is not to be understood as an excuse for 'anything-goes postmodernism'. Rather it encourages the use of a judicious mix of theory and other approaches so as to avoid some of the all-too-familiar end results that plague many investigations.

See also: **Audiences, Content analysis, Effects, Ethnography, Participant observation**

Further reading: Berger (2000); Corner (1998)

METONYMY

A term from rhetoric where part stands for whole. 'The Crown' stands for the monarchy. Metonym works the other way round also, where whole stands for part. 'The USA' might refer to the government of that country, or its basketball team or a presidential opinion. Metonymy may be used to identify a significant function ('hand' for labourer, 'squeeze' for partner). Along with **metaphor**, metonym was thought by the linguist Roman Jakobson to be a fundamental mode of meaning-creation. Where metaphor works though choice substitution ('ice' for 'diamonds'), metonym works along the chain of signification (the syntagm as opposed to the paradigm). Jakobson thought that realistic novels were metonymic – part of life standing for its entirety. News is metonymic on the same principle (whereas drama may be metaphoric).

MODE OF ADDRESS

A concept referring to those processes that take place within a text to establish a relationship between the addresser and the addressee. It refs to how both media texts and media organisations address audiences. While it originates from the study of face-to-face communication, mode of address can also refer to textual features beyond verbal language.

Mode of address is reliant on the genre in which it appears. In everyday communication, the way the same story is related will often alter when told to a friend, a parent, a policeofficer or via an office document. So it is with media texts, where the mode of address will alter between, for example, news and current affairs and game shows. While there are differences in the processes involved, mode of address allows media texts to invent a fictional image of their preferred audience. **Discourse** analysis is useful here in uncovering the characteristics of this imagined viewer.

Relevant to notions of address is Althusser's theory of **interpellation**. Interpellation refers to how subjects are 'hailed' by the discourse of a text. Consider the example of sports reporting. Here, interpellation works through the ideology of nation (or city, etc.). The commentator's mode of address assumes or even requires (hails) a *national subject*. To understand the force of interpellation, then, you only have to watch sports coverage from someone else's nation or city – they are clearly not addressing you at all, and what is more, they are getting excited about things that are unimportant; it's all too obviously ideology. The Althusserian position is that all media discourse is ideological in this way, because no matter what it is about, it must employ a mode of address that interpellates a subject.

Consideration of mode of address need not be limited to individual texts. Entire television stations will utilise different modes of address in order to differentiate themselves and make unique the types of programming they offer. This feature can be noted most obviously in a station's own promotional advertising. The same can be said of newspapers, where what differs between one title and another is not the content (they cover the same stories) but the mode of address – one is aimed at women, one at lads, another at business leaders and so on. Thus the difference between the *Daily Mail*, the *Sun* and *The Financial Times* is at least in part a difference of mode of address creating a special relationship between addresser and addressee through discursive strategies.

See also: **Genre, Ideology, Interpellation**

MORAL PANIC

A term used to describe public anxiety about a perceived deviancy or threat from within a culture itself that is thought to challenge generally accepted societal norms, values and interests. The term moral panic was originally employed by Jock Young (1971) and Stanley Cohen (1980) in studies of deviancy in the media. They argued that the media played an ideological role, both contributing to and amplifying the active construction of certain kinds of meaning (McRobbie, 1994: 203).

The problem with moral panic theory is that is assumes that the media are involved in misrepresentation or distortion of opinion. However, as Lumby (1999b) points out, this suggests that there is some place outside of the mediasphere where rational debate and opinion are being informed in direct contrast to the media's construction. But by now the media are fully integrated participants in the process of public opinion and policy formation; they don't 'amplify' anxieties generated elsewhere, but *orchestrate* them. Thus, evidence of what looks like a moral panic needs to take account of the extent to which particular media are campaigning on an issue, whether it be juvenile crime or the 'outing' of paedophiles.

See also: **Discourse, Public sphere**

Further reading: Cohen (1980); Thornton (1994)

MOTIVATION (OF THE SHOT)

The arrangement of props and actions in a film or video shot to suggest the source of diegetic features (see **deixis**). Light is motivated if a window, table lamp, candle, extraterrestrial being or other source is shown on screen as well as the light that apparently emanates from it. However – and this is the point for analysts – it is extremely rare to find that the scene actually is lit from the motivating source; motivation is a convention designed to promote naturalism (verisimilitude).

Motivation is among the distinctive features of a genre, contributing to its aesthetics. TV soap opera, for instance, has become associated with unmotivated studio lighting; lots of it, pouring down on the glistening heads of the characters, brightening colours but flattening the scene. Subtly motivated lighting, conversely, is often associated with high-budget drama series, precisely to set apart such (filmed) shows from the 'cheaper' look of studio (video) productions.

Hartley and Montgomery (1985) found the term *motivation* useful to distinguish between different kinds of news camerawork. Motivated news filming is where the camera 'defers' to the action and participants, following their movements by panning, reframing, etc. Unmotivated news camerawork, conversely, imposes itself on the scene without reference to what participants are actually doing. Often this is by means of a close-up shot on an apparently insignificant detail, followed by a reframing zoom-out/pan to a wide shot of the main action. Where both motivated and unmotivated news camerawork are co-present in one news item, and applied to opposing parties in an industrial dispute, the argument is that this is a form of visual bias, producing an ideological preference for those treated 'deferentially'.

Further reading: Hartley (1992a); Hartley and Montgomery (1985)

MODERN/MODERNISM/MODERNITY

Modernity may be thought of as a period, modernism as an ideological attitude towards that period. Like all historical phenomena, modernity developed unevenly. It 'began' at rather different times over about half a millennium, depending on the area under scrutiny.

- *Economic* modernity began in the 1400s in the city-republics of Italy, with the invention of banking, joint-stock companies, international trade and, therefore, of capitalism.
- *Technological* modernity may be traced even further back to 'early modern' inventions that were made in medieval times, but without which modernity could not have taken the course that it did. These included the plough, the compass, gunpowder and printing in Europe from the 1200s to 1450s. Technologies of exploration, mapping and navigation, associated with a range of maritime nations from the 1400s to 1600s – Genoa, Portugal, Spain, the Dutch, England – were also 'modern' applications of medieval technologies.
- *Literary* modernity began with secular drama presented to an unknown audience for profit (Shakespeare), the novel (Cervantes) and realism (both journalistic and literary); these developments occurred at the beginning of the seventeenth century.
- *Scientific* modernity began with the scientific revolution of the seventeenth century, associated with Galileo and Francis Bacon, and

with the Royal Society, founded in 1662.

- *Philosophical* modernity began with the Enlightenment, centred on the eighteenth-century philosophers of France.
- *Political* modernity began with the transfer of sovereignty from monarch to people. After an interrupted English experiment (1645–1660), it was inaugurated successfully, i.e. continuously, in the American (1776) and French (1789) Revolutions.
- *Industrial* modernity began with the Industrial Revolution, associated with the 'steam age' and manufacturing pioneered in England from about 1780 to 1830.
- *Cultural* modernity came of age in the nineteenth century, when all these influences were fused and generalised internationally, with the great metropolitan cities, rapid communication systems, industrial workforces, popular entertainments and the beginnings of media, tourism, department stores and mechanised warfare. Here was where New York began to outshine its European antecedents.

Modernism as an artistic or literary movement was associated with the intellectual and artistic reaction to the last of the developments noted above; it was influential at the turn of the twentieth century.

There was also, perhaps more importantly, a 'small-m' modernism that turned the historical amalgam of modernity (as above) into a kind of manifesto. This was modernism as the pursuit of modern ideals – reason, truth, progress, science, secularism, popular sovereignty, open society, technology and communication. Such an *ideology* of modernism contrasted with the *condition* of modernity by its partisanship, and it tended to become more pronounced the more it felt itself threatened. Threats to modernism of this sort came from three directions:

- pre-modern thought – magical systems, traditional authority, private realities;
- modernity's own 'dark side' – the horrors that reason and science could unleash, from the Holocaust to Hiroshima, Apartheid to colonialism, exploitation by market, gender, race, class, etc.
- postmodernism – 'high' modernists saw 'postmodern' developments as undermining truth and reason in the name of relativism and irrealism, displacing the hope of progress in the rush for identity, which was seen as retribalising modern societies.

See also: **Culture wars, Meaning, Postmodern/postmodernism/ postmodernity**

MP3

A compression technology that allows for the storing and transmitting of audio data, usually music. Evolving from the development of digital television, MP3 technology provides the means for transferring digital audio to data that can be translated by computer software. The original intention for this technology was a means of saving valuable information space held on hard drives and CD ROMs. This certainly has been achieved – for example, thirteen hours of MP3 files can now be stored on a CD compared to traditional digital audio only allowing for seventy-four minutes.

MP3 files not only provide an efficient means of storing audio information but also for transmitting it. It is here that most discussion concerning MP3s is centred. Prior to a court order closing down online music distributor Napster in 2001, MP3 users were able to traffic and trade favoured songs, artists and genres with other users with a speed and an ease that were previously unknown. Intervention from the music industry, however, has attempted to halt this activity, with copyright infringement cited as the legal rationale.

While the debate over intellectual **copyright** continues to impinge on the future uses of MP3s, musicians continue to argue the importance of this new technology. For newer artists MP3s provide a means of distributing their music without the need for record label and distributive support. Established artists too are seeing the potential for establishing a direct link between themselves and their fans without the need for support from the music industry. The threat to the music industry as a result of these possibilities suggests that further debates concerning MP3s will not be based on technological possibility, but rather how to control, regulate and benefit economically from the distribution possibilities.

See also: **Online music distribution**

Further reading: Hacker (2000)

MULTI-ACCENTUALITY

A property of signs, consisting in the capacity every sign has to signify more than one meaning, depending on the circumstances of its use. The term was coined by Volosinov (1973) as part of an argument which sought to show how the meaning of signs is fixed not by the abstract system of language (**langue**), but by the **dialogic** interaction of social relations within which the potential for meaning is fixed.

In principle multi-accentuality is a property of all signs, but in practice most signs are not constantly the object of active struggle. However, the concept remains useful in accounting for such phenomena as anti-languages or languages of resistance such as those of slaves in the West Indies in the eighteenth and nineteenth centuries, which are characterised by complete inversions of existing signs and their values (thus 'black' is inverted to become the sign for 'good', 'powerful', 'sacred', and so on). Feminism too has demonstrated that apparently inert signs ('he', 'man', 'mankind') are ideologically loaded and represent social power relations.

MULTICULTURALISM

Diversity of population and culture as public policy. The advent of multiculturalism as a governmental programme signified a deliberate departure in the way that nation-states historically have chosen to depict themselves. Rather than projecting an image of the nation as a unified, culturally homogenous group, multiculturalism recognises that contemporary society is made up of distinct and diverse groups. The official policies of multiculturalism aim to manage cultural diversity through welfare, culture and social justice initiatives. The intention is to move away from 'assimilation' of migrants or Indigenous people towards wider social acceptance of difference as something legitimate and valuable.

Multiculturalism emerged in the latter half of the twentieth primarily as a response to political demands from **ethnic** minorities. Countries facing populations that contained distinctive cultural groups as a result of migration policies began to accept that assimilation was either not possible or not desired for a large proportion of groups. Migration, as a result, took on new significance. It was no longer simply a means to population growth, but something culturally significant requiring government recognition and assistance.

In the 1970s Australia and Canada officially declared themselves multiculturalist societies. Considerable infrastructure was erected to support these policies, including, in Australia, the SBS or Special Broadcasting Service, a national radio and television network dedicated to 'free-to-air' broadcasting of materials in languages other than English and English-language programming that promotes multicultural aims. SBS television, run on a shoestring compared to established public broadcasters (in Australia, the ABC), is a wonder of world television.

Early works on multiculturalism advocated 'toleration' as a means of living peacefully in a society made up of disparate groups (Walzer, 1997). These have been replaced by demands for public affirmation and respect for difference, as toleration can have the negative implication of 'conceding the validity of society's disapproval and relying on its self-restraint' (Parekh, 2000: 1).

Some people of colour have rejected multiculturalism as cosmetic and even part of entertainment culture, arguing that it has not had sufficient effect on the living conditions of people in non-white neighbourhoods. As Joan Morgan put it in the American context, multiculturalism *can* come over as another 'brand' of white consumerism:

> What white American racism offers to people of color, under the guise of multiculturalism, is an invitation to a dinner where we are expected to lay out a cultural smorgasbord while white America shows up with a very big fork.

(Morgan, 1994: 34)

See also: **Diaspora, Ethnic/ethnicity, Nation**

Further reading: Castels *et al.* (1988); Rajchman (1995)

MULTIMEDIA

The term multimedia was used originally to describe audio-visual presentations that consisted of slide presentations synchronised with sound (Wise, 2000) – in other words, the very same mode of exhibition as the magic lantern shows of the nineteenth century. The literal definition of the term as the processing and presentation of communication by more than one medium (audio *and* visual) still holds true but has been extended and complicated in contemporary use.

It is now most widely used to refer to communication that is mediated by computer technologies and that utilises a repertoire of graphics, text, sound, animation or video. This includes web sites, video games, digital television, electronic books and CD ROMs. The boundaries of multimedia's definition are far-reaching and unspecified in literature on the subject. A common characteristic, however, is the appearance of cohesion, or 'seamlessness'. The integration of images, text, audio and video within multimedia is often made possible by digital technology, although it may also involve analogue media.

Multimedia has liberated the way in which ideas are presented. The sci-fi dream of being able to layer sensory experiences in the recreation of real or imagined worlds – complete with taste, sound, touch and visual images – may not be fully realised yet, but due to multimedia developments it appears to be getting closer.

See also: **Digital/analogue distribution, New media technologies**

MYTH

Myth is generally understood to be a form of **narrative** that is shared amongst members of a traditional community or culture. In communications studies myth is understood as a means of disguising or masking ambiguities within a culture, and to a certain extent its role can be understood as ideological. Its theoretical application is usually anthropological, psychoanalytical and/or semiotic.

The anthropological understanding of myths is influenced by the work of Claude Lévi-Strauss, who argued that myths are unique to specific cultures and are used as a means of explaining the workings of the world: they are thinking machines. He argued that these explanatory narratives worked to 'deal with contradictions in experience, to explain the apparently inexplicable, and to justify the inevitable' (Turner, 1993: 72). The contradictions inherent in human existence were thought through in myths using **binary opposition**, simplifying the process of 'being' into an either/or scenario. To this end, myth worked to **ex-nominate** the gaps that can be understood to exist *between* such oppositions.

The psychoanalytical approach carries with it a similar thesis in that it is concerned with how myths seek to teach universal morals albeit on a more 'internal' level. The work of Jung is influential here, as he developed what he termed *archetypes* that he thought were common to all myths. Jung argued that the archetypical characters in myths guide individuals into behaving in certain ways, and proffer, for instance, preferred types of gendered behaviour as a means for reaching our ideal humanity (see O'Shaughnessy, 1999: 147–154). Like Lévi-Strauss' understanding, Jung's also is based on a series of binary oppositions as a means of masking contradictions.

The **semiotic** understanding of myths is one that is influenced by the work of Barthes (1973: 117) who argued that myth was a mode of **signification**. He argued that in myth, the link between the signifier and the signified was motivated (unlike the arbitrary model that underpins semiotics), so that a culturally constructed sign becomes a signifier, thus allowing what is signified to be naturalised.

Contemporary examples of this form of mythical analysis can be applied to leisure-wear brand names. The name of Nike for instance has come to signify an attitude, status and class that are beyond what might otherwise be signified by sports apparel (i.e. practically nothing). In examples such as this, and in many contemporary advertisements, myth works to mask its very own contradictions – which in the case of Nike is largely the price of, for example, a sports shoe in comparison to the values of those who supposedly wear them. Myth works to naturalise contradictions such as these and attempts to turn something that is cultural (a shoe) into something natural ('just doing it').

See also: **Narrative, Semiotics/semiology**

Further reading: O'Shaughnessy (1999)

NANOTECHNOLOGY *see* biotechnology

NAPSTER *see* MP3, online music distribution

NARRATIVE

Narrative is continuous story. It has two facets. The first is the *chain* or plot. Plot tends to move between an opening equilibrium that is disrupted, precipitating the action that goes through the usual tribulations, towards a new or restored equilibrium. Or, as the old Three-Act Play had it: Act One: Get a man up a tree; Act Two: Throw stones at him; Act Three: Get him down again. The second facet of narrative involves *choice* or presentation – the way the story is realised or told. It is this facet, and the devices and surprises chosen in it, that are often the focus of textual analysis.

Narratives are understood to reveal the work of ideology and discourse in both plot and presentation; chain and choice. In the former, narrative is driven by a series of questions and answers in the movement between opening and closing equilibrium. Which character or discourse underpins these questions is often referred to as the point of view that leads to a preferred reading of the text. The resolution of these questions will often involve putting forward dominant cultural beliefs.

In the presentation of a narrative, what types of individuals are chosen as heroes, victims, villains or innocents may reproduce common cultural assumptions about such individuals. Accusations of stereotypes arise in analysis of narrative presentation, especially in relation to raced or gendered characters. It is narrative's use of shared cultural assumptions that leads to the suggestion that all narratives are ideological.

Narrative analysis is applicable to more than traditional film practices. It is a central function in photographic images and print advertising, where the reader of an image is invited to make sense of what happened before the image was captured and what will happen after.

Narrative is also applicable to non-fictional genres such as television news. In a similar way to soap operas, news does not explicitly begin with a stable situation, but rather assumes there has been one. The nightly news broadcast can be thought of as presenting the ongoing disruptions to this presumed equilibrium through the representation of question and answers. Like other narratives the techniques used in television news are 'meaningful because they are conventional rather than natural' (Taylor and Willis, 1999: 67). Attention to the narratives of news reporting reveals that they negotiate cultural values and beliefs in a way that is directly comparable to fictional narrative.

See also: **Discourse, Genre, Myth, Representation, Structuralism**

Further reading: Bordwell and Thompson (2001)

NASDAQ

The world's largest electronic stock exchange or securities market, founded in the US and launched in 1971. Its business is capital formation by share trading. Nasdaq was the focus of the '**dot.com**' boom and subsequently the 'tech wreck' of 1999–2000. It remains the barometer for the 'new economy': companies in the private and public sector trading including electronics, e-commerce, the Internet, interactive technologies and applications. Nasdaq had its big bubble (boom and bust) year in 1999–2000 and was restructured and floated as a for-profit company later in 2000. In the meantime it had linked with new and existing stock exchanges in Hong Kong,

Japan, Europe and Canada as part of a globalising strategy extending to Asia, Latin America and the Middle East. Nasdaq was designed to build 'the world's first truly global stock market – digital and Internet-accessible, open to anyone anywhere in the world, 24 hours a day' (*http://www.nasdaq.com/about/about_nasdaq.stm*).

NATION

An 'imagined community' which is understood as distinct and separate from all other nations. 'Nation' is a relational term; like any **sign**, one nation consists in being what the others are not. The concept belongs in fact to the realm of political signification: nations have no essential or intrinsic properties; each is a discursive construct whose identity consists in its difference from others.

'Nation' is often used to mean *nation-state* – a sovereign state with its own government, boundaries, defence forces, etc., and symbolic markers of nationhood such as a flag, an anthem, local currency, a head of state, membership of the UN and so on. But there are many nations that are not also nation-states. Some states encompass more than one nation (e.g., Wales, Scotland and Northern Ireland in the UK). Then there are nations which exceed national frontiers (e.g., China) or those incorporated in several other states (e.g., Kurdistan). And there are some nations without a state or any territory at all (e.g., Palestine).

If territory does not define a nation, then neither does race or ethnicity, and nor does language or culture. Most modern nations are multiracial, multilingual and multicultural to some degree, if not always in official policy, and they are getting more so. The dictionary or common-sense definition of a nation as being a large number of people of common ethnic descent, language and history, inhabiting a territory bounded by defined limits, is thus seriously at odds with the facts.

In fact, when nations are regarded as ethnic, coupling them to the state – and putting nineteenth-century liberalism's innocent-looking hyphen in the term 'nation-state' – can have disastrous consequences. States that couple statehood with *ethnic* nationhood can literally fail. For instance, Sri Lanka installed a Singhalese *state*, inevitably precipitating separatism and eventually war with the Tamil nation living on the island. Fiji has endured years of instability because native Fijians want a native Fijian *state*, despite the numerical majority of people of Indian origin living in Fiji. Singapore on the other hand avoided that fate by maintaining an ethnically neutral state.

A nation may be ethnic, but a state ought not to be. 'Ethnic cleansing' is the latest technique for trying to make a state and a nation coterminous. 'Balkanisation' is a term for the process of dissolution of a state into (often warring) statelets based on ethnicity. Rwanda in 1994 showed what can happen when a *state* apparatus is used to impose *ethnic* national ends. Many nation-states produce less bloody but nevertheless real internal tensions by coupling the nation to the state. For instance, despite the Indigenous nations living within it, and its very diverse multicultural population, Australia's official national icons, myths and heroes are relentlessly white and Anglo-Celtic.

This may explain why important critics such as Paul Gilroy believe that 'nation' is an irredeemable term and that nationalism is always racist (Gilroy, 1987, 1993). In the context of black activism and the dispersal of African and Afro-Caribbean people around the nations bordering the Atlantic Ocean from South America to Scotland, such a view has force.

Even so, there are nationalisms that work from socialist principles – in Wales for instance. And some post-colonial or decolonising countries have produced non-racist nationalisms that could be a model for others – Singapore for one. Indigenous ethno-nationalisms are 'mixed' in this context: they are emancipatory movements, but rely on ethnic descent to identify those in need of emancipation, and are not normally 'independence movements' as such. They seek recognition of ethnic nationhood within a larger nation-state. Perhaps they point the way towards nationalisms that can recognise race without succumbing to racism.

Clearly 'nation' refers not to the external world of 'facts' but to a symbolic referent – an 'imagined community' (Anderson, 1983), which is maintained by a wide variety of discursive institutions, ranging from national literatures and languages to national curricula in education. There are of course national inflections in all areas of economic, political, cultural and discursive life; but certain institutions play a more prominent and routine role in creating and sustaining an evolving referent for the concept and its subjects. Among the more important of these are the media.

Participation in the nation is 'imagined' because no one can know more than an infinitesimal number of the other citizens of their nation, but it is a 'community' because everyone has complete confidence in the simultaneous co-existence of all the others. This sense of community is built and sustained by the quotidian rhythms of print and electronic media output, along with periodic national ceremonies which are themselves communicated through the media.

With increased migration and mobility, these symbolic markers of a nation can be the only common 'heritage' it has. Certainly, such markers are ever-more prevalent in the media, a common motif in advertisements, continuity and the like to propose a euphoric unity among groups which otherwise display few common traits. Here, the nation has been appropriated as a 'user-friendly' metaphor through which *multi-national* firms mobilise not citizens but consumers. However, it is more vital than ever to make such markers ethnically inclusive.

See also: **Ethnic/ethnicity**

Further reading: Anderson (1983); Hartley (1992a)

NATURALISING

The process of representing the cultural and historical as natural. Naturalising is a distinctive feature of ideological **discourses**. The ideological productivity of naturalisation is that circumstances and meanings that are socially, historically, economically and culturally determined (and hence open to change) are 'experienced' as natural – that is, inevitable, timeless, universal, genetic (and hence unarguable).

Naturalisation is the prize in modern cultural and signifying struggles; class or male supremacy, for example, is expressed as natural, and conversely resistance to that supremacy is represented as unnatural. So socialist and feminist discourses have to contend both with the naturalised discourses that continuously encourage us to understand social relations in ways that reproduce class and gender inequalities, and with the difficulty of establishing *as* natural (or as not unnatural) their alternative discourses and representations. Naturalising, then, is a force in the maintenance of hegemony.

See also: **Hegemony**

NATURALISM

A term which is often used as a synonym for realism. It first became influential in the theatre, where it referred to those modernist plays, especially Ibsen's, which tried to do away with signs and replace them with the objects that such signs had stood for. Thus, a play set in a living room would be staged with a living room on the stage –

aspidistras, chintz curtains and all. Speeches would be written not as staged speeches, but as if they were 'actually happening'. Actors would not represent their characters, but become them (this became codified as 'method' acting). Of course, everyone on stage has to pretend the audience was not there, since audiences aren't generally to be found in people's living rooms. So this kind of theatre is voyeuristic from the point of view of the audience, a point of view known as the 'fourth wall', since that is the perspective the audience uses to view the play.

Clearly naturalism was a gift for cinema, and even more for the domesticated medium of television, where the camera and crew replace the audience in the setting, so you don't even have a sense of 'being in the theatre' to put alongside 'being in that person's living room'. The ideological productivity of the naturalist conventions is considerable, because the 'reality' of the objects and interaction represented allows the representation itself to appear as innocent, self-effacing. Our attention is devoted to looking 'through' the screen and into the setting, so that any sense we might make of the drama appears to arise directly from the scene depicted, and not from its representation. It comes across more imperatively than something clearly constructed or 'handled' according to recognised conventions. And that, of course, is the point. Television exploits naturalism on the set to promote the naturalisation of images/representations on the screen.

NATURE

The material world as a whole together with its determining forces; the inherent or essential qualities of an object which determine its form, substance and behaviour. Because it is a multidiscursive concept which defies attempts to give it a precise referent, the term should be used with care in analytical work. At the very least the nature of an object, or the material world of nature, or the word nature itself, should not be taken as self-evident with respect to any qualities, properties or characteristics whatsoever: these natures are the object of study, not the premise.

Nature is often contrasted with culture; the non-human as opposed to the human. However, this non-human nature is often taken to be an inherent or essential quality of the human itself – as in human nature. In such usages the concept appears ultimately to be a secularisation of the category of God – a non-human agency which is beyond our control but which determines our characteristics and behaviour. In this sense, nature is an ideological category.

The other main way in which nature is used in analytical discourses is as the material properties of an object. Hence the nature of something is contrasted with whatever conceptions of it might be available (the nature of the planet earth is contrasted with conceptions of it as flat). Nature in this sense is the proper object of study for science: the attempt to reveal or discover by analysis the 'true' nature (determining properties) of an object of study.

Further reading: Eagleton (2000)

NET RADIO

Radio, since its creation, has been understood as a broadcast medium, transmitted from a central tower and receivable by radio equipment within the signal's limited reach. Net radio has none of these technical characteristics. It is made possible by streaming technologies that carry the audio information across the **Internet** and is receivable through computers via telecommunications infrastructure. As it is carried over the Internet, it can be received anywhere in the world where such technology is available.

Net radio is what Marshall McLuhan (1964) called a 'rearviewmirrorist' invention. In its first years, television content was developed that mimicked existing radio and theatre formats. Net radio is only conceived of, referred to and marketed *as radio* in order to satisfy the desire of audiences, and producers, for a reference point. By attaching an existing label to a new technology we are able to create a familiarity with something that might otherwise be a radically different, and difficult, concept to grasp. However, as with the early days of television, by breaking free from **rearviewmirrorism**, audio Internet content may reach new levels of innovation. Some net radio stations already allow listeners to create their own listening programme – a significant departure from the broadcast radio format where listeners are restricted to the station's selection (see also Hartley, 1992a).

NETWORK SOCIETY

In the late twentieth century, a historical shift occurred in the configurations of social organisation. Statism and capitalism – around which existing social principles were ordered – were both fundamentally redefined through the development of information technologies. Manuel Castells (1996) named this new social landscape the 'network society'.

Networks are interconnected systems that exchange data selectively and intentionally. They dissolve centralised power and institutionalised hierarchy. Access to a network requires the ability to decipher, to understand the technology and its rules. In the network society, economic and political transactions are conducted by organisations that are arranged as information networks. Globalised (and largely digitised) markets shifts capital strategically around the world at a rapid speed. Nation-states strive to become network states, influential through their partnerships (the EU, the UN, trade agreements, etc.) rather than their autonomy. Individuals group around identities of religion, ethnicity and nation instead of central, institutional powers. The Internet – a decentralised communications network – has become a primary tool for community interaction.

Information technologies are at the centre of the network society. Microelectronics, communication technologies and genetic engineering signify a shift to a new technological paradigm characterised by connectivity and information. Whereas the technologies of the industrial age were created to accelerate the manufacturing of material goods, the technologies of the network society are used in the production and distribution of knowledge and information. **Biotechnology** and **nanotechnology** represent the extension of this cycle. These technologies manipulate the organic, coordinating the information of life at the molecular level.

Within the new paradigm, information technologies are used to create increasing returns within the network. Bob Metcalf, pioneer of the network technology that led to the development of the Internet, realised that networks increase exponentially with each new addition. Therefore, with telephone services, each new person with access to the phone line would significantly increase the possible pairings between all callers (Kelly, 1998).

However, the network is selective and strategic by nature. An individual's or a group's place within a network will have consequences for their ability to generate wealth and to communicate effectively with others within the network. Individuals, localities and nation-states are susceptible to exclusion from the network, to being disenfranchised. For Castells, choosing or being forced to live outside the network is associated with fundamentalism. Rejection of the network may motivate al-Qaida terrorism, which may therefore be said to be a product of its extension across the world.

See also: **Globalisation, Information society/information economy**

Further reading: Escobar (2000)

NEW ECONOMY

The capitalisation and commercialisation of information and know-ledge, especially via the use of ICT and new interactive media. Alan Greenspan, Chairman of the US Federal Reserve Bank, described this as a shift to a new 'weightless' economy. As Diane Coyle explains:

> whether it is software code, genetic codes, the creative content of a film or a piece of music, the design of a new pair of sunglasses or the vigilance of a security guard or helpfulness of a shop assistant, value no longer lies in three-dimensional objects in space.
>
> (Coyle, 1998: x)

The value is in **intangibles**, especially information.

Although manufacturing is still necessary, much of this activity has been redistributed to the less economically powerful nations or adapted to new technologies in order to increase efficiency (Giddens, 1994). In this way, the new economy consists of the *knowledge* and *service industries*. Skills, personality, knowledge, intelligence, information and the technology to mobilise such qualities are at the centre of the new economy.

For some it brings with it increasing risk (Beck, 1992), requiring new attention to the cultivation of social capital and trust (Giddens, 2000; Leadbeater, 1997). When economists and social theorists use the term new economy they are referring to the large shifts that have come about through globalisation and information technologies. The **network society**, the **information society** and the **knowledge society** all describe the new configurations that influence and make up the new economy.

See also: **Globalisation**

Further reading: Kelly (1998); Quah (1997); Tapscott (1995)

NEW MEDIA POLICIES

New media technologies such as the Internet are proving to be a challenge to once reliable policy mechanisms imposed by governments within their national territories. Because of media convergence, content and competition, regulatory concerns are not restricted to the Internet. For example, interactive television services are capable of giving viewers access to the World Wide Web through their television set. This not only presents concerns in the area of content regulation and classification processes, it may also complicate existing ownership and competition safeguards. Through broadband technology, the broadcaster may be able to direct viewers to additional (Internet) channels. Alternatively, the new technology may allow new players into the broadcasting market surreptitiously through the Internet.

In the past, media policy has been directed at ensuring universal, affordable access to media communications and upholding principles of democracy, opportunity, fairness and security (Collins and Murroni, 1996). Media businesses have enjoyed monopoly, or market dominance, only in exchange for meeting government public interest requirements (sometimes termed 'quid pro quo'). These policies have been industry specific, often with separate regulatory agencies overseeing their application.

Some policy analysts maintain that with convergence, the only regulatory measures required for the media should be generic (rather than industry specific) competition policy. In this scenario, a single regulator with a directive to ensure competition and prevent dominance by one or few players would act as a watchdog on all aspects of economic activity (and not simply the media industry). Collins and Murroni maintain that 'competition policy is not sufficient to establish a robust civil society animated by vigorous debate. Nor will it establish easy access for citizens to the information necessary to fully participate in political and social life' (1996: 167). Much of the debate around new media policies centres on these concerns: whether the role of government is actively to provide and nurture a diverse, universal and healthy **mediasphere**, or whether the market is more capable of achieving this if left to its own devices.

Deregulation of the media industry could arguably be justified as a result of media convergence and the new issues of whether regulation is possible in all cases. However, it is more likely that the forecasted economic rewards of media deregulation in the new media environment are driving new media policies, as many of these dilemmas remain hypothetical due to current industry structures and consumer preferences.

Since the mid-1990s, governments in developed countries have been drawing up visionary blueprints, or strategies, that will improve their ability to participate within the **information economy** (Gore, 1999). The original vision for new media policies was delivered in the US under the title National Information Infrastructure (NII). Intended as a broadband communications network, the NII was based on principles of:

- private investment
- competition
- economic progress,
- the advancement of democracy
- providing better solutions to environmental issues

As Barr points out, 'these five now consistently appear in so many economic development national blueprints that they have virtually become international communications policy benchmarks' (Barr, 2000: 171).

NEW MEDIA TECHNOLOGIES

The first new media technology we know about was writing, invented about 3100 BC in Egypt and Sumaria, and separately in China around the same time, and never subsequently extinguished, no matter what changes in civilisation ensued. Thus writing is as much a communications technology as the telephone: both are used to distribute ideas between people. Technologies are the systems and machinery that we use for getting things done (Green, 1994). Advances in communication technologies have had immense consequences for cultural, economic and political life, determining the ways in which information is processed, transferred and creatively expressed.

Although technologies have always had a transformative impact upon society, the current interest in communications technology – in creating and advancing it, deploying and theorising it – seems unprecedented (Barr, 2000: 21). The new media technologies are said to have 'reshaped the material basis for society' (Castells, 1996: 1), enabling the globalisation process through their capacity to distribute information at a rapid pace and volume. Important discourses on economic shifts (the **new economy**, or the **knowledge economy**) and cultural possibilities (**cyberdemocracy**, **cyborg** and **virtual communities**) all point to the significance of change brought about by new media technologies.

A key characteristic of new communication technologies is digitalisation. As discussed by Feldman (1997), digital technology is compressible, able to be manipulated and networked, dense and impartial. Its density means that large amounts of digital information can be stored in a small space – what would otherwise take up shelves of printed books can be stored on a single CD. If it is still not dense enough, large files of information (such as video) can be compressed and then decompressed when required. As it is manipulable, the information can be reshaped easily, allowing for interactive services. Audiences can alter signals at the delivery point in order to specify what it is they wish to see, thus creating their own content. The networking ability of digital media means that information can be distributed to numerous users at once. All these characteristics combined have radically altered the speed and capabilities of media technology.

A significant result of digitalisation is that information can now also be transferred across otherwise distinct platforms. This means that the traditional media (television, radio, print) are no longer required to retain their separate identities. Print media content, for instance, can be received through a web site on a computer or a digital television set, with links to audio (radio-like content) or video (television-like content). The impact of media convergence on incumbent media institutions and industry structures is proving immense.

Media studies itself has changed significantly as a result of new media technologies. Apart from a range of new theoretical concerns arising from the advent of digital media, media studies is becoming increasingly 'hands-on'. As media production is now possible from the desktop, the distinction between those who do media and those who analyse it is becoming increasingly blurred.

See also: **Convergence, Digital/analogue distribution, Information society/information economy, Network society**

NEWS VALUES

Those professional codes used in the selection, construction and presentation of news. News values do not necessarily relate to individual journalists, who themselves are subject to personal values, beliefs and attitudes. Rather, the concept relates to the corporations that produce industrialised news. Within these environments, news values work to unify varying ideological stances amongst journalists and **gatekeepers** under the notion of objectivity. Understanding the implications of these procedures demonstrates how news is a creative product, rather than a mere reflection of reality.

Professionals generally justify the selection of stories not by reference to news values, but first by reference to the story itself – it has to be inherently newsworthy – and second to the demands of the audience – the story has to serve the public interest or satisfy their curiosity.

It is the notion of what makes a story newsworthy that has gained most critical attention (see for example Galtang and Ruge, 1973; Cohen and Young, 1973; Hartley, 1982). While the studies that have been undertaken point to some recurring themes within news practices, these should not be taken as definitive. As with all forms of research, each project is informed by differing approaches, assumptions and methods. That said, the following categories may be helpful, as long as it is recognised that news values are about news *stories* and not the events themselves.

- News values prioritise stories about events that are recent, sudden, unambiguous, predictable, relevant and close (to the relevant culture/class/location).
- Priority is given to stories about the economy, government politics, industry and business, foreign affairs and domestic affairs – either of conflict or human interest – disasters and sport.
- Priority is given to elite nations (the US, the UK, Europe, etc.) and elite people (celebrities).
- News values often involve appeals to dominant ideologies and discourses. What is cultural and/or historical will be represented as natural and consensual.
- News stories need to appeal to readers/viewers so they must be commonsensical, entertaining and dramatic (like fiction), and visual.

See also: **Bias, Gatekeeper, Infotainment, Objectivity**

Further reading: Hartley (1982); Watson (1998)

NOISE

A concept associated with traditional communication theory. Noise refers to the interference that is experienced during the transfer of information between a sender and a receiver. Aside from its literal meaning, the concept refers to those outside influences that may alter or disrupt the original meaning of the information being sent.

Noise can be either mechanical or semantic. The former includes static interference on radio and television, as well as crackle over the phone. Semantic noise refers to confusion over the meaning of the message. This can be caused by language and cultural differences as well the use of jargon or slang that may not be familiar to the receiver.

While not central to contemporary media studies, the term is nevertheless useful for communication practices such as public relations. Here, noise refers to a broad range of interference to optimum communication such as lobby and interest groups, as well as competing discourse.

OBJECTIVITY

Within the media claims to objectivity revolve around non-fictional genres such as news, current affairs and documentary. The general idea is that despite the processes and techniques of production, and the personal views of the production team, a given sequence portrays an accurate rendering of an objective situation that exists independently of its representation in that sequence. Clearly there are important issues at stake here, for on the reputation for objectivity rests the reputation and credibility of broadcasting and news organisations. But at the same time the claim of objectivity can itself be ideological – seeking to impose a particular perspective on a situation that may be imported into it by the producer or organisation. In other words, in the end, paradoxically, media objectivity is not about 'reality' or 'truth', so much as it is about trust between addresser and addressee.

Documentary often employs an ethnographic discourse as a means of claiming objectivity (see **ethnography**). Ethnography, however, is itself a method whose outcomes may well be influenced by the ideologies and subjectivity of the researcher. In news and current affairs, suspected lack of objectivity attracts accusations of **bias**. But like other genres, news is constructed through **representation**. Additionally, codes and conventions unique to news and current affairs limit what gets reported, who gets to speak and who is excluded. Rather than understand this as falling short of the ideals of objectivity, it is useful instead to consider, for instance, generic boundaries, the role of **gatekeepers** and consensual **news values**. In other words, objectivity can be honestly striven for by professionals, but is still, on-screen, an *effect* of semiotic and other textual strategies.

ONLINE

If someone is online they have entered a digital communications network. The term is most frequently used in reference to the Internet, whereby a modem carries information to and from the online user via telecommunications infrastructure (the 'line'). When devices such as printers are online, they are ready to receive data from a separate source such as a computer.

See also: **Connectivity, Internet**

ONLINE MUSIC DISTRIBUTION

Made possible by **MP3** technology, online music distributors provide a forum where users can swap and download music files of their favoured artists. The most famous of these, Napster, offered a free facility to its users to download and swap MP3s before trading was suspended in 2001. The music industry claimed that online music would deprive both the industry and artists of the income required to keep popular music alive, just as they did when recordable sound cassettes arrived in the late 1970s. Yet this industry, using **intellectual property** rights, now stands to benefit most from the new system of content delivery.

Recent developments in online music distribution suggest that it is not so much the *availability* of music on the Internet that concerns the music industry majors but rather the fact that it is *free*. Napster, having been bankrupted previously as pirates, was relaunched on a subscription-only basis with funding from industry giant Bertelsmann. The other music label giants have also got in on the act. Both *PressPlay* (a joint venture between Sony and Universal) and *MusicNet* (funded partially by Warner, EMI and Bertelsmann) offer subscription-based services but with more stipulations than during the previous era of file sharing. *PressPlay*, for example, allows 50 downloads per month, with only two tracks per artist permitted in that period. Additionally, if subscription lapses, tracks that have been downloaded are no longer accessible.

The shift from copying to borrowing or hiring music is not all that is apparent in the post-Napster environment of online music distribution. The business practices of the music industry are now under scrutiny due to accusations that they are impeding fair competition in the online market by restricting the supply and licence of major label music to other online distributors (Healy, 2001; Myers, 2002). It seems the liberating promise of online music distribution has been replaced by the same dichotomy that plagues the offline music business. Major recording labels not only have the major artists contracted to them but ensure the right to distribution of this content lies solely within their power.

See also: **Copyright, Intellectual property, MP3**

ORALITY

That which characterises speech; a culture characterised by the primacy of speech over other forms of signification. Usually opposed to literacy, orality refers to those aspects of a culture's way of life that are attributable to its investment in the resources of spoken language. These may include formal ways of organising thought (myth) or knowledge (magic); or they may be associated with rhetorical and other systems for fixing and transmitting sense.

The idea that oral cultures are fundamentally different from literate ones at the level of social and individual consciousness is associated with Marshall McLuhan, and may be followed up in Ong (1982). The analysis of oral systems of thought has occupied social anthropologists for years, and is perhaps best approached via the work of Lévi-Strauss (see Leach 1976; Sturrock 1979), whose structural method revolutionised Western thinking about 'primitive' myths, analysing them as a form of reasoning appropriate to oral societies.

Despite its official promotion and pervasive presence in industrial societies, literacy nevertheless has to co-exist with an abiding orality in certain crucial guttural spheres – perhaps the most obvious of which is the early socialisation of infants (see Lotman, 1990).

See also: **Literacy**

ORIENTALISM

A term used to describe a way of imaging what was traditionally known as the East. Developed by Edward Said (1979), a Palestinian intellectual living in the US, Orientalism refers to those practices, writings, policies, philosophies and ideologies that sought to construct a sense of the Orient. Said argues that Orientalism is to be found in both historical and academic accounts largely arising from Britain and France, and more recently the US. It is not to be understood as a form of racism; rather, it arises from the intention of understanding disparate and different cultures. Orientalism is a discourse.

As a discourse, Orientalism says little about the Orient. Said argued that through a discursive conception of the Orient, the West was able to construct an image of its own identity. That is, the West was the negative of 'Oriental', comprising what the 'Other' did not. In this sense, Orientalism involves a binary opposition that finds the West as central in modern, enlightened thought, and the Orient as the mysterious and often dangerous Other. Like all oppositions, this binary relies on a series of cultural constructions that in this instance can be understood as biological essentialism, as well as racial, religious and cultural prejudices.

The concept of Orientalism is useful for analysing media. *Indiana Jones and the Temple of Doom* provides an example where the white (Western) American hero is understood as noble, brave, strong, sexual and of consummate ability. In contrast, Oriental characters in the movie are either helpless victims awaiting the arrival of the hero or villains who enslave their own people.

Said (1985) argued that contemporary versions of Orientalism are to do with Arab and Islamic cultures. Certainly this concern seems apparent in the reporting on events such as the Gulf War as well as the US's post-September 11, 2001 'War Against Terrorism'. Here, the generalisation and grouping together of religious and national cultures that are collectively perceived as a threat to world order require critical consideration.

The use of the concept of Orientalism need not be restricted to discussing national or religious cultures. Some, such as Brennan (2001: 95) argue that the same concept can be applied to the category of youth. Here youth are cast as the helpless Other and the world of adulthood collectively imagined as responsible, enlightened and able. With the amount of intellectual discourse devoted to youth studies, it may be pertinent to revisit Said's call for 'a plurality of terrains, multiple experiences and different constituencies' (1985: 105). Youth, like the Orient, is often only captured through a discourse that relies on generalisations. It is the implications of these generalisations that are central to the theory of Orientalism.

See also: **Discourse, Ideology, Race, Representation**

Further reading: Said (1979)

PARADIGM

In **semiotics**, a paradigm is the notional set of signs from which a particular **sign** is chosen to be included in a syntagmatic combination. Like **syntagm**, paradigmatic selection involves a set of choices, but unlike the former, a paradigm is a set of signs that are interchangeable within a given context. Importantly, all 'units in a paradigm must have something in common [and] they must share characteristics that determine their membership of that paradigm' (Fiske, 1990: 57). Menus are paradigmatic lists: diners choose individual dishes from each section of the menu, the sequence of such dishes making the syntagm of the meal.

Paradigmatic analysis is useful in examination of **representations**, and in particular for ascertaining what signs have been chosen at the expense of others. Words, images, even colours, are chosen from a potential set: sometimes such choices are highly significant, for instance the decision about whether to use the term 'soldier', 'terrorist', 'freedom fighter' or 'armed man' in a news story.

The concept of paradigm is useful also in film studies where the sets of signs that are considered include characters and settings, as well as technical elements such as camera angle and lighting. In the depiction of characters for instance, the selection of certain traits and features that are assigned to figures of ethnicity and gender may have implications for how the narrative is read and what final meaning is attributed to those who are represented within its framework. Considering the paradigmatic selection within a text may reveal particular discursive strategies and ideologies at work.

See also: **Representation, Semiotics, Structuralism, Syntagm**

PAROLE

In Saussurian linguistics, the activity of speaking. The term was used by Saussure to separate out those variable and accidental aspects of speech that were to be excluded from the focus of linguistic inquiry. As such, parole needs to be understood in relation to its contrasting term, **langue**. Parole amounts to individual instances of speaking; langue to the abstract system that underlies it. Although what people actually do when speaking may be of interest to the physiologist or the behavioural psychologist, it cannot form the basis of linguistic study, because – for Saussure – it was subject to too much random fluctuation. Instead, linguistics should focus on the underlying sets of rules and conventions that make parole possible and guarantee its intelligibility.

There is nonetheless a close and complementary relationship between langue and parole. Parole may be seen as a continual implementation of the underlying system constituted in the langue; but conversely the continual practice of speaking adorns and adjusts the langue, moulding it gradually into a different form. No single individual can control or shape the langue; but generations of speakers can and do alter it from one historically specific state to another.

Like many of the terms originally developed in Saussure's lectures between 1906 and 1911, langue and parole achieved new currency during the 1960s and 1970s with the emergence of semiology as the study of sign systems (see **semiotics**). In this study a particular film or fashion garment could be seen as an individual instance of parole against the backdrop of the underlying system of film language or fashion codes. One difficulty with this application of the term is that it was much more difficult to think of ways in which film as a system of **signification** was available for study except through its parole, whereas language was more generally available through introspection because of its mental basis.

See also: **Code, Langue**

Further reading: Culler (1976); Montgomery (1986); Saussure (1974)

PARTICIPANT OBSERVATION

A method used in the social sciences to study the lived practices of a community or collective of some sort in a 'natural' environment, i.e. outside a laboratory or experimental context. Participant observation is a form of ethnography that has been used in media studies as a means of understanding how selected audiences make sense of and utilise media texts in their daily routines. Research of this kind seeks to garner a greater understanding of individuals through the submersion of the researcher into the lives of their research subjects.

See also: **Audiences, Ethnography, Methodology**

Further reading: Hansen *et al.* (1998)

PERFORMANCE

The semiotics of self. The concept of performance has gained ground in recent cultural analysis; it encompasses both institutionalised, professional performances (drama, ritual), and a non-psychologistic approach to individual people's self-presentation and interaction. It also seems to suffuse American popular culture and everyday encounters.

The appeal of performance as a general analytic category is twofold. First, its very generality: the term has been applied not only to what actors and other professionals do but also to the 'performance' of unrehearsed cultural practices in everyday life, to the actions of audiences, spectators and readers. Although performances in everyday life will differ markedly from theatrical or media performances, there are sufficient connections to make comparison worthwhile. You can analyse the differences between fictional and public performance (drama and politics); between acting conventions (naturalistic and ritualistic); between media (cinema and television); between genres (soap opera and Shakespeare); and so on.

Second, the concept of performance directs the analyst's attention not to the internal psychological state or even the behaviour of a given player, but to formal, rule-governed actions which are appropriate to the given performative genre. If you start looking at ordinary encounters in this way, from doctor–patient interviews to telephone calls, it is clear that there are performative protocols in play that require skill and creativity in the manipulation of space, movement, voice, timing, turn-taking, gesture, costume and the rest of the repertoire of enactment.

PERSUASION

The act of motivating or influencing the behaviour, opinions, values and beliefs of groups and individuals. Persuasion in the media is both political (political parties, lobbyists, interest groups, spin) and commercial (advertising, product placement, public relations). In communication practices such as marketing and PR, persuasion techniques are designed to 'influence *how* receivers choose or decide which information to process' (Ross, 1990: 4)

The genre of public service advertising is an example of the employment of persuasion techniques. Such campaigns are concerned with influencing and changing the attitudes of the public in relation to issues such as health and safety. In Australia in the 1980s, the actor Yul Brynner, who was suffering the effects of throat cancer, urged individuals to give up smoking, knowing that by the time people saw the ad he would be dead. DeFleur and Ball-Rokeach (1989: 214) call this 'social learning theory', whereby the use of a well-known public figure is thought to encourage behavioural modification.

Within this genre, however, it is the Threat (Hovland *et al.*, 1961: 60) or the Fear Appeal (Severin and Tankard, 2001: 159) that is most apparent. Advertising that discourages drink driving, speeding or unsafe sex will often employ this technique. Here, the persuasive address is aided by the depiction or description of the unfavourable consequences that will result should the receiver fail to adhere to the communicated information.

By examining the techniques of persuasive communication, what motivates nominated groups and individuals becomes apparent. How receivers choose which information to process will depend on the discourses, ideologies and values that are contained within these communications.

See also: **Discourse, Ideology**

Further reading: Ross (1990); Severin and Tankard (2001)

PHATIC COMMUNICATION

Communication designed to open or maintain contact between addresser and addressee. Its classic form is the greeting: 'Hello; G'day; Hi!' Phatic communication was identified by Roman Jakobson as one of the six functions of language. It is content-free: when someone passes you in the corridor and inquires 'How are you?', it would be a breach of manners to take the question as having content and actually to tell them what a bad day you've had.

Phatic communication is used 'ideologically' by broadcasting organisations. News anchors will say 'Good evening' to a camera, but (hopefully) be heard by viewers as establishing communication. The more populist and entertainment-oriented the show, the more it will distend phatic communication. Some weather people include more phatic communication in their updates than information about the weather – a truism made lethal by Nicole Kidman as the not-so-airhead weather-girl Suzanne Stone Maretto in the 1995 film *To Die For*. Game show hosts will engage in phatic communication with both contestants and viewers, at least in the non-competitive, fun versions of such shows. Their warm and friendly linguistic performance slides into corporate marketing, because the TV channel itself is associated with the openness and other-orientation characteristic of phatic communication.

See also: **Language, functions of**

PHONEMIC/PHONETIC

A useful conceptual distinction between two kinds of elements in a signifying system – one capable of generating meaning, the other not. The terms are borrowed from linguistics, but are applicable to any sign system. In linguistics, a *phoneme* is one of a limited number of sounds (in English there are about forty of them) that are *recognised* as part of the system of such sounds. Verbal utterance is based on the selection and combination of groups of these phonemes in a rule-governed order.

Phonetic, on the other hand, describes the sounds *actually made* by a speaker. The point about this is twofold:

- Each speaker will use her or his physiological, regional, contextual and other resources to produce a *unique* version of the generally recognised phoneme. No one says 'I' in quite the same way as anyone else, but everyone in a speech community will recognise the phoneme 'I' when used by a native speaker.
- All languages recognise as 'the same' phoneme sounds that are actually different. For instance, the 'k' sound in the spoken words 'kin' and 'ink' *sound* 'the same' to the speaker and the hearer. But they are *actually* different sounds, produced in slightly different parts of the mouth. Try it.

The conceptual point about this is again twofold:

- If we paid attention to the sounds we all *actually* make rather than the ones that are *recognised by the language* there is little chance we would be able to make sense of anything – there are too many differences.
- The power of language (as opposed to actuality) is so great that it is difficult for us to perceive anything outside its recognised elements: you may flatly disagree that the 'k' sounds are different, but an oscilloscope would not.

There is no mystery about this property of language. Following Saussure, we can say that phonemes are abstract and they belong to **langue**, whereas phonetics are concrete and belong to **parole**.

See also: **Difference, Phonology**

Further reading: Hawkes (1977)

PHONOLOGY

The branch of linguistics devoted to studying the sound patterns of a language. The human vocal organs are capable of producing an extremely rich array of different sounds. Each language, however, draws for communicative effect upon only a small portion of this total range. Phonology examines which particular units of possible sound constitute the basic meaningful set for any one language. It does so in the first instance by building up contrasting pairs of sounds on the principle that for any one language certain sounds will cause changes in the meaning of words, whereas other sounds will not. In English if we change the initial sound of /pig/ from /p/ to /b/ we end up changing one word into another – changing *pig* to *big*. By using this test, known as the minimal pairs test, it is possible to discover which sound substitutions cause a difference in meaning. Each change in meaning isolates a new element of the basic sound structure of the language, each element being known as a phoneme. Thus the minimal pair

> *pig* versus *big* isolates the phonemes /p/ and /b/
> *pig* versus *pin* isolates the phonemes /g/ and /n/
> *ten* versus *den* isolates the phonemes /t/ and /d/
> *rip* versus *lip* isolates the phonemes /r/ and /l/

and so on. The total inventory of phonemes built up using this method is *language-specific*. The contrast between /r/ and /1/ in English, for instance, is not matched by an identical contrast in Chinese **dialects**.

Phonological analysis is to be distinguished from phonetic analysis, where the emphasis is on the description and classification of speech sounds independent of meaning.

PIDGIN

A synthetic, simplified language of a type that sometimes develops between groups who lack a language in common, in order to facilitate contact between them. Many recorded examples of pidgins involve contact between an invading European colonial or mercantile power, and Indigenous communities. Initially the pidgin serves primarily for contact between the groups for quite specialised purposes such as trade. In these circumstances the pidgin borrows key vocabulary items from the language of the invading power to cover crucial areas of meaning such as number or livestock. This borrowed vocabulary is used with a highly simplified grammar in which word order is fixed, inflections are dropped, fewer prepositions are used, and so on. Pronunciation is likely to owe much to local sound patterns.

However, it is possible for the restricted purposes of the original pidgin to become extended, even after the withdrawal of the colonial power, if the pidgin proves useful for communication between local communities, especially where these communities speak mutually unintelligible languages. In Cameroon on the west coast of Africa there are at least two hundred vernacular languages for a population of less than eight million. Although French and English are maintained as official languages, there also exists an important link language – Cameroon Pidgin English – which is common amongst all sectors of the population, is widely distributed amongst the two hundred **ethnic** groups and has been spoken in the area for at least 150 years. Under such conditions quite significant developments can take place within the pidgin, increasing its complexity and extending its functions, including its use for written communication.

See also: **Dialect**

Further reading: Mulhauser (1986); Todd (1984)

POLYSEMY/POLYSEMIC

Refers to the ability of a **sign** to have multiple meanings. This concept recognises that meaning is not reproduced by referral to an essence, but rather is achieved through the difference of one sign from another. Furthermore, the polysemic nature of the sign confirms that there is no natural relation between its components, the signifier and the signified, but rather that this relationship is arbitrary. To take the example of a black dress as a sign, depending on the context in which it appears it may signify evening attire, a sexy outfit or a costume of mourning.

This should not be taken as an excuse to assume that analysis is impossible due to the nature of the sign. Barthes' (1973) notion of 'anchorage' argues that strategies are employed in all texts to anchor the preferred **meaning** or in other cases suggest one meaning as being more applicable than others. In advertising this may be the words that appear alongside the images in the text, and in film as well as television, it may be expectations of genre which limit potential multiple meanings. Barthes claimed that anchorage is necessarily an ideological imperative through which the polysemic nature of the sign is controlled. Writers such as Fiske (1987), on the other hand, understand polysemy as part of the pleasure, and indeed one of the required features, of media that strive to reach a mass and diverse audience.

See also: **Semiotics/semiology, Sign**

POPULAR/POPULAR CULTURE

Of people in general; for people in general; well liked by people in general. 'Popular' is often synonymous with 'good' in ordinary conversation, but this is an inversion of its earlier pejorative connotations. In its original form, popular was used to distinguish the mass of the people (not 'people in general') from the titled, wealthy or educated classes. Not surprisingly, since most writers on the subject were either members or clients of the latter three classes, its synonyms were gross, base, vile, riffraff, common, low, vulgar, plebeian, cheap (*OED*).

From these inauspicious beginnings the term has to some extent been 'decolonised', principally through its usage in democratic politics in and since the nineteenth century. However, it still retains sufficient traces of its history to be a **multi-accentual** term: the popularity of something may be taken either as an indication of its positive or of its negative value, depending on your alignment to 'the people'.

Thus the concept is not exempt from politics, which has in fact dogged its usage within the sphere of cultural analysis. The popularity (ubiquitousness) of the mass media in particular has resulted in a recurring ambiguity in both academic and public debate about whether the products of the media are good because they are popular, or bad because they are popular (the 'more means worse' or **dumbing down** view of popularity).

The ambiguity is not simply a matter of the personal prejudices of the critic. It is implicit in the position of those people and products that can be described as popular. It has two aspects. First, there is ambiguity about the extent to which popular culture is *imposed on* people in general (by media corporations or state agencies), or *derived from* their own experiences, tastes, habits, and so on. Second, there is ambiguity about the extent to which popular culture is merely an expression of a powerless and subordinate class position, or an autonomous and potentially liberating source of alternative ways of seeing and doing that can be opposed to dominant or official culture.

These ambiguities have an important bearing on the study of *popular culture*, since they make it very hard to specify an easily agreed object of study. What 'counts' as popular culture depends to some extent on whether you are interested in what meanings are produced *by* or *for* 'the people', and whether you take these meanings as evidence of 'what the public wants' or of 'what the public gets'. Further, the study of popular culture requires some attention to cultures other than popular ones – especially that known as *high culture*. However, discussion centred on differences between popular and high culture has traditionally focused on matters of taste and artistic merit. For instance, there is an implicit valuation in distinctions such as those between 'serious' and 'pop' music, which are frequently institutionalised in the form of entire radio networks (Radio 3 and Radio 1 in the UK), or between creative genius (high culture) and commercial consumption (popular). These distinctions appear at first to derive from the qualities of the works associated with each type: Mozart writes 'better' music than a chart-topping pop group, and moreover Mozart's music is not tied to time, nation or class – it is seen as an expression of human genius in general. In short, the accepted (or at least the established) evaluations of different cultural products are naturalised: accounted for as intrinsic properties of the product and not as a result of their assignation to different cultural categories.

What is at stake in the attempt to specify popular culture is the status of these naturalised evaluations. For they may themselves be explained as an ideological strategy whereby class relations (supremacy and subordination) may be 'lived' as natural differences. In fact the study of popular culture cannot get very far without some attempt to relate the social production and reproduction of meanings to the economic and political divisions and antagonisms of class.

The recognition of a relation between class and culture has led to further issues. First, attention has broadened beyond its original focus on such obviously cultural artefacts as texts, to include practices, lifestyles and 'lived culture' – especially in the ethnographic study of subcultures. Second, there has been a rediscovery of 'cultural politics', often associated with the work of Gramsci (1971) and his concepts of hegemony and the 'national-popular'. Finally, attention to class has led to consideration of the complex relations that exist between this and, especially, gender and ethnic relations.

See also: **Class, Cultural studies, Culture, Ideology, Subculture**

Further reading: Fiske (1989a, 1989b); Frow (1995, 1997); Turner (1990)

POSTMODERN/POSTMODERNISM/ POSTMODERNITY

A social epoch, and an aesthetic movement, contrasted with modernity. The concept of the postmodern has become widely used in public discourse, often with its original theoretical assumptions ignored or misunderstood. It is therefore useful to consider the term in two ways – as a condition of society (postmodernity) and as a textual practice (postmodernism).

The concept of postmodernity seeks to describe the contemporary era or epoch. It has two central characteristics. First, the end of mass markets and a change in the economic conditions that were associated with modernity. Thwaites *et al.* (1994: 210) argue this change began following World War II with Western Europe and Japan rebuilding their own economies and relying less on US production and technologies. Through these emerging economies, the development of information technologies became prominent. It is with the development of these technologies that the concepts of production and consumption become less straightforward. The contemporary understanding of this shift is represented by theories of the **new economy**.

These changes to economic structure are seen as part of the end of meta-narratives, the second notion that is central to discussions of postmodernity. Whereas modernity was characterised by the unity of the human race in the rational pursuit of truth and enlightenment, postmodernity sees the two World Wars as ending this utopian vision. The mass genocide that characterised these events fractured the concept of a universalised 'we'. Our present epoch is now instead characterised by petit-narratives or identities characterised by, for example, nation, gender, ethnicity and sexuality.

Postmodernism in comparison is concerned with aesthetic practices that seek to articulate the condition associated with postmodernity. Frow (1997) argues that postmodernism is a genre of theory writing, not a description of the world.

See also: **Bricolage, Modern/modernism/modernity**

Further reading: Easthope and McGowan (1992); McRobbie (1994); Morley (1996)

POST-BROADCAST MEDIA

A distinction can be made between broadcast era and post-broadcast media. It may assist in thinking about the social implications of technological change. It includes such contrasts as:

Broadcast media	Post-broadcast media
analogue	digital
one-to-many	many-to-many
mass	interactive
television	computer
media	telecommunications
centralised	dispersed
standardised	customised
public	private
sit back	sit forward
'passive' consumer	active user

Post-broadcast media allow for users rather than consumers, and through interactivity allow those users to produce or 'write' in the given application (from games to web sites, video-streaming to online journals), whereas broadcast-era 'literacy' confined audiences to 'read-only' status.

POWER

Power has been theorised in two competing ways by Marxism and Foucault, and both are influential for cultural and media studies. At the same time the word retains much of its force as a term from ordinary language.

The latter usage derives from theories of political economy, which understood power as emanating from the monarch – a single source of power, the exercise of which was founded on threat of death, both internal (execution) and external (war). Monarchical power did not have to be exercised by a *monarch* – the system still worked when 'abstracted' to, for example, the law (internal) and the state (external).

Fundamentally this concept of power was based on *scarcity*; there was not enough of it to go around. If you wanted it, you had to take it from someone who had it. If you didn't have it, you were confined to your 'lack' of it by repression (ultimately, fear of death). This conceptualisation probably remains at the heart of the common-sense (ordinary language) use of the term.

The classic political economy approach (power as a scarce resource) was the mental map inherited by Marxism, which shifted the focus from ethno-territorial sovereignty to the social landscape of industrialisation. The Marxists saw power as emanating from productive forces, i.e. capital and labour. They understood that, compared to previous epochs (feudalism, slavery), capitalism was a progressive force in society, and also that without capital there would be no working or 'productive' class. But despite this Marxism persisted in thinking about the relations between these two forces as a zero-sum game whereby one side had power and the other side lacked it. So for Marxism class antagonism took the form of one class dominating and repressing another, using the ultimate fear of death (coercion) as well as intermediate strategies of sovereignty, such as the law, divide and rule, patronage, **hegemony**, etc. The point was that power was still something to be taken from someone else, and exercised over them. In contemporary cultural theory, the model persists, but the place of 'class' in 'class struggle' has been taken over by any of a number of *soi disant* oppressed or repressed groups, from women and ethnic populations to people identified by their sexual preference, age or identity.

Foucault broke with this scenario in order to take seriously the effects of modernisation, and the changes brought about by the productive force of both capital and labour, acting on both the natural and the social world, in an expansive cycle of growth. His own work focused on studies of *madness*, *incarceration* and *sexuality*. From these he formulated theories of *truth* (knowledge), *power* (how 'we constitute ourselves as subjects acting on others') and *the self* (ethics) (see Foucault, 1984: 351–352).

Foucault's theory of power was not based on *scarcity*, but *plenty*, and not on fear of *death* but on the 'plenitude of the possible' (1984: 267). He abandoned the idea of power as sovereignty. Instead, he introduced the idea that power was 'taking charge of life':

> Power would no longer be dealing simply with legal subjects over whom the ultimate dominion was death, but with living beings, and the mastery it would be able to exercise over them would have to be applied at the level of life itself; it was the taking charge of life, more than the threat of death, that gave power its access even to the body.

> (Foucault, 1984: 265)

The management of *life* required *knowledge*-power, not pain of death. This kind of power was dispersed throughout the productive forces and institutions of modernising societies; it was manifest not in gallows and armies but in knowledge, and in the organisation and administration of bodies. It was exercised in the techniques developed in institutions and discourses to govern – and so make productive – whole populations. Hence power could be seen in the minutiae of everyday transactions, in private life, and in the technologies mobilised to evaluate, measure, appraise, hierarchise – and so to *produce* – 'normal' society. This was what Foucault called 'governmentality'.

Even the actions of those (including cultural critics) who sought to oppose traditional (sovereign) power had to be understood within these terms. For Foucault there was no 'outside' to power, a place from which one could take a swing at those who 'had' it. But the exercise of power in knowledge, discourse, institution, technique, administration, management, bureaucracy, and the rest was never complete; it generated its own resistances, and these needed to be understood for worthwhile political contestation to occur. Politics was conducted at the level of understanding how selves were formed and acted on others, including intellectual selves.

In communication, cultural and media studies the Marxist and Foucauldian conceptualisations of power have both been influential. Marxist-derived approaches have focused on the adversarial aspect of power: on 'struggle'. Foucauldian approaches have focused on knowledge, truth, discourse, self, sexuality and governmentality as sites of power. Many commentators regard power as constitutive of cultural studies, being a fundamental aspect of any study of meaning.

Further reading: Bennett (1992, 1998)

PRAGMATICS

The study of the interpretation of utterances and more specifically how the context of situation influences their meaning. Traditionally the study of meaning in linguistics has focused upon the meaning of words or sentences as if meaning inhered within the linguistic expression itself and was ultimately determined by the linguistic system. Pragmatics, however, emphasises the role of context in determining meaning. In fact, of course, it has long been recognised that linguistic items such as deictics and other *indexical expressions* depend for their meaning on the context of situation. In particular, deictics such as the personal pronouns 'I' and 'You' and indexical expressions such as 'tomorrow' all depend for their meaning on the circumstances in which they are uttered. Thus, the precise meaning of 'I'll visit you tomorrow' will vary depending upon who actually is speaking to whom, and on when the utterance takes place.

But in any case, even apart from **deixis**, many words have multiple senses. Even a simple item such as 'coach' has several senses, including 'a mode of transport' and 'someone who trains people in a particular sport'. Its use, therefore, in an utterance such as 'Look out for the coach' is potentially ambiguous, and we rely upon context to select the relevant sense.

Pragmatic issues, however, go far beyond issues of word meaning to include consideration of complicated kinds of contextual effect where the meaning of an utterance is much more than what is literally said. If in a review of an opera we read that 'Mr Jones sang a series of notes which corresponded to those of an aria from *Rigoletto*' we infer that he sang badly, *even though the utterance does not actually say so*. Similarly, if while driving in a strange town we ask someone, 'Is there anywhere we can get petrol round here?' and they reply 'There's a garage just round the corner', we assume that it is the type of garage that sells petrol (not that it is one for parking your car) and that it is open. These kinds of inferences that go beyond the literal meaning of what is said are known as **implicatures**.

A further kind of contextual effect relates to the notion of **speech act**. *Directives*, for instance, are a commonly occurring type of speech act designed to get someone to do something. An utterance such as 'Play the piano, Elton' is likely to be a directive whatever the circumstances of its occurrence. But utterances such as 'Would you mind playing the piano, Elton?', 'Can you play the piano, Elton?', 'The piano, Elton', etc., may or may not prove to be directives depending on the context of situation. If a teacher in a music lesson says to a pupil, 'Can you play the piano, Elton?', with the piano waiting for someone to play it, then it is most likely to be heard as a directive. If, on the other hand, a group of acquaintances are discussing what instruments they can play and one asks of another 'Can you play the piano, Elton?' then s/he would most likely be heard as requesting information rather than making a directive. In this way, what an utterance is heard as doing (in other words, what speech act it is performing) can vary according to its context of situation.

The aim of pragmatics is in the first place to describe these various kinds of contextual effect; but more significantly it aims to explain how language users actually make sense of each other's utterances in the face of the various kinds of indeterminancy and ambiguity outlined above.

The contribution of pragmatics to communication studies is potentially considerable, although not always realised, since it goes to the heart of some of the most troubling issues surrounding **text** and interpretation (e.g., 'Where is meaning – in the text; or in the context?'). At the same time, however, pragmatics has become closely associated more recently with the interests of cognitive science and the study of artificial intelligence. Such links tend to produce a strong emphasis on the supposed rationality of communicators, and on the universality of the interpretative procedures that they adopt, so that much work remains to be done on the socially structured distribution and organisation of pragmatic knowledge and procedures.

See also: **Conversation analysis, Meaning, Semantics, Speech act**

Further reading: Leech (1983); Levinson (1983)

PRIVATISATION

An economic strategy entailing the release of a government-owned asset into private hands (or a reduction in government share-holding). Gayle and Goodrich (1990) include in it the replacement of budgeted public services by private market mechanisms within the definition of privatisation practices, such as state management contracts, user charges, lease-purchase arrangements and tax reduction to stimulate private sector investment.

Developments within the telecommunications industry highlight the issues surrounding privatisation. Economists originally believed that telecommunications was a 'natural monopoly', meaning that one 'telco' would be able to provide infrastructure and services more efficiently than competing providers. As the infrastructure costs of telecommunications are high, government was called upon to ensure that infrastructure was provided to remote locations even if it was considered economically unattractive. In the US the telecommunications provider was privately owned and heavily regulated. In most other countries, it was government owned and ran telecommunications.

In 1982 this began to change. The US introduced legislation that would allow the telecommunications monopoly AT&T to participate in the new ICT markets if it agreed to allow new players into the telecommunications industry. In the UK, British Telecom was sold to a private company and a new competitor, Mercury, was allowed to enter the market. Whereas the US was instituting competition policy and **deregulation**, the UK was implementing a policy of privatisation.

In the case of telecommunications, technological change had altered the way that the market was functioning causing the 'natural monopoly' model to be called into question. It was assumed in the UK that private industry would be motivated towards greater service and product innovation. Competition, it was expected, would bring prices down, resolving market failures. This both did and did not happen, in different contexts.

However, there is doubt about whether privatisation on the whole resulted in greater efficiencies (Barr, 2000). Further, many on the left believe that the up-front money derived from the sale of public assets would be less than the long-term dividends that could be spent on public infrastructure and services if the government were to retain ownership and profits.

Privatisation is not the same as deregulation; nor should it be assumed that privatisation results in less regulation. In many instances, governments have set up regulatory authorities to ensure that privatised industries continue to meet public needs; for instance, meeting universal service obligations (USO) in the telecommunications industry. As a result, regulators have taken on a greater role in governance following liberalisation policies and, as Collins and

Murroni (1996) point out, are often intervening in operations and management to a greater extent than governments have in the past.

Privatisation has been a driver of **globalisation**. This raises concerns that we will experience a scenario whereby a handful of privately owned global corporations with the capital to buy publicly owned utilities will replace national publicly owned enterprises. Government, in this scenario, would be forced to bargain increasingly with private companies.

See also: **Anti-globalisation, Deregulation, Globalisation**

PROPAGANDA

'Propagation' – derived from the organisation set up by the Roman Catholic Church in 1622 to propagate that faith in the aftermath of the Reformation and the rise of Protestantism; propagation in *adversarial* or competitive circumstances. This sense of propaganda was later deployed by totalitarian regimes of both left and right – communist and fascist – who took pains to make the 'propagation' of state ideology a matter of policy, not chance. Where communist governments had not been established, the task of 'agit-prop' – 'agitation and propaganda' – was assigned to trustworthy militants. Small wonder that liberal democracies, especially those founded in Protestant countries, regarded propaganda as a 'term of reproach applied to secret associations for the spread of opinions and principles which are viewed by most governments with horror and aversion' (*OED*).

But the governments protested too much. Soon everyone was at it. Propaganda under the guise of 'government information' is a staple of contemporary life, and its privatised form, PR and advertising, is a mainstay of the contemporary economy.

Propaganda is still controversial because it suffuses the media of public enlightenment, especially news. It may take the banal form of PR handouts that get reproduced verbatim in the local give-away paper or it may take a much more expensive and sophisticated form – political and commercial campaigns, for instance. So much so that wise readers and viewers regard everything they see and read as propaganda for something, always in someone's interest, whether in the factual or fictional media. There is a continuing need to ask, 'Who says?'

Scepticism about news and fictional realism is healthy, and requires some work by the reader or viewer, but simply to dismiss propaganda out of hand or to seek to 'ban' or control it, or to purge it from the media, would be to miss the point. For all communication has some sort of **spin**, especially communication addressed to a large, anonymous public from across demographic boundaries. The wise reader might prefer to see propaganda as a genre rather than as an infestation; it is better to know it than to knock it. The generic characteristics of propaganda (compared to realism in both fact and fiction) include the following.

- News and fiction draw attention *into* the text, seeking to resolve conflicts diegetically, within the story. Propaganda directs attention *beyond* the text, seeking to provoke conflict in the reader.
- News and fiction are images of the past, in which the action is completed. Propaganda aligns the reader with the future, towards actions yet to occur. News and fiction continue existing meanings. Propaganda seeks to change the future.
- News and fiction position the reader as uncommitted, even passive recipients or consumers. Propaganda calls the reader towards participation.
- News and realist fiction seek to convey the impression that they are true, unauthored, real. Propaganda seeks to produce faithfulness in a relationship between addresser and addressee.
- News and fiction employ transparency and verisimilitude to produce the effect that techniques used in the communication are 'not there'. Propaganda can experiment with a much broader palette of rhetorical and visual techniques, and draw attention to its own communicative status.
- News is diegetic. Propaganda is dialogic.

Propaganda can still be politically controversial, especially in its clandestine form. After the events of September 11, 2001, the US Defense Department set up an 'office of strategic influence', which planned to feed information, some of it false, to foreign news agencies, in an attempt to influence public opinion across the world (especially the Islamic world) in favour of the US-led 'war on terrorism'. The plan caused outrage within and beyond the US when it was revealed in February 2002, and the 'office of strategic influence' was 'restructured'.

Further reading: Hartley (1992a: 51–55)

PROXEMICS

The semiotics of space. E. T. Hall (1973) posited that space may be intimate (near), social (middling) or public (distant). People's *proximity* to one another will communicate their mutual status – lovers will 'naturally' stand nearer each other than strangers. There are reputed to be different proxemic standards in different countries, resulting in some nationalities gaining a reputation for aloofness (their relaxed social space when standing is longer than an arm's-length: 'Swedes') or for over-familiarity (they habitually stand closer than arm's-length: 'Latins'). Adhering to proxemic standards in a given context is a good test of politeness; failing to do so can cause offence (invading one's personal space; being stand-offish) or it can be exploited (politicians and sales reps). Proxemic codes can be observed both in behaviour and in the organisation and architecture of public spaces, which can be manipulated for public or commercial ends. VIPs tend to be surrounded by more space than regular folk, a truism exploited by the organisers of public spectacles from Nuremberg and the Olympics (think of the winners' podia) to Oscars night and the Presidential inauguration.

PUBLIC

Pre-dating the use of the terms **nation** and nationality, the 'public' described the population of a city-state in classical times. The people comprising the public could gather in a single space within sight of each other (in Greek: *agora*, in Roman: *forum*). It was here that free citizens argued, legislated and adjudicated, both in their own interests and on behalf on others who were not free – slaves, women, foreigners, children.

With the growth of polities to many times the size of these classical antecedents, the public was 'abstracted' or virtualised – it was either an imagined community or could gather together only by *representative* means. However, the notion of the public has survived, sustaining public governmental, media and academic interests, among others. For the existence of the unseen public is the warrant that allows such institutions to speak and act on behalf of unknowable audiences, construed as the public. They seek to *represent* public opinion, public service (broadcasting), the public interest, etc.

As Bonney and Wilson (1983: 77) have argued, the idea of a public interest presupposes that there is 'a single public with a unified set of interests'. Public interest, like the construction of the public, is based on inclusion and exclusion. Those who have not been included as part of the contemporary mediated public may include youth, gays and lesbians, and the disabled. It is groups such as these that are recognised by newer theoretical paradigms such as **cultural citizenship** that involve a move from the conception of a unified public to a notion of public*s*. But even then, in many countries the line of exclusion is still drawn at migrants, especially those fleeing zones of turbulence in the Middle East and Africa. They 'belong' to no public and are treated as if that status made them not migrants or refugees but criminals.

See also: **Cultural citizenship, Public sphere**

Further reading: Hartley (1992b)

PUBLIC SERVICE BROADCASTING

Publicly funded broadcasting services. By extension, *all* broadcasting in countries with a public service broadcasting regime, for example, the UK, where the BBC is the archetypal public broadcaster but the commercial channels ITV, Channel 4 and S4C, also have 'public service' obligations in their enabling statutes – and in their culture. At the heart of conceptions of public service broadcasting is the notion that a healthy **public sphere** is required in order to produce democratic conditions (Garnham, 1986). By remaining outside of market influences, public service broadcasting provides a much needed public forum within which information dissemination can occur, aiding in the stimulation of public debate.

Public service broadcasting plays a significant role in shaping national identity by creating and reinforcing cultural products and practices. Its attempt to provide quality content for the nation has placed public service broadcasting in the problematic position of having to assume what it is that citizens should know and enjoy as citizens of a particular country.

In having to negotiate the provision of what could be considered 'quality' content, public service broadcasting directs itself towards an audience that is presupposed, fixed and homogenous. It presumes that citizens are consensual in the public service broadcasting culture (and hence in the national interest) and, more often than not, that they are a speaker of the national language. As a consequence, public service broadcasting has attracted criticism for denying difference within the national community, for being elitist, assuming a commonality and excluding interests, cultures and tastes that do not conform to the privileged depiction of the public service broadcasting citizen (Hawkins, 1999).

In recent years, theorists have challenged the assumption that public service broadcasting has an exclusive claim in creating the conditions necessary for democracy. As Keane writes, the case for public service broadcasting is weakened by 'its unconvincing attempt to justify publicly the public service model against its enemies' (1991: 116). Although public service broadcasting has played a large part in the development of innovative television, commercially produced programmes have also extended our public debates, our acceptance of difference and our national identities (see Hartley, 1992a).

Further reading: Murdock (1992)

PUBLIC SPHERE

Jürgen Habermas' theorisation of the public sphere, most thoroughly explored in his work *The Structural Transformation of the Public Sphere* (translated 1989), was an attempt to find possibilities through which democracy could be realised. Influenced by his experience of fascism and his apprenticeship with the **Frankfurt School** as Adorno's research assistant, Habermas held little hope of being able to identify a political philosophy that could resolve the consequences of capitalism or state control (Calhoun, 1992). As such, the public sphere is not an attempt at a prescriptive political theory, but a conception of the conditions within which healthy and just political conditions may be realised.

The public sphere is the arena within which debate occurs; it is the generation of ideas, shared knowledge and the construction of opinion that occurs when people assemble and discuss. Although real and experienced, the public sphere cannot be located in particular place or identified as an object. It 'cannot be conceived as an institution and certainly not as an organisation', writes Habermas, rather it is 'a network for communicating information and points of view' (Habermas, 1996: 360). The public sphere is where ideas and information are shared. It is where public opinions are formed as a result of communication.

For Habermas, the public sphere was most constructive when not influenced by commercial interests or state control. In its original conception, the public sphere must be insulated from the interests of such dominant powers if it is to be a corrective to them. Only in this way can it effectively produce democratic conditions. This was a weakness, for it allowed no function of the public sphere to be assigned to commercial organisations and media (whether the latter were public service media owned by the state or private commercial media).

Media theorists (for example, Garnham, 1986; Price, 1995) have used Habermas' public sphere to explain the importance of communication for the processes of democracy. If we accept that communication is important for democracy, Garnham points out, the next question is how to position this goal within 'the conditions of large-scale societies in which both social and communicative relations are inevitably mediated through both time and space' (Garnham, 1986: 365). This is the democratic nature of the media in today's world – they exist as an arena for knowledge exchange on a large scale, from which people are able to gain the information necessary to participate fully as citizens.

Feminist perspectives on Habermas' work have highlighted the exclusionary, elitist nature of the public sphere's original conception. Habermas' public sphere was based primarily on the process of debate and knowledge exchange. The participants' status was not a factor in the success or character of the public sphere. In response, Fraser (1992) asserts that it is unrealistic to assume that the historical exclusion of women, or the racial and property criteria needed to participate in the public sphere, can be overlooked. Rather, the likelihood is that ignoring group differences will lead to the exclusion of some groups from participation within the public sphere. For Fraser the solution is to see not a singular public sphere but a number of public sphericules, through which groups interact, contest and withdraw to when they so desire. In viewing the public sphere theory in this way, it is possible to offset the reality that participatory privileges are something to be enjoyed only by members of the dominant group.

Further reading: Calhoun (1992); Fraser (1992); Habermas (1996); Price (1995)

RACE

Race is a system of categorisation that classifies populations by reference to physical attributes such as skin colour and other perceived bodily distinctions. An implication of such a system is that different races inherit common behavioural and emotional traits. Yet the concept of race is itself, like the concept of **nation**, *relational* – each race is to some extent a product of its difference from others in the system. It is clear that over time and in different circumstances the system changes, altering such fundamental matters as the number of races that are recognised, and therefore the way that different characteristics and attributes can be distributed and distinguished.

Thus, there is a great element of *culture* in what counts as race. Race is a *meaningful* category, rather than a biological given; the ideals and characteristics of races are not natural but are constantly reproduced in language, historical ideologies and discourses, images and other cultural practices.

In media and cultural studies, writing on race emerged alongside **identity politics**. Concerned with what were perceived to be limited representations of raced identities in the media, text analysis was undertaken in an attempt to chart the relationship between societal attitudes and raced characters. Work by Bogle (1989) and Jhally and Lewis (1992), for example, argued that representations relied on stereotypes and promoted a form of implicit racism. While important in highlighting the limits of raced representations, this form of investigation often relied on a binary of positive/negative images. Binaries such as these seemed to suggest that there was indeed a paradigm of positive characteristics that are representative of a given race. But neither good policy nor good media content could come out of a demand for 'more positive images' to redress the balance.

Said's (1979) concept of **Orientalism** offered a theoretical means of addressing this problem. He argued that race was a discourse that served to shape how Europeans understood themselves through assigning undesirable characteristics to other races. By constructing the inhabitants of the Orient as savage, uncivilised and exotic, Europe imagined itself as brave, cultured and noble. Said's model could not necessarily be applied to other nation/race dynamics, but it does reinforce the notion that characteristics of race are constructed, and are often less a 'construction' of the race to whom they are applied than of the people who create and sustain the discourse. This has lead to post-colonial and post-structuralist work that continues to move away from the essentialism inherent in previous writing on race, in favour of an approach that recognises the socially constructed and dialogic nature of the categories.

Race is constantly under reconstruction. In the nineteenth century the term was virtually synonymous with 'nation' – one could write of the Czech or Belgian or Bantu 'race'. Later, race was reduced to three global categories – 'caucasian', 'mongoloid' and 'negroid'. Later still, different jurisdictions struggled to place their populations into categories that reflected their own circumstances, rather than squeeze people into a universal standard. Hollinger (2000: 199) discusses how in the US an 'ethno-racial pentagon', based on historically assigned racial categories, is designed to allow the enforcement of anti-discrimination and affirmative action policies of the federal government. Consisting of five categories – European, African, Hispanic, Asian and Indigenous – the 'pentagon' has 'come to replicate the popular colour-consciousness of the past: black, white, red, yellow and brown' (Hollinger, 2000: 202). Certainly, despite its desire for bureaucratic accuracy and neutrality, the categorisation of race in this way is problematic, not least owing to internal differences within and between each of the categories, and the difficulty of moving between them, which has major implications for 'mixed families'. Two of the 'races' – Hispanics and Europeans – would both be regarded as 'white' in other contexts.

The use of the 'pentagon' as an anti-discriminatory tool in US federal policy clearly moves beyond the idea of race as a universal to recognise histories of both culture and discrimination. Thus it demonstrates that the category of race, for theoretical or governmental purposes, cannot be separated from historical and cultural contexts (see Hall, 1997; Hartley and McKee, 2000).

Because it is historical and therefore culturally specific rather than universal, the 'pentagon' model would not make sense outside of the US. In Africa, Europe, Asia or Australia, the demographic make-up of the population is different. Australia for instance has no Hispanic category. But it does make a distinction between 'Anglo-Celtic' and 'multicultural' Australians – the latter being those who migrated after World War II, first from Southern Europe (Malta, Greece, former Yugoslavia, Italy) and later from Asia (Vietnam and Cambodia in particular). Australia thus has a racial 'diamond', not a pentagon: Indigenous, Anglo-Celtic, multicultural, Asian.

The current historical period is characterised by a re-proliferation of the races, an attempt to arrive at non-discriminatory descriptive categories for governmental purposes and different racial categories in different jurisdictions. On the streets, there remains the working through of quite different racial policies rooted in popular prejudice and residual supremacist theories, and sometimes also inter-ethnic competition, such as disputes between populations where both are regarded as racial minorities, for example, Korean and Black or Hispanic Americans. How the bureaucratisation of race in multi-cultural policy may affect the outcome of these skirmishes remains to be seen. In communication and cultural studies, and in the media, it is important to follow the development of debates, policies and coverage of race, but not to assume that race describes any essential properties or attributes.

See also: **Diaspora, Ethnic/ethnicity, Identity politics, Orientalism, Representation**

Further reading: Baker *et al.* (1996); Carrington (2001); Gilroy (1987, 1993); Gray (2000)

READER/READERSHIP

Readerships are the *product* of media industries: they are populations gathered without regard to otherwise powerful distinctions of territory, demographics and wealth and constituted as the readership of newspapers, which is then available to serve as a **metonym** for the nation or society as a whole. Readerships (which in this usage includes audiences) are the largest communities ever assembled, albeit virtually. This is why the term 'reader' or 'readership' has often been used to describe audiences for audio-visual as well as print-based media.

The public is, first and foremost, a reading public, and audiences engage in 'reading' – i.e. an active, literate encounter with semiotic materials – not only via traditional print literacy but also in relation to audio-visual media such as television and film. Readers and audiences are the 'product' of media in a more commodified sense, their aggregated purchasing power being sold to advertisers by media organisations.

REALISM

A mode of representation of the world, both material and psychological. Historically, it was understood to imply a sense of objectivity in the arts, sciences and in literature. However, realism may also be used in a wider sense, as for example when intellectual movements such as Marxism and feminism, and textual systems such as journalism, are cast as 'realist' endeavours (as opposed to as textual or metaphysical knowledge). Realism is therefore intimately bound up with modernism.

In media analysis, realism may be understood not as an aim but as a convention. It *aims* to naturalise the modes of production that are necessarily part of any cultural text by drawing attention to the *verisimilitude* of the characters, action, plot, etc., rather than to the apparatus of its own narration: its rhetorical device is to pretend that the telling is not there, there is only the tale. By familiarisation and habituation to realist genres, **readerships** also contribute to the effect by agreeing to read within the claims of the convention.

This naturalising process is often understood as ideological, since realism in fact and fiction alike is assisted by **semiotic** tricks. Understanding it as convention moves beyond a fruitless search for a text's proximity to the real. Rather, it draws attention to the signs and techniques that have been employed for the reader to understand the text as real. In film and television drama these may include the use of a linear narrative, **mode of address** and technical aspects such as continuity and editing. The conventions of **genre** are also understood to inform the representation of realism. Science fiction, for example, through the use of special effects, is able to create its own sense of the real owing to the rules that govern the genre: it is therefore quite normal to have 'realistic' portrayals of scenarios that everyone knows are 'really' impossible.

Such conventions then become a sort of pact between film-makers and their audiences. For instance, even though sound cannot travel through space, it is standard practice to apply sound effects (whooshes, engine noises) to spacecraft in movies – they are by general agreement more 'realistic' as a result. That realism is as much ideology as objectivity can be demonstrated by noting that its own conventions evolve over time, and what was greeted as shockingly realistic in one decade looks mannerist or kitsch in the next.

Realism is reliant on shared value judgements. What texts are accepted as belonging to this category will depend on the use of those conventions that have been accepted as realistic. These conventions are the signifying aspect of realism.

See also: **Aesthetics, Diegesis**

Further reading: Stam (2000)

REALITY TV

A recent generic phenomenon of television broadcasting, reality TV is difficult to define owing to the rapid development of programmes of this nature, and also because in both journalistic reviews and academic criticism different types of show have been bundled together under this banner. Some who have investigated its conventions suggest that the terms 'factual television' (see Dovey, 2001) or 'popular factual entertainment' (see Roscoe, 2001) do more justice to a type of programming that encompasses everything from confrontational chat shows to surveillance entertainment such as *Big Brother* and *Survivor*.

Examples of reality TV can be traced to the early 1990s and the emergence of programmes that traded on the reality of the everyday tasks of the emergency services. Shows such as *Cops* and *999* often masqueraded as investigative journalism and found justification and legitimation by using the rhetoric of 'public service' to describe their role (Roscoe, 2001: 10). This is most evident in shows such as *Cops*, which transformed the 'crime-stoppers' genre into drama.

Another emergent form of reality TV is docu-soap. This hybrid differs from documentary in that it prioritises entertainment over social commentary (Bruzzi, 2001: 132). It shares with other 'reality' formats the presentation of the everyday as entertainment. One innovation arising from this development is that 'ordinary people' are doing the talking – 'real' folk get to be stars (Roscoe, 2001: 11).

Some of the criticism aimed at this type of programming stems from the loss of the expert's role. The rise of shows that foreground ordinary people is characterised as **dumbing down**. Typical of such attacks, Kronig (2000: 47) argues that reality TV is a 'triumph of emotional sensationalism over serious issues from politics to science', echoing the cry that documentary film and its supposed representation of the real are being forsaken in favour of this obviously 'unreal' genre.

Reality TV makes no attempt to hide the extent to which reality is a product of its production values, which have increased in proportion to the genre's popularity (for example, *Big Brother, Survivor, Popstars*). Indeed, Roscoe argues that the audience of these shows are well aware of their artificial nature, and that part of the pleasure for viewers is in evaluating the performance of participants – a pleasure that is particularly rewarding during moments when the performance breaks down (2001: 14). It is at such moments that a different kind of 'reality' pokes through. Tears, back-stabbing, injury and facial expression in the moment of defeat are all examples of what Roscoe calls 'flickers of authenticity'.

Combining elements of, for example, documentary, soap opera and quiz shows, reality TV demonstrates the continuum of television formats and the hybridity of programming. Further research in the area should therefore seek to understand how these changes are related to the changing experiences of the audience as well as the policy and economic decisions underpinning television production.

Further reading: Dovey (2000)

REARVIEWMIRRORISM

A term coined by Marshall McLuhan (1964), rearviewmirrorism occurs where a new technology or medium imitates the one it is destined to supplant. Early printed books such as the Gutenberg Bible looked like medieval manuscripts. The first house in the UK made of concrete (Gregynog Hall in Wales) was designed to look like Tudor half-timbering. The first photographs borrowed composition and genre conventions from painting and portraiture. Early television was watched in a darkened room, as if it were cinema. Digital media aspired to look like analogue, e.g. computer-generated faces and hair were celebrated for looking 'real' (like those film). The implication of the term is that new media need to establish their own form and aesthetic as quickly and confidently as possible, rather than looking behind them.

Further reading: Hartley (1992a, 1999)

REDUNDANCY

Predictability in communication secured by repetition. Radio presenters are trained to say things three times: 'tell'em you're going to tell'em; tell them; then tell'em you told'em'. *Teletubbies* is built on the idea that toddlers require things to be repeated four times, so on the show everything is, including the characters themselves – communicatively, three of them are redundant, but they are indispensable to ensure successful communication. There are six marines in the famous 1945 Rosenthal photograph of the planting of the American flag at Iwo Jima. This is one of the most copied images of the twentieth century, but many versions make do with only four figures. Two can hardly be seen in the original, but their limbs and arms 'redundantly' repeat the stance of their more visible comrades, making an effect whose power can be measured by comparison with the pale imitations.

Built-in redundancy is necessary for increased intelligibility. Too much information interferes with clarity. Reader-oriented, as opposed to subject-oriented, communication, whether via speech, writing or audio-visual production, tends towards greater redundancy. Scientific papers in specialist journals strive for low redundancy, but are very hard to read. Mass communication, it follows, is highly redundant in these terms, but it is not by that token '**dumbed down**'; it is, rather, sensitive to the fact that audiences do not share codes with communicators or with each other.

REFERENT

A term used in semiotic analysis that describes what the **sign** stands for; whether an event, a condition or an object. The referent is a part of the signifying system of language, rather than a property of the independently existing external world of nature. So, for instance, there are *beaches* the world over, with various identifiable properties, but the referent of the word 'beach' will differ in different languages, depending on both the structure of the language and the historical significance of the beach in that culture.

REGISTER

Stylistic variation in language according to its context of situation. The selection of words and structures by the language user is influenced strongly by features of the situation. Indeed, utterances typically carry the imprint of their context so markedly and we are so attuned to contextual variation that we can often infer features of the original context of situation from quite fragmentary, isolated linguistic examples. For instance, most readers will feel confident that they can reconstruct the original context of situation for the following examples:

(1) I'm going to give you a prescription for the pain.

(2) New Tubifast. The tubular dressing retention bandage.
     No sticking. No tying. No pinning.

And so it will come as no surprise to hear that (1) is from a doctor–patient interview and (2) from a magazine advertisement. What is more difficult to explain is how we recognise the original context in each case. Why, for example is (1) not from an exchange in a pharmacy, and why is (2) not from a discussion between two nurses in casualty?

The fine-tuning that goes on between language and its context of situation operates along three independent parameters. First, the activity or topic on which the talk is based influences the kind of language used, particularly in the selection of vocabulary. Second, the nature of the social relationship will affect the language: talk between friends, for instance, is likely to avoid formal expressions, unless for ironic effect. Finally the medium of communication adopted – whether face-to-face speech, written text, telephone, dictaphone, etc. – will affect the way all utterances are formed. These three parameters are known as *field*, *tenor* and *mode*, respectively. Collectively they shape the register of a particular text.

See also: **Genre**

Further reading: Halliday (1978); Montgomery (1986)

REGULATION

Government guides and shapes the conduct of institutions, individuals, the market and culture through regulation. Regulations are administrative rather than legislative instruments, but they are backed by statute. The rules are intended to provide a framework that will bring about stability and prevent disorder.

Government regulation is justified as necessary for the promotion of the public good, in overcoming inequality and deprivation or possible harm. It is also intended to stabilise industry and advance particular activities. The word 'protection' has been used to describe the purpose of regulation. The need for protection can be seen in rules that uphold the consumer's interest by means of price control or quality control, or in regulation that guards workers from exploitation or unsafe practices (Groenewegen, 1991). Regulatory controls within the media determine issues of ownership, content and licensing, shaping cultural consumption and production. Although regulation differs from country to country, regulatory media requirements may include: local content rules that require broadcasters to screen a minimum number of hours of locally produced material, ratings and classifications that prohibit certain content from being shown to children and ownership rules to prevent a monopoly or an oligopoly from occurring.

As regulation often has direct or indirect consequences for the distribution of wealth, it is seen by some as interference in the workings of the market. **Deregulation** is based on the assumption that the market alone 'can do better' and is advocated, in many cases, on the grounds of regulatory failure.

One approach within cultural studies has been to interpret and engage with the institutional frameworks that govern culture, including regulatory frameworks and process. Bennett (1992: 397) maintains that cultural practices should be seen as governmental, and defined in terms of 'the specificity of the governmental tasks and programs in which those practices come to be inscribed'. 'Government' in this context is taken to mean the action of governing, controlling, ordering, commanding and systematising. As Rose (1999: 3) writes, it is 'the invention, contestation, operationalisation and transformation of more or less rationalised schemes, programmes, techniques and devices which seek to shape conduct so as to achieve certain ends'. In this sense, regulation is an explicit framework that informs and influences conventions and interaction. Regulation can be seen within a wider set of established spoken and unspoken rules, boundaries and codes through which we are urged to curb behaviour and negotiate communication (see also Foucault, 1977; Cunningham, 1992; Hawkins, 1993).

RHETORIC

The practice of using language to persuade or influence others and the language that results from this practice; the formal study of oratory, exposition, persuasion. Rhetoric was a formal branch of learning in medieval Europe; one of the seven liberal arts or sciences, the others being grammar, logic (dialectics), then arithmetic, geometry, astronomy and music. It fell into serious disrepute and did not survive the Reformation. Rhetorical figures have survived, however, along with certain rhetorical terms (see for example, **metaphor**) that have achieved the status of ordinary language.

Since **structuralism** began to disclose how much of what we know and experience is structured by the **sign** systems we inhabit and encounter, there has been a noticeable revival of interest in rhetoric. There are two good reasons for this. First, rhetoric as a branch of learning requires us to attend to the sign system itself (whether verbal or visual), and to concentrate on the devices and strategies that operate in texts themselves – it offers a well-established and elaborate set of terms and classifications that we can use to see how sense is made, not by reference to imponderables such as authorial intentions or 'truth to life' but by reference to actual discourses.

Second, if rhetoric did not already exist it would no doubt have to be invented, since so many of the various forms of cultural production with which we are surrounded are by themselves highly rhetorical. Publicity, advertising, newspapers, television, academic books, government statements and so on, all exploit rhetorical figures to tempt us to see things their way. If we have available a means to unpick these strategies we can begin to take a more critical and less intimidated stance towards them.

Further reading: Dyer (1982: chs 1 and 8) for a modern application of rhetorical analysis to advertising; Ong (1982: 108–112) for an account of its history

REPRESENTATION

In politics, representation means that a chosen few stand for the people as a whole as their 'representatives' in Congress or parliament. Similarly, in language, media and communication, representations are words, pictures, sounds, sequences, stories, etc., that 'stand for' ideas, emotions, facts, etc. Representations rely on existing and culturally understood signs and images, on the learnt reciprocity of language and various signifying or textual systems. It is through this 'stand in' function of the sign that we know and learn reality.

Representations are the concrete form (signifiers) taken by abstract concepts. Some are banal or uncontroversial – for example, how rain is represented in the movies, since real rain is both hard to see on camera and hard to produce on cue. But some representations go to the heart of cultural and political life – for example, gender, nation, age, class, etc. Since representations inevitably involve a process of selection in which certain signs are privileged over others, it matters how such concepts are represented in news media, movies, or even in ordinary conversation. In fact, Dyer (1993: 1) claims how 'we are seen determines in part how we are treated; how we treat others is based on how we see them [and] such seeing comes from representation'. It should come as no surprise then that the way representations are regulated through various media, genres and within various discourses, has been given considerable attention.

Race and gender are examples of how analysis has sought to subvert traditions that were seen to involve an inaccurate representation.

Analysis of representations of race in the cinema suggested an implicit racism could be found (see Bogle, 1989). In the case of gender, innumerable studies have found demeaning images of women, and some have argued that it is possible to overturn these by substituting such negative representations with 'positive images' (see Artel and Wengraf, 1990). Clearly representations articulate with cultural power, but the demand for 'positive images' did not get far because of course not everyone would agree on what counted as a 'negative' or 'positive' representation. As Lumby (1997: 4) rightly asks: 'Is a sexist or demeaning image something universal which anyone with the right feminist consciousness can spot?' Are 'bad girls' positive or negative images? Seeking to redress the imbalance by producing more positive representations of women was also futile if the underlying material conditions went unreformed – negative images may be *accurate*, in other words.

When considering media representations, rather than looking for accuracy, it is perhaps more useful to understand the discourses that support the image in question. Furthermore, one cannot assume that all people read all representations in the same way. Any analysis should be careful not to accuse an image of being patronising or demeaning, because such a judgement speaks on behalf of a group who may not feel the same way.

See also: **Gender, Identity, Race**

Further reading: Lumby (1997)

SEMANTICS

The study of meaning from a linguistic perspective. Semantics aims to analyse and explain how meanings are expressed in language. Current inquiry seems to be organised around three important distinctions.

Sense versus reference. The meaning of a linguistic expression – a word, for instance – can be treated in terms of its connection with extra-linguistic reality. Thus, the meaning of the word 'chair' lies in its capacity to refer outwards from the language to objects such as the one on which you may be sitting as you read this entry. From a different perspective, however, the meaning of a word can be considered in terms of its relationship to other words in the language. Thus, the meaning of the word 'chair' lies in its relationship with other words such as 'furniture', 'table', 'seat', 'bench', etc. A famous example of the distinction between sense and reference is the way in which, objectively, the same planet – Venus – can be referred to equally appropriately as 'the morning star' and 'the evening star', since it has the capacity to shine brightly both in the morning sky and in the evening sky. Consequently, the two expressions – 'the morning star' and 'the evening star' – have an identical referent, although the sense of each expression is of course quite different. More attention in semantics has been given to the area of sense relations than to that of reference, in line with Wittgenstein's dictum: 'the meaning of a word is its use in the language'.

But ignoring either side of the contrast between sense and reference tends to lead to unbalanced theories of meaning, and this can have consequences that go beyond the domains of linguistic theory. It is worth noting, for instance, that rival aesthetic theories can be divided into two camps depending upon whether they tend to favour one or the other side of the distinction between reference and sense: realist theories favour art that appears to mirror or reflect reality in as direct a way as possible; other more Formalist theories, however, stress the conventionality of artistic representation and see art, and more particularly literature, as a continual experiment with meaning (or 'sense'). Contemporary literary theory tends to be very strong on the conventional bases of meaning, so much so that at times it seems to deny the possibility of any reality at all outside language. At the very least, it insists that reality is not mediated to us directly, but is constructed through acts of meanings, so that we have no direct access to it outside of language. One pitfall of this position is that it can lead to a species of idealism in which reality is spoken into existence through language, and arguments about interpretation become avowedly subjective, to the exclusion of culture and history as material process.

In modern semantics sense relations have been treated in terms of the following major relationships that words can have with each other.

- *Synonomy*: expressions which can be used in identical ways are considered synonymous, by which criterion an expression such as *to ponder* is held to be synonymous with *to meditate*, or *loutish* is held to be synonymous with *uncouth*.
- *Antonymy*: expressions which reverse the meaning of each other in some way are considered to be antonymous. Thus, the pairs *woman/man*, *fast/slow*, *up/down*, *good/bad* all express relations of antonymy.
- *Hyponomy*: expressions may also operate in hierarchical relations of

meaning where the meaning of one expression includes that of another. Thus, the expression 'dog' is a hyponym of the expression 'animal', the latter being a superordinate term for a range of co-hyponyms with *dog*, such as *cat, monkey, giraffe, rabbit*. *Dog* itself, of course, is a superordinate term for another range of hyponyms such as *terrier, hound, retriever,* etc.

Synonymy, antonymy and *hyponomy* consist, therefore, of differing kinds of sense relations possible within the vocabulary of a language. They provide a way of conceptualising the construction of meaning as it goes on within the linguistic system. In this respect it is worth emphasising that they display linguistic and not 'real-world' classification. There is no reason in real world why terms for animals should be organised in the particular types of sense relation adopted in English, as becomes immediately apparent when comparisons in particular areas of meaning are made between languages. According to Whorf (1956), the Hopi tribe of North America used one word *masaytaka* to designate all flying objects except birds. Thus, they actually designated an insect, an aeroplane and an aviator by the same word, whereas English provides quite separate lexical items.

Word meaning versus sentence meaning. Other approaches to the meaning of words involve notions such as semantic features and collocation. Whatever approach is adopted, however, it does not seem possible to account for the meaning of a sentence merely by building upwards from the individual words that make it up. Otherwise 'Man bites dog' would mean the same thing as 'Dog bites man'. Nonetheless, it seems possible that there may be parallels between the kind of sense relation we have described between words and those that exist between sentences. A sense relation such as synonymy, for instance, may be considered to hold not only between individual words but also between whole sentences. Thus 'Sidney sold the book to Sheila' may be considered to be synonymous with 'Sheila bought the book from Sidney', and the same kind of relation can be claimed between 'The police arrested the miners' and 'The miners were arrested by the police'. Other kinds of relationship that can hold between sentences are those of *entailment* and *presupposition*. *Entailment* is a relation whereby, given two sentences A and B, A semantically entails B if under all conditions in which A is true, B is also true. Thus, a sentence such as 'Achilles killed Hector' entails 'Hector is dead'. In such cases B follows from A as a logical consequence. If it is true that Achilles killed Hector, then Hector must as a logical consequence be dead. *Pre-suppositional* relations are somewhat different. Basically, whereas negation will alter a sentence's entailments, it will leave presuppositions in place. Consider the sentence: (i) 'Sidney managed to stop in time'. From this we may infer both that (ii) 'Sidney stopped in time' and also that (iii) 'Sidney tried to stop in time'. These inferred sentences, however, do not behave in quite the same way. Sentence (ii) 'Sidney stopped in time' is a logical consequence of sentence (i) – an entailment – and it does not survive under the negation of (i) – 'Sidney did not manage to stop in time'. Sentence (iii), however, is a presupposition, and whilst the original entailment now no longer holds, the presupposition that (iii) 'Sidney tried to stop in time' still survives intact.

These kinds of distinctions are important for the analysis of meaning in all kinds of discourse. Ideological claims, for instance, are often promoted implicitly rather than explicitly, covertly rather than overtly; and they often need to be recovered from the presuppositions or entailments of a discourse rather than from its surface assertions. Thus, when a Ministry of Defence pamphlet urged that 'Britain must do everything in its power … to deter Russia from further acts of aggression', various unargued propositions were merely presupposed; notably, for example: (i) 'Britain has power' and (ii) 'Russia is committing acts of aggression'.

Text versus context. The third major area of inquiry and debate is addressed to issues such as how much of meaning is created and carried by the linguistic system and how much and in what way it is determined by crucial characteristics of the context in which any utterance is grounded. Indeed, some aspects of meaning previously considered to be semantic – i.e., part of the linguistic system itself – are now being treated as part of **pragmatics**.

The history of linguistics during the last sixty years can be read in terms of a continual deferral of the study of meaning. Indeed, the progression during this time has been very much from the smaller units of linguistic organisation, such as the phoneme to the larger, such as the *sentence* or text; it has also been a progression from substance (phonology) to significance (semantics). Meaning, however, has at last come centre stage, and the last ten years has seen an immense burgeoning of work in both semantics and pragmatics. Meaning, of course, cannot be other than the ultimate goal of linguistic inquiry, and findings in this area undoubtedly have important consequences for associated areas of scholarship such as media studies, literary criticism, interpretive sociology or cognitive science, in all of which issues of meaning are often at the centre of debate.

See also: **Discourse, Multi-accentuality, Pragmatics, Semiotics/ semiology, Speech act**

Further reading: Lyons (1981)

SEMIOSPHERE

The 'semiotic space necessary for the existence and functioning of languages', which is both the 'result and the condition for the development of culture' (Lotman, 1990: 123–125). The term was coined by Yuri Lotman, on the model of the 'biosphere'. Unlike Saussure, who sought the smallest signifying unit in language, Lotman was convinced that communication could not occur without the *system* in place first; he thought *dialogue* was a precondition for language, not the other way round. So he wrote that the 'smallest functioning mechanism' of meaning-generation is 'the whole semiotic space of the culture in question' (Lotman, 1990: 125). Hence the semiosphere is the enabling structure that allows asymmetric or mutually untranslatable messages – like the communication between mother (language of smiles) and baby (looks and burbles) – to work as communication.

Further reading: Hartley (1996); Hartley and McKee (2000)

SEMIOTICS/SEMIOLOGY

Semiotics is the study of **signs**. It seeks to understand how language is made meaningful and how meaning can then be communicated in society. Semiotics is not to be found in the text itself, but rather it should be understood as a **methodology**. Accordingly, it is not a discipline in its own right, but its influence on institutionalised ways of approaching media texts has been considerable.

Swiss linguist Ferdinand de Saussure is often considered to be the founder of semiotics, along with other figures such as the American philosopher of language C. S. Pierce, the Italian semiotic theorist Umberto Eco and the Soviet theorist of language Valentin Volosinov (who may have been the literary writer Bakhtin).

Saussure proposed an approach and terminology that was itself very influential on **structuralism** when his theory of language was taken up later on by such writers as Roland Barthes and Claude Lévi-Strauss. Saussurian semiotics approaches language 'synchronically', as a phenomenon existing in the here and now, rather than 'diachronically' (as did the then-ascendant discipline of philology). He was interested in its structure and the rules that allowed utterances to be generated, not in existing words. He proposed that language works as a *system of difference*, in which what any one element means (its 'value' in the system) is arbitrary, consisting precisely in being what the others are not.

This idea was taken up and applied in contexts going well beyond the realm of spoken language. Anthropologists looked at the structure of myths using Saussurian concepts. Barthes used them to analyse both literary and popular cultural texts, particularly via his *Mythologies* (1973). He led the way for those working in media and cultural studies to begin to apply semiotic terms to the analysis of everything from advertising (see for example Williamson, 1978) to ideology.

In fact following developments in France in the 1950s and 1960s, in the 1970s semiotics was knitted together with Marxism and psycho-analytical approaches by intellectuals working in the Birmingham tradition of cultural studies and the *Screen* tradition of cinema studies respectively. It was this from this conjunction that the emancipatory potential of semiotics was proposed: it could help to 'demystify' dominant ideologies and assist in the effort to understand how commonsensical representations of an apparently unarguable reality were in fact constructed, often in line with existing arrangements of power.

Fiske (1990: 40) argues that semiotics has three main areas of study.

- The sign: for example, an utterance, word or image. This is broken down into two components that make up the sign – the signifier and the signified – the former being sound, letters or image that make up the material form of the sign, the latter representing its associated mental meaning.
- The codes and systems into which signs are organised. Codes involve 'choice and chain' – **paradigm** and **syntagm**.
- The culture within which these signs and codes operate. Meaning is dependent upon shared structures of understanding. As Saussure put it, signs have a 'life in society'.

Recognising that meaning was dependent on, for instance, shared cultural codes (which are also understood to be historically located and subject to change), meant that audiences could no longer simply be thought of as passive receivers. Semiotics gave them something to do. The reader of a text was active in the meaning-making process, bringing with them cultural experiences, discourses and ideologies for the process of making sense. Semiotics was a good technique for making this largely spontaneous, untutored activity more self-reflexive and critical.

See also: **Sign, Signification**

Further reading: Barthes (1973); O'Shaughnessy (1999)

SIGN

A concept drawn from **semiotics**, a sign is anything that stands for something else in the production of meaning. It may include words, photographs, sounds and gestures. A sign has three characteristics:

- it must have a physical form – you can see, hear, smell, and/or touch it;
- it must refer to something other than itself;
- it must be used and recognised as a sign; that is, it be an element in a shared cultural code or system.

According to Saussure's theory of semiotics, a sign is made of two equal parts:

- *The signifier*. This works at the level of *denotation*. It is objective (a material thing). Using the oft-quoted example of a red rose, the flower itself is the signifier.
- *The signified*. This works at the level of *connotation*. It is subjective (a 'mentifact' not an 'artefact'). The signified is the concept referred to by the signifier. In the instance of the red rose, what is signified may be love, passion or the Labour Party.

As you can see by this example, the signified of the sign can sometimes have more than one meaning (**polysemy**), but this is often tempered by the context within which the sign is represented. A red rose means one thing if given to a lover on Valentine's day, another if given to a parent. In another semiotic system, a red rose means 'the Labour Party'.

Signs function not through their essential nature but through their relative position in the ordering of other signs and **codes**. In fact Saussure argued that there is no intrinsic value in a sign, rather, its meaning arises from its difference from other signs within the system. So, in the above example, we know that the rose is a rose by distinguishing it from others in the paradigm of flowers – it is not a lily or a daffodil. Applying this idea to human relations, in the rules of gender, the sign 'male' only makes sense through differentiation from 'female' – there are no necessary positive content to maleness.

As the above examples demonstrate, the meaning of a sign is cultural. As such the sign is an unstable entity that relies not only on contextual knowledge but also on the knowledge of other available signs within that context.

See also: **Paradigm, Semiotics, Signification, Syntagm**

SIGNIFICATION

In semiotic analysis, signification is the output of **signs**. Signification is as it were the content or import of communication.

Roland Barthes argued that there were in fact three levels of signification:

- the denotative (this is a tree);
- the connotative (tree connotes nature);
- the mythical (nature is bountiful).

To summarise, an image of a tree can *signify* 'bountiful nature'.

Barthes used the example of photography to demonstrate *denotation*. The photograph denotes what was in front of the camera when the image was captured. But *how* the image is photographed, and what abstract values may be associated with the resultant picture, are a matter of connotation. A photograph of a face denotes that face, but what is *connoted* will depend on the genre of photography (surveillance, fashion, news, art) and on stylistic manipulations of composition, colour, etc. – the same face can connote 'criminal', 'beauty' and 'supermodel'.

The mythical level of signification can also be termed the ideological. At this level, signification is dependent on shared cultural values and beliefs. Consider the use of images of countryside in advertising. Signification here depends on the myth or ideology that opposes city and country: the country is signified as more pure and innocent than the urban lifestyle. Such myths are specific to certain cultures, and they are arguable: 'countryside' may connote something quite different to a confirmed city-dweller. Whilst the process of signification is universal, the meanings that are generated in the process will be culturally specific.

See also: **Referent, Semiotics, Sign**

Further reading: Fiske (1990)

SIT UP/SIT BACK

A common-sense way of distinguishing 'passive' screen consumption as an audience member for leisure entertainment (sit back), from 'active' interaction with a screen with keyboard, as a user, for either entertainment or instrumental purposes (sit up). The boundary between these modes is eroding rapidly with interactive digital television, datacasting and video-/sound-streaming. People can interact (via remote control devices) even as they sit back; they can be entertained, by streamed video, DVD or gaming, as they sit up. Thus the apparent distinction serves usefully to connect the two modes of 'sitting', or audiencing, superseding broadcast-era presumptions about audiences and consumers as inactive.

SPEECH ACT

The action performed by an utterance as part of an interaction. The concept developed out of the work of the philosopher J. L. Austin, who demonstrated that many utterances are significant not so much in terms of what they say, but rather in terms of what they do. Indeed, in the case of many utterances it makes more sense to ask, 'What is this utterance trying to do?' than to ask, 'Is what it says true or false?' – as may be seen if we consider the following fairly unremarkable examples of everyday utterances:

'I bet he won't turn up.'
'Stop here on the left.'
'Hello.'
'Please keep your seat belts fastened.'
'Okay.'

'Sod off' (or words to that effect).
'I now declare the Garden Festival open.'

These utterances exemplify a whole range of speech acts, including those of *betting, commanding, greeting, requesting an action, acknowledging, insulting,* and so on. None of them is limited to asserting some kind of propositional truth. This kind of observation led Austin to the conclusion that stating or asserting (in ways that can be judged true or false) is only one of many kinds of action (or speech act) that language makes possible – actions as diverse as warning, promising, naming, exemplifying, commenting and challenging. Significantly, for many of these actions it is difficult to envisage how else they might be performed except in words. Since Austin's pioneering work, most attention has been devoted to trying to identify a determinate range of speech acts, and also to specifying precisely the recognition criteria for the most common speech acts, such as questions or commands.

The concept is an important one for communication and cultural studies, partly as a way of countering simplistic linear flow models of communication that see it simply in terms of 'information transfer' or 'exchanging ideas'. It has also been influential in studies of social interaction by providing an analytic tool for a variety of research traditions ranging from discourse analysis to the ethnography of communication.

See also: **Discourse, Language, functions of, Pragmatics**

Further reading: Austin (1962); Montgomery (1986); Searle (1969)

SPEECH COMMUNITY

A group of people who share a common language or linguistic variety. A speech community in the strongest sense will also display common ways of using the shared language and common attitudes towards it within a given society. The term is important for highlighting the way in which language exists not just as an abstract system, codified in grammar books and dictionaries; it is integral to everyday social life and belongs ultimately to its community of users. It is they who make and remake it in their everyday encounters.

At the same time it is a term beset with difficulties. First, the reference to 'speech' recalls earlier societies based on face-to-face contact, and this seems inappropriate for societies in which print and electronic means of communication have opened up a whole range of mediated transactions that do not rely on speech. Some linguists now use the term *language community* instead.

Second, the reference to 'community' seems something of a misnomer under late capitalism. This is not just a question of the division of labour. In the case of UK society, for example, it is now clearer than ever that gross inequalities of material advantage continue to accumulate around the divisions of **ethnicity**, **gender**, **class** and region. And if the society displays not only diversity but also fundamental division, then verbal practices themselves will not just be held in common, but will come to operate actively in opposition to each other.

See also: **Standard language**

Further reading: Montgomery (1986)

SPIN

The management of news by professional publicists and media agencies, both independent and attached to governments or ministries. The professionalisation of public communication in general. 'Spin doctors' became familiar in the UK during the 1990s, and were especially associated with the very tight control of their public image that was exercised by the New Labour Party prior to the election of the Blair government in 1997 (and subsequently). The dark arts of media manipulation were used not only externally, to control as much as possible the flow, even the style, of information used by journalists, but also internally, to make sure Labour politicians themselves remained 'on message' at all times.

Commercial publicists such as Max Clifford also achieved celebrity status during the same era. Clifford specialised in selling scandalous stories about private lives to tabloids. If the private life in question was that of a political high flier, and preferably a Tory, so much the better. Clifford presented himself as a champion of the 'little person'. Not only did they deserve to win (through his contacts with the media) the full value of the 'intellectual property' their gossip or scandal could command, but in addition, the impact of revelations on the careers of the high and mighty – often catastrophic – was seen as exerting a kind of moral justice. Indeed, the dying days of the Conservative government under John Major were dogged by sleaze and scandal, some of which undoubtedly contributed to their trouncing in the

1997 election. Hence, 'spin' could work both ways – as official manipulation to protect the government and as the revenge of the disenfranchised, to 'keep them honest'.

One of its more peculiar claims to fame was that spin could cause an event to occur before it happened. Part of the art of spin was to use selected briefings, leaks and media releases to provoke coverage in the press and on the morning radio and TV shows *before* the publication of something risky – for example, a critical report or less-than-perfect figures on the economy.

STANDARD LANGUAGE

A dialect that has assumed ascendancy within a language community to such an extent that its internal rules become the standard of correctness for the whole community. A standard language tends to have abrogated more prestige and authority to itself than the varieties with which it competes, principally because it usually emerges from the **dialect** of the dominant group. The emergence of a standard language is often related to the process of nation-building; and just as nations are imaginary communities within the social sphere, so standard languages are imaginary systems within the linguistic sphere – not many of us actually speak the standard language, although most of us either think that we do or believe that we should. Their imaginary nature is suppressed by elaborate processes of codification in prescriptive grammar books, guides to usage and dictionaries. All these help to give the standard a spurious air of reality, perhaps with a greater degree of success than that achieved in the UK by the Queen's televised speech at Christmas, which attempts to convince us that we all belong to one nation (or Commonwealth).

See also: **Dialect**

Further reading: Leith (1983); Milroy and Milroy (1987)

STAR/STARDOM

The study of stars arises from film studies. Stars demonstrate the relation between production and consumption, and between producers and consumers. Unlike the notion of **celebrity**, the concept of star is specific to cinema history. It originated with Hollywood film production.

Richard Dyer (1998: 1) argues that stars are studied for both sociological and semiotic reasons.

- *Sociologically*, stardom can be studied to see how stars fit into the industry and economics of Hollywood, and how their image for fans and consumers sustains the business. So, for instance, sociological analysis may investigate whether the phenomenon is a result of production (it is driven by the film-makers) or of consumption (it is what the audience demands) (Dyer, 1998: 9). Such analysis tends to confirm that the function of stars is necessarily ideological.
- The *semiotic* approach to stars differs from the sociological as it focuses on reception rather than production: on experience and meaning, not on the maintenance of the system. Here stars are signs that work intertextually to anchor a preferred reading or meaning of the narrative.

Dyer's own work goes beyond both sociological and semiotic analyses by describing what can be referred to as the cultural function of stars. Dyer argues that stars are definers of general ideas in society. Through their representations of, for example, work, sexuality, ethnicity and gender, they circulate ideas about what makes an individual (1987: 8). For instance, Marilyn Monroe (as a star not a person) signifies a particular type of femininity and whiteness, or as Dyer himself argues, 'an exemplary figure of the situation of women in patriarchal capitalism' (1987: x). To this end stars perform a function for the audience by representing certain types of behaviour and going some way to working through the complexities of subjectivity.

The study of stars is similar to the study of celebrity as both paradigms often work towards uncovering how individuals stand as signs. Additionally, the study of stars works towards understanding how the dynamics of economics, industry and audience can be understood as contributing to contemporary notions of subjectivity.

See also: **Celebrity, Identification, Intertextuality, Sign**

Further reading: Dyer (1998); Gledhill (1991)

STEREOTYPE

A stereotype is a fixed impression. The word comes from the printing process, where rows of type are literally fixed on a plate (called the

215

stereotype) which then makes an impression on paper. Thence, the term also implies monotonous regularity – each page printed from a stereotype is always the same.

Stereotype has entered public life (via social psychology) as a term that is used to describe how fixed qualities or traits may be attributed to groups in the way they are represented in various media. It is usually applied to negative impressions or pernicious representational techniques. In other words, negative portrayals of people of colour may be said to be stereotyping them. But, conversely, the word stereotyping is not used to describe equally fixed and equally fantastic *positive* portrayals – for example, of American heroes and buddies.

McKee (2001: 425) argues that it is constructive to understand stereotypes as reflecting a dominant mode of representation rather than seeking to judge them on their accuracy. This is useful as it opens up the field of analysis; stereotypes are not so much failed representations of an external reality as textual devices that play a role in the economy of narration. For instance, stereotypes can be understood as a concise means of delineating character. Their use is also intertextual. As Dyer (1993: 15) argues: 'stereotypes always carry within their very representation an implicit narrative'. Certainly the genre of comedy has always relied on stereotypical characters; 'comic stereotypes' should thus be considered within the conventions of genre rather than as realistic portrayals.

See also: **Representation**

Further reading: McKee (2001)

STREAMING

Streaming is a technology most widely used for its capacity to efficiently download information from the Internet. Without high-speed Internet access (**broadband**), downloading large multimedia files can be time-consuming. Streaming applications such as browsers and plug-ins begin displaying the information (such as an audio or video file) before it has finished downloading. The information is not delivered as a single unit but gradually through a continuous stream.

See also: **Net radio**

STRUCTURALISM

An intellectual enterprise characterised by attention to the systems, relations and forms – the structures – that make meaning possible in any cultural activity or artefact. It is associated with a number of French writers who became influential in and after the 1960s.

Structuralism is not an *interpretative* approach to meaning. Unlike certain well-established kinds of literary and cultural criticism, it does not seek to reveal the hidden, essential or intrinsic meaning of a text or artefact. On the contrary, structuralists refuse the very idea of essential or intrinsic meaning, together with the notion that individual texts or individual people are the source of the meanings they generate. Structuralism is an analytical or *theoretical* enterprise, dedicated to the systematic elaboration of the rules and constraints that work, like the rules of a language, to make the generation of meanings possible in the first place.

Thus early structuralism was distinguished by the use of Saussurian linguistics and its terminology: especially the notions of signifier and signified; **langue** and **parole**; **synchronic** and **diachronic**; **paradigm** and **syntagm**. These and other distinctive features of a language structure were used to show how disparate and apparently unorganised phenomena were actually instances of the same structural patterns and relations, just as all the different things that can be said in speech depend on the rules and constraints of langue. Further, structuralism was dedicated to showing how such structures were to be found in all kinds of cultural activity. Thus there are structuralist analyses of architecture, fashion, food, kinship networks and the unconscious, as well as of the more obvious signifying 'systems' of cinema, television and literature.

The most prominent names in structuralism are Roland Barthes (criticism) and Claude Lévi-Strauss (anthropology). Other influential writers associated with the enterprise are Louis Althusser (Marxist theory), Jacques Lacan (psychoanalysis) and Michel Foucault (studies of sexuality, madness and incarceration in terms of theories of power, discourse and knowledge) (see Sturrock, 1979).

During the 1970s structuralism underwent a transformation. This was due partly to the proliferation of different positions within the enterprise, which eventually became too diverse to be understood as a unitary approach. It was also brought about by the unease expressed by some of structuralism's original proponents that structuralism was becoming itself the very type of intellectual orthodoxy it was originally set up to challenge. The outcome of this transformation was to produce at least three rather different fields of study.

- *Semiotics*, which had hitherto been synonymous with structuralism but which became established as a major strand within the study of popular culture.
- *Deconstruction*, which is overwhelmingly a mode of literary analysis, derived from the writings of Jacques Derrida. Derrida, a philosopher, showed how the philosophical assumptions that underlie writings are not by any means the guarantors of their meaning – on the contrary, the discourses in which such assumptions are presented systematically undermine the philosophy. This approach has given rise to an entire *deconstructionist* movement that is particularly influential in literary studies in the US. In this guise, the approach is a 'method' whose only precept is to take nothing for granted – doubt and questioning raised to the level of doctrine. Deconstruction is, then, one of structuralism's logical conclusions. Structuralism sought to challenge the common-sense assumption that meanings are the result of their author's intentions, or that language is simply a referential nomenclature (an instrument that simply names an already-existing world). Deconstruction takes these notions further, and concerns itself solely with the signifier (not the signified or the socially 'fixed' sign). Applied to the study of literature, deconstruction has produced a characteristic form of criticism in which the verbal virtuosity of the critic is as much in evidence as reflections on the object of study. The object of study (a work of literature, for instance) is in fact given no especially privileged status; it is not a warrant for its own reading. On the contrary, deconstruction is dedicated to teasing out the repressed, marginalised and absent in the chosen discourse.
- *Post-structuralism*, hard in practice to separate from structuralism. It is more alert to psychoanalytical theories and the role of pleasure in producing and regulating meanings than was the highly rationalist early structuralism. Post-structuralism is also more concerned with the *external* structures (social process, class, gender and ethnic divisions, historical changes) that make meaning possible than the early version, which was concerned mostly with *internal* or 'immanent' textual structures. Hence structuralism shifted its focus from the text to the reader, but this should not be taken as a radical break – post-structuralism is implicit in structuralism itself.

Structuralism has been seen as a characteristically twentieth-century way of understanding the world. The nineteenth century was notable in many different fields for work that sought causes and origins (Darwinism, Marxism, Freudianism) as the framework of explanation. Structuralism shares with other twentieth-century enterprises – in physics and astronomy especially – attention to relations and systems as the framework for explanation. Instead of treating the world as an aggregate of things with their own intrinsic properties, structuralism and physics respectively seek to account for the social and physical world as a system of relations in which the properties of a 'thing' (be it an atom, a sign or an individual) derive from its internal and external relations.

See also: **Difference, Discourse, Postmodern, Semiotics**

Further reading: Culler (1983); Hawkes (1977); Norris (1982); Sturrock (1979)

STYLE

The display of difference. Style can be understood as the combining of pre-existing **codes** and conventions in the formation of identity. While style can be personal, it also refers to cultural and historical identity. Meyer (1987: 34) distinguishes among cultural styles (as discerned by anthropologists, for instance), the style of an epoch (Baroque, Renaissance), as well as **aesthetic** styles (impressionism, surrealism).

The production and consumption of fashion illustrate the functioning of style in contemporary culture. Fashion is one of the means by which individuals mark out notions of the self and personal identity. Yet fashion, like all aspects of style, is constrained by rules, codes and conventions. As much as an individual's writing style is guided by the rules of grammar, so fashion design is restricted as well as enabled by the function of clothing. Nevertheless, top fashion designers may push the limits of what is wearable by showcasing outfits that can't be worn on the high street. Here they are acting as visionaries of style, not designers of clothes. They are the R&D arm of the consciousness industry, much like radical film-making styles such as surrealism or French new wave. Such avant-garde movements challenge and change what is possible in their medium.

Style is concerned with distinctiveness, another aspect of fashion. This is not limited to appearing personally different from those who surround us; it may differentiate between being at home and being 'on display' in public (Wilson, 1985: 27). Entwisle (1997) has suggested that 'power dressing' in the 1980s was a means for the ambitious to signifying their difference from clerical or secretarial workers. Style serves not only to differentiate, but also to forge an identity. Identity through style is also reliant on similarity. For a style to be recognisable, an outfit must belong to a paradigm. Individuals from various subcultures such as punks, Goths and skinheads, while visibly 'different', can (especially to the uninitiated) 'look all the same'. The paradigm allows individual difference within collective uniformity. With reference to aesthetics and identity formation, style relies on choice and combination (or chain); it works in much the same way as **genre**.

See also: **Bricolage, Genre, Subculture**

Further reading: Hebdige (1978, 1988); Lang (1987); on fashion, see Bruzzi and Gibson (2000); Craik (1994); McRobbie (1999, 1999); Wilson (1995)

SUBCULTURE

A group of individuals who share particular interests, ideologies and practices. As the prefix *sub* indicates, such groups are understood to form their identity in opposition to a dominant or 'parent' culture. Early subcultural studies noted that this opposition was carried out through various means, but the most visible was **style**. Recent work in the area suggests that this relationship is no longer as explicit, arguing that traditional definitions of subcultures rely on particular historical circumstances.

Hebdige's (1979) study of teddy boys, mods, rockers and punks is understood as one of the founding texts of subcultural studies. He argues that subcultures make their identity visible by the incorporation of specific style and leisure choices. Punks, for example, used safety pins, make-up and extravagant clothing and supported a particular genre of music as a means of representing their identity. For Hebdige, subcultural groups' use of style and leisure was a form of symbolic politics, 'making their values visible in a society saturated by codes and symbols of the dominant culture' (Shuker, 1994: 238). The formation of identity and a visible challenge to the **hegemony** of the straight society are the aims of subcultures.

Central to Hebdige's thesis is the notion of resistance, specifically in relation to parent or mass culture. But as he stated, one of the greatest challenges to this resistance is 'ideological recuperation', whereby a subculture begins to lose its sense of difference as its style is incorporated into commercial culture (Hebdige, 1979: 97). One of the ways this is achieved is via media exposure. Although disapproving stories in the press may work to create and legitimise subcultures (see Cohen, 1980), approving reports 'are the subcultural kiss of death' (Thornton, 1995: 6). Punk's initial impact was reported in the media in terms similar to a **moral panic**, but before too long punk fashion had spread and the appearance of punks themselves on London postcards signalled the process of recuperation as described by Hebdige had begun.

More recent theorists of subcultures such as Thornton (1995: 3) argue that communities are being formed not so much out of resistance, but out of shared tastes and interests. Thornton uses the term 'taste cultures' to describe the grouping of individuals who listen to dance music and go to raves and dance clubs. She insists that although taste cultures, like subcultures, are bound together through certain commonalities, they are less reliant on the models of resistance put forward by Hebdige. Here, music, drugs and leisure (dance clubs/ parties) rather than style are central to meaning-making, with opposition directed towards mainstream popular music, rather than more generally towards the parent culture.

The move from subcultures to taste cultures recognises that marginal communities are not necessarily always concerned with resistance. Whilst Hebdige (1988) himself declared the death of subcultural significance along with that of the punk movement, studies of the relationship between identity and leisure choices continue (see Gelder and Thornton, 1997). What is apparent in more recent work is that style and leisure are still employed as symbols in youth practices, and are done so as marks of distinction amongst various taste cultures or scenes. Resistance is useless.

See also: **Bricolage, Style**

Further reading: Gelder and Thornton (1997); Thornton (1995)

SUBJECTIVITY

Selfhood. Cultural studies was perhaps more interested in subjectivity than in culture during the 1970s and after. It became a central focus of attention during this period for political and cultural reasons, to do with the rise of **identity politics**. At the same time, structuralism and its aftermath suggested that subjectivity was not a natural but historical and cultural phenomenon, produced out of the resources of language and culture, rather than simply being 'given' by nature. Thus, subjectivity was implicated in new theories of **power**.

Stuart Hall (1994) argues that there have been five decentring shifts in the concept of identity since Enlightenment that have informed our contemporary understanding of 'the subject'.

- *Marxism* demonstrated how individuals were subject to conditions not of their own making (Hall, 1994: 120). Marxist theory undermined the notion that was a universal essence to mankind by arguing instead that individuals were products of social relations such as those required to accommodate the expanding force of capitalism. Marxism's refusal of essential human nature suggested that ethics and morals could no longer be thought of as being universal; rather they were acquired or produced by one's position in society, and indeed had a political functionality in maintaining those positions.
- *Freud*'s 'discovery' of the unconscious (Hall, 1994: 121). Freud argued that an infant's being is formed in relation to others, suggesting that identity was something that was learned rather than existing as an innate essence. Theorists such as Lacan and Kristeva have continued the psychoanalytic path, arguing that identification and subject-formation are an ongoing process conducted in negotiation with the unconscious. Although psychoanalysis is often criticised for its irrecoverable object of study, it has been enormously influential in theorising subjectivity, not least because it was the first to show how reason did not rule the roost in the human imagination.
- *Saussurian* semiotics and structuralism marked another shift in the way we imagine the self. Saussurian approaches to language led to the structuralist contention that we cannot know ourselves outside of language, that it *constitutes* our reality – in a sense, language speaks us. The subject is positioned in language.
- *Foucault*'s reworking of the notions of power, truth and the self (Hall, 1994: 123). For Foucault the individual is 'subject to institutions of power, such as governments, and subject to discourses, such as theories of the person' (Miller, 1993: xvii). Subjectivity was constructed and administered through discourses, including those that investigated what it means to be human (science) and what it means to be social (government). It is these that 'discipline' subjects, making them manageable, knowable and restrainable.
- *Feminism* (Hall, 1994: 124). Feminism gendered the subject. What was widely assumed to be true or universal turned out not to be

true for women. Activism by women was a major contributor to the rise of identity politics.

One would want to add that a sixth decentring has occurred via post-colonial and 'subaltern' studies, which have worked to decentre the Western, universal subject and to introduce the notion of the hybrid, multicultural, 'subaltern' and colonised subject (see Gilroy, 1987, 1993).

See also: **Identity politics**

Further reading: Hall (1994); Miller (1993)

SYMBOL

Symbols may be simple non-verbal signs: something visual standing for something other than itself, as in the way a road sign may use a simplified image to symbolise a bicycle, roadworks and the like. But symbols can also be much more complex artefacts and mentifacts, operating at the most elaborate levels of literary and visual culture. In communication and cultural studies, the study of symbols is used in the following ways.

- In the theory of *semiotics* developed by C. S. Peirce, the term symbol is used instead of the word sign. Using the term symbol he argues there is no relationship between the signifier and the signified (see Leeds-Hurwitz, 1993). What meaning is derived is purely reliant on shared cultural connotations. This is most explicit in the use of national flags, where what the object itself signifies is symbolic rather than natural. Language too acts symbolically, as when a collection of letters come to represent an agreed-upon meaning.
- In *psychoanalysis* (in dialogue with earlier theories of symbolism in *art* and *literature*), symbolism refers to the act of representing something that has been repressed by the unconscious. For Freud, matters of sexuality, birth and maternal relationships are all aspects of the self that are repressed. Psychoanalytic theory posits the 'return of the repressed' through symbols in representation. Sci-fi horror films, for example, replete with hideous monsters, dark corridors and launching spacecrafts represent a form of symbolism for the unspoken and unspeakable (see Creed, 1990).
- The *sociological* theory of 'symbolic interactionism' argues that through symbolic communication we come to know ourselves and

others around us (see Bilton *et al.*, 1987). This was an important development within a discipline that had previously studied only observable behaviour. What this theory recognised was that between communication and response there existed the communication and interpretation of symbols. As a method symbolic interactionism will consider, for example, language, behaviour and body language. Giddens (1993: 716) notes that when 'we interact with others, we constantly look for clues about what type of behaviour is appropriate in the context and about how to interpret what others intend'. Accordingly there is a need for shared cultural consensus of meaning. Giddens uses the example of the first date to demonstrate how two individuals, while remaining aware of their own behaviour, will engage in interpreting the other's behaviour in order to reveal their true opinions. The possibility of romance in this example is revealed both through language and through symbolic communication (see Blumer, 1969).

SYNTAGM

A 'chain' of signs which are combined or organised in a meaningful order from a paradigmatic set of choices. Some examples of syntagm arrangements include a sentence, which is a syntagm of words (signs) or a melody that is a syntagm of notes (also signs). In these examples we can understand how the meaning of the sign in these arrangements can be informed by the elements that surround it.

Combination is rule-governed. Choice of food from a menu involves a syntagmatic process that guides the order in which different foods are eaten (no custard *with* beef, although you may eat it *after* beef). Different cuisines have different rules of combination and sequence, so a Chinese meal (properly done) involves a syntagmatic chain of dishes that bears no resemblance to a Western meal.

Analysis of syntagmatic structure is rare in contemporary media studies. However, the study of narrative continues to carry on this tradition to some extent. Within film narrative, syntagm analysis looks at how events are combined into sequences and how sequences are then ordered into the story through temporal succession (one event follows another) and causality (one event makes another happen). Narrative analysis of this kind demonstrates the syntagmatic choice and the combination of signs within this arrangement is imperative to an understanding of how meaning is constructed.

See also: **Narrative, Paradigm, Semiotics, Sign**

SYNCHRONIC

One of a pair of terms – the other is **diachronic** – taken from the work of Saussure. They refer in this context to two different, but not mutually exclusive, ways of conducting semiotic/linguistic analysis. Synchronic analysis concentrates on the state of language (**langue**) at one moment. Diachronic analysis concentrates on the changes in a given language over time.

Saussure was strongly convinced of the need for synchronic analysis – the attempt to take language as a structured whole and understand its internal relations. Synchronic analysis is essentially abstract since it is empirically impossible to stop a language (much less langue) in its tracks and observe its state. But abstraction was just what Saussure favoured, since his argument was that people had become so bogged down in the empirical fact of particular languages and their word-stores (philology) that there was no developed theory of language-in-general from which to make sense of the empirical data.

Synchronic analysis has become the norm in much semiotic work, where the emphasis has been on isolating the elements (signs) and their internal relationships within an abstract system (codes) of many different sign systems. Saussure predicted that synchronic analysis would eventually lead to a more theoretically adequate diachronic analysis, or even to a combination of the two, which he dubbed *panchronic*. This may be the situation now developing in **semiotics**, where more attention is being paid to the historical development of particular media and institutionalised discourses than was hitherto the case.

See also: **Diachronic, Discourse, Langue, Paradigm, Parole, Sign, Signification, Syntagm**

TECHNOLOGICAL DETERMINISM

The doctrine that social change is determined by technological invention. For instance, Marshall McLuhan (1964) thought that modernity was caused by the invention of printing. Technological determinism is contradicted by Marxism, political economy and other such movements, which award the determining role to the economy.

Communication and media studies have a bet each way in this context, since it is clear that technological development, whilst driven by economic forces, nevertheless opens up possibilities not predicted by them. A simple example is the use of mobile phones for text-messaging, a 'cultural form' that was not predicted by the inventors of that technology, but which secured its commercial viability. Here the technology itself was significant (it could do things not intended). But equally, the example indicates that technology by itself is inert – it has to be taken up by users. Thus, it seems that determination is multiple: economic direction by business and government, combined with the potentiality and capacity of technological inventions themselves, combined with their success or otherwise in the public arena, are all 'determining' forces.

TEXT/TEXTUAL ANALYSIS

A text traditionally refers to a sequence of writing, bounded by the medium on which it is written – page, scroll, stone. The term is inherited from Judeo-Christian traditions of textual exegesis, whereby scholars would take sections of holy or religious texts and explain them, either verbally (sermons) or in writing (concordances). The skill of explication of difficult passages of significant texts was secularised in the form of literary criticism, which began to take hold in the eighteenth century, when religious texts tended to be supplanted by national literatures. But the *technique* of study and commentary remained the same, and so therefore did the concept of 'text'.

In the contemporary era, three developments have coincided to extend enormously what might be encompassed by the term 'text'.

- mass education brought a universal, not merely an elite, readership to texts of all kinds, and thus increased both the need and the opportunity for exegesis;
- continental philosophy, especially that associated with Derrida and the deconstruction movement in the US, contended that humans only know anything by *textualising* the world, and that therefore there is nothing 'beyond' the text;
- contemporary audio-visual media extended *verbal* textuality into visual, aural, and sequential forms – you could buy a video as easily as a book.

It became possible to perform 'textual exegesis' on completely non-written 'texts' such as movies, TV shows, news photos, magazines, web sites, etc. Working back over the three developments noted above, texts became formidable. In a secular era of popular sovereignty the 'textual' media were held to be the bearers of significant meanings about democracy, subjectivity, identity, ideology, fantasy, etc. There seemed to be a philosophical warrant for taking textual evidence seriously, not just as 'representing' the human condition but as getting about as close to reality as can be got. And contemporary life is promiscuously textual. Viewing, reading and listening suffuse everyday activities rather than being a distinct and relatively rare special event (such as 'going to the theatre'). It requires a universal 'literacy', and the study of 'texts' is one means by which citizens of media can become self-reflexive in that context.

Once the pattern was set almost anything could be a text, or be subjected to textual analysis, including live events and actions. Some anthropologists have objected to this exorbitation of the text. But on the other hand, humans cause just about everything they touch or do to signify in one way or another, so to trace the process of meaning creation, transmission and interpretation may well involve looking at customs, buildings, media and bodies as well as papyrus and stone.

Textual analysis is a particularist, empirical, analytical methodology that is central to the work of cultural and media studies. It involves examining the formal internal features and contextual location of a text to ascertain what readings or meanings can be obtained from it. It is not a tool to find the correct interpretation of a text, rather it is used to understand what interpretations are possible. Textual analysis is interested in the cultural and political implications of representations, not only in how meaning is constructed. Remembering that one of the aims of undertaking textual analysis is to understand the variety of meanings made possible by a text, it is essential to consider the context in which the text is received. This is not the same as context in an **ethnographic** sense, where the researcher aims to understand the space in which a person reads a text. Rather, context in textual analysis refers to the wider world of textuality. For example, this can refer to conventions of genre, the intertextuality of an actor, the narrative of the text, as well as discourses that are evoked in discussions of the subject in other media texts. It is the interplay of meanings both inside and outside the text that textual analysis works towards uncovering, and a way of understanding the variety of interpretations likely to be generated by such an analysis.

See also: **Aberrant decoding, Meaning, Methodology**

TEXTUAL SYSTEM

A content industry plus a readership (or audience) and a cultural form, sustained in complex mutual relationship across a number of appropriate media, over an extended historical time. The paradigm example of a textual system is journalism. Hartley claims that journalism, as the sense-making practice of modernity, is the most important textual system of that period (Hartley, 1996: 31–35). Drama is also a textual system, and its survival into modernity suggests the limits of the truth-seeking rationality of modernism.

The most important *textual* feature of journalism is that it counts as true. The most important component of its *system* is the creation of readerships and publics that count as coterminous with the entire nation or society, and the connection of those readers to other systems, for instance politics, economics, social control and the **semiosphere**. The most important textual feature of drama is that it is imaginary – *not true*. Drama's *system* includes the audience, production and exhibition venues, including both 'live' (theatrical) and media (cinema and TV) outlets. Also included are the technology, institutions and practices required to sustain drama – 'Hollywood', for example.

Study of a textual system must be interdisciplinary, both *textually* (using semiotics, content and genre analysis, ideology, pleasure) and *socially* (using quantitative, generalising methods, ethnography, policy analysis, history, etc.), in order to connect the minutiae of communication with the structures, institutions, economics and history so communicated (see **aberrant decoding**).

TEXTUALITY

The empirical trace left by semiosis. That is, any object from which communicative **text** can be recovered. Textuality is a condition of contemporary life.

TRANSITIVITY

Transitivity is a way of describing the relationship between participants and processes in the construction of clauses – basically, 'who (or what) does what to whom (or what)'. Transitivity relations and the roles of participants depend crucially upon the kind of process encoded by the main verb in the clause. For English, four fundamental types of process may be distinguished (for a more complete and complex treatment see Fawcett, 1980 and Halliday, 1985):

- *material:* 'John broke the lock';
- *mental:* 'She understood immediately';
- *verbal:* 'Michael said he was hungry';
- *relational:* 'The main course is excellent'.

Material action processes (realised by verbs such as 'break', 'wipe', 'dig', 'unbolt') are associated with inherent roles such as an AGENT (someone or something to perform the action), and an AFFECTED (ENTITY) (someone or something on the receiving end of the action). Thus:

John	broke	the lock
AGENT	PROCESS	AFFECTED

There need, of course, be no necessary correspondence between the participant role AGENT and the syntactic element 'subject'. The passive makes possible one obvious kind of non-congruence:

The lock	was broken	by John
AFFECTED	PROCESS	AGENT
Subject	Predicator	

The passive thereby allows the topicalisation or thematisation of the AFFECTED.

It also allows the deletion or non-statement of the AGENT:

The lock	was broken
AFFECTED	PROCESS

Mental processes (realised by verbs such as 'know', 'feel', 'think', 'believe') are associated with inherent roles such as SENSER (the one who performs the act of 'knowing', 'thinking' or 'feeling') and PHENOMENON (that which is experienced by the SENSER). Thus:

James	considered	the problem
SENSER	PROCESS	PHENOMENON

Mary	understood	the message
SENSER	PROCESS	PHENOMENON

The message	amazed	me
PHENOMENON	PROCESS	SENSER

Quite commonly, the PHENOMENON will not be realised in the surface structure of the clause, but there may be some reference to the CIRCUMSTANCES of the action:

The doctor	thought	hard
SENSER	PROCESS	CIRCUMSTANCE

Mary	understood	immediately
SENSER	PROCESS	CIRCUMSTANCE

Verbal processes are processes of saying, though this comes in many forms ('suggest', 'promise', 'inquire', 'tell', 'inform'). Typical participant roles are SAYER, VERBIAGE and RECIPIENT. Thus:

I	said	it was time to leave
SAYER	PROCESS	VERBIAGE

I	told	him	it was time to leave
SAYER	PROCESS	RECIPIENT	VERBIAGE

Relational processes in their simplest form involve some entity that is identified by reference to some attribute. The process may be realised by verbs such as 'become', 'seem', 'be', 'have'; and typical roles are IDENTIFIER and IDENTIFIED.

The sky	is	blue
IDENTIFIED	PROCESS	IDENTIFIER

Other important roles are those of POSSESSOR and POS-SESSED:

He	had	no money
POSSESSOR	PROCESS	POSSESSED

Any event or relationship in the 'real world' is filtered through and given linguistic shape by means of one or another of the types of process outlined above. Transitivity relations, therefore, go to the heart of the linguistic construction and mediation of experience. And the patterning of transitivity choices in any one text can reveal crucial predispositions towards the construction of experience along certain lines rather than others. Analysis of transitivity, therefore, makes available an important tool for exploring the ideological dimensions of text.

See also: **Ideology, Semantics**

Further reading: Halliday (1985); Montgomery (1986)

VIRTUAL COMMUNITIES

The network of the Internet provides the possibility for increased **connectivity** between people. Communication through Internet forums (such as e-mail, chat rooms, graphical worlds and discussion lists) allows people to participate within multiple social networks, known as 'virtual communities'. Interaction within the virtual environment is mediated through technology rather than face-to-face. Meeting people can be achieved easily, despite distance. Language differences can be overcome through software applications designed to translate messages. As a result, particular communities can be formed in the virtual world that might otherwise not exist.

The rise of virtual communities has been understood by some as providing the means to greater community participation. In the early days of the Internet, Howard Rheingold wrote that discovering the Whole Earth 'Lectronic Link (WELL) 'was like discovering a cozy little world that had been flourishing without me, hidden within the walls of my house; an entire cast of characters welcomed me to the troupe with great merriment as soon as I found the secret door' (Rheingold, 1994: 2). The virtual community here is depicted as a mythical hope regained – the ecstatic realisation of a long-held desire for a sense of belonging. Such portrayals of virtual communities re-state the large body of communitarian theory that sees community participation as a means to greater social cohesion and personal fulfilment (see for example Putnam, 2000). Virtual communitarians depart from their traditional communitarian predecessors by viewing technology as a promise – a means to achieve the ideal of community, rather than a contributor to its demise.

Analysis of virtual communities focuses largely on issues of identity formation. Cyberspace strips away signifiers such as clothes, age, gender and ethnicity. Individuals are able to create alternate identities and to remake themselves, if momentarily, through fictional histories, by renaming themselves and switching gender ('cross-dressing' online). For some this holds emancipatory potential, allowing people to escape prejudices, fears and repression experienced IRL ('in real life'). For others, virtual communities are problematic substitutes for face-to-face communication. Lack of accountability and the facelessness of individuals within virtual communities can lead to practices that may not be risked within the norms of real face-to-face social relationships. In this way, virtual communities have raised the question of whether a stable and constant identity is a necessary or desirable requirement for community participation (Smith and Kollock, 1999).

The Internet may provide new possibilities for communication but it is not separate from other aspects of people's social life, work and community activities. People bring experiences and attitudes gained from face-to-face communication to their virtual communities. Hierarchies and prejudices are mostly reproduced online rather than resolved. As with communities that are constituted through face-to-face communication, virtual communities can be closed, insular, fundamentalist and motivated by hate. Virtual communities are not implicitly positive.

However, as Avital Ronell has pointed out, virtual communities have led to a rethinking of the conditions necessary to create community: 'In the absence of the polis, something like VR [virtual reality] obligates us to pose ethical questions about contact, memory, the prosthetic subject, and it teaches us to dislocate our proper place' (1996: 126). Virtual communitarians contribute to the established body of community theory by demonstrating that community is not tied to geographic locations but can exist through mediated communication.

See also: **Cyberdemocracy, Cyborg, Internet**

VIRTUALITY

Virtuality is a **cyborg** phenomenon, experienced by the individual whose identity is extended or manipulated through her/his interaction with technology. Underlying the concept of virtuality is the presumption that technology can take us out of ourselves, allow us to create a new identity by manipulating information and allow us to wander through landscapes that are divorced from the material reality that we usually inhabit.

A standard definition of *virtual reality* is 'interactive graphic simulations' (McKie, 1994). However, *virtuality* has been defined by Hayles (1999: 69) as 'the cultural perception that material objects are interpenetrated by information patterns'. This complex definition is intended to illustrate the fact that virtuality as a concept depends upon the cultural construction of a binary opposition between information and materiality.

As a result of this conceptual distinction, information is something separate from the material world that may one day allow us to transcend it. Sci-fi fantasies of being able to take on a new body, or to rematerialise in a different place ('beam me up Scottie') are an expression of this cultural assumption/ideal. This historical construction has resulted in the cultural perception that computer media are 'disembodying' technologies. Hayles traces the creation of this binary opposition back to communication theory and Shannon's assertion that the information has no content or necessary connection with meaning in itself, that only when it is encoded in a signal for transmission does it take on a material form (Shannon and Weaver, 1949). With information decontextualised, it can be cast as promising to take us beyond the physical world, hinting at the possibility of immortality. Not unlike the traditional spirit–body distinction of religious belief, that sees an essence beyond physical presence, virtuality is a belief that it is possible to exist beyond the body.

However, virtuality is not a physical fact but a rhetorical accomplishment. Richard Doyle's analysis of DNA as the 'rhetorical software' of the human body serves as an example. Following scientific discourse, it was long considered (and still is in non-scientific circles) that the gene contained the original information that produced the body, despite the fact that the body contains the gene and not the other way around. This 'impossible inversion' is similar to the dichotomy between information and materiality that is created through discourses on virtual reality (Hayles, 1999). To believe that computers are capable of removing us from the material world is to deny the fact that information and materiality are not mutually exclusive.

In fact, information depends upon the material world for its distribution and use. Here, the rhetorical disembodiment of virtuality takes a different form, invoking the 'weightlessness' of the **new economy**, where **intangibles** rule the roost.

See also: **Cyborg, Virtual communities**

Further reading: Rheingold (1992); Stone (2001); Wark (1994)

VIOLENCE

Physical attack or abuse, normally interpersonal, but also person-to-object (and in some scenarios, vice versa). It can include domestic violence and interpersonal violence, as well as acts of war. What counts as violence requires both context and cultural agreement. Sports contain forms of violent behaviour that are not so labelled, for instance boxing, wrestling, ice hockey and gridiron. But in another context, much less aggressive acts may 'count' as violence – aggression in children's TV shows, for instance.

Violence in society is often attributed to the effects of the media, with each new form of medium attracting criticism for the escalation of this unwanted social behaviour. Comic books, film, television, video games and the Internet have all endured public disquiet about their content and its supposed effects. However, as Goldstein argues, the debate over violent entertainment focuses 'only on its *production* while ignoring its public *reception*' (1998a: 1, emphasis in original), thus leaving the possible pleasurable effects of this form of entertainment out of the equation. O'Shaughnessy, for example, argues that violent entertainment provides a form of fantasy for viewers, allowing 'us to explore and understand our sexual and violent feelings' (1999: 29).

Whether or not depictions of violence provide some form of exploration for viewers is rarely questioned. Methodologies such as the effects model prefer instead to assume that 'violence is an abstractable unit whose presence can be counted and whose influence can be studied' (Barker and Petley, 2001: 3). This model ignores 'the moral codes that different audiences bring to bear as they watch' (2001: 7) as well as the context in which a violent act is represented. As Cerulo (1998: 13) notes, a young boy's torture of small domestic animals will be considered a violent act, yet the same experimentation carried out in the context of the laboratory is considered a scientific one. The same is true of representations of violence. Contextual consideration in content analysis along with ethnography and historical considerations may prove more enlightening in under-standing how and why people use forms of violent entertainment (see Goldstein, 1998b).

Finally, it is worth noting that increased representations of violence do not necessarily say anything about society's attitudes towards these acts. As Casey *et al.* rightly note, 'unlike many forms of comedy or drama, violence requires little translation and therefore travels well'

(2002: 252). The proliferation of representations of violence may have more do to with cross-cultural textual exchange than with the media reflecting or creating a violent society.

See also: **Content analysis, Effects, Methodology, Representation**

Further reading: Barker and Petley (2001); Goldstein (1998b)

WALLED GARDEN

A metaphorical term used to describe strategies employed by **Internet** service providers (ISPs) to encourage online users to stay within the confines of their own or affiliated sites. As the metaphor suggests, a walled garden is built to identify ownership of that area. The garden itself (the ISP's service) is an attractive closed environment that entices you to stay; to leave you must actively seek out the gate.

Walled gardens are used in some cases to prevent users from certain content, for instance, to keep library catalogue users from browsing beyond catalogue use, or to protect children from content deemed unsuitable, in which case they are protected by a 'firewall'. But mostly they are a business strategy used to promote use of an ISP's services and as a means for Internet business to form strategic partnerships with other services by offering them their customers.

Aufderheide (2002) lists a number of such strategies including:

- monitoring the controls of information by privileging one provider over another;
- controlling the first screen a user encounters;
- controlling the frame around the image;
- monitoring and controlling the speed, amount and kind of data a user sends;
- providing content that discourages users from travelling outside them or even from knowing about other options.

Salzer (1999) identifies further methods of **gatekeeping**, in the form of 'service bundling'. These are anti-competitive, and certainly at odds with the Internet's 'End-to-End' architectural principle. These include:

- ISPs restricting customers from running their own Internet service;
- limiting the amount of video streaming the customer may use (a means to prevent Internet TV services conflicting with existing cable television services);

- determining which backbone is in use if they are under contract to a certain carrier (which may slow down user connection speed);
- filtering data;
- preventing customers from developing home networks between computer units.

Furthermore, by not carrying e-mail traffic from addresses assigned by a different provider, ISPs can prevent the customer from using another service simultaneously.

See also: **Broadband, Internet**

Further reading: Miller (2000)

WORLD TRADE ORGANISATION

The World Trade Organisation, or WTO, was formed out of the General Agreement on Tariffs and Trade (GATT) in 1994. GATT had been in existence since the post-World War II period and consists of a collection of contractual arrangements between consenting countries intended to lower tariff barriers imposed on imported goods by states. As GATT began to extend its attention to other aspects of trade protectionism, its primarily voluntaristic dispute resolution processes and limited scope were seen to require further means of ensuring adherence to agreements. In contrast to its predecessor, the WTO is a member organisation with a consistent set of rules intended to govern all trade relations rather than a set of separate agreements. It is wider in scope, applies to more countries and has greater force (Croome, 1999). Including aspirants, the WTO membership numbers over 160, making its influence and reach practically universal.

The mission of the WTO is to promote free trade and free markets. By entering into free trade agreements, members must open their markets to other signatories. As members agree to abide by its rules and obligations when they join, the WTO acts a legal framework for the processes of economic globalisation. WTO membership, it is argued, is beneficial for less economically powerful and developing countries in that it provides them with advantages that they may not be able to negotiate through bilateral trading agreements. It is also promoted as a defence against the activities of larger nations and transnational corporations (Arup, 2000). However, free trade can favour already industrialised nations who have reached a status of prosperity due to previous economic regimes of domestic protectionism. Due to WTO membership, developing countries may be restricted from instituting economic policies that are essential in order to move them beyond their pre-industrial status. Compliance with some WTO free trade measures may in fact be increasing the gap between rich and poor countries.

Free trade agreements are placing new pressures upon cultural policies in a number of countries. As signatories or WTO members, governments are finding that some existing policies have been made redundant by international trade commitments.

In December 2001 China joined the WTO. The effect of this event on world trade, and the international dialogue between China and the hitherto Anglophone, American-dominated world of culture, media and communication, are going to be one of the most important and interesting developments of the twenty-first century.

WORLD WIDE WEB *see* Internet

BIBLIOGRAPHY

Acs, Z. and Audretsch, D. (1990) *Innovation and Small Firms*, Cambridge, Massachusetts, MIT Press.

Althusser, L. (1971) *Lenin and Philosophy and Other Essays*, Harmondsworth, Penguin.

Amad, P. (1994) *Radical Inauthenticity and Cultural Anxiety: The Benetton Advertising Phenomenon,* MA thesis, University of Melbourne, Department of English.

Anderson, B. (1983) *Imagined Communities*, London, Verso.

Ang, I. (1985) *Watching Dallas: Soap Opera and the Melodramatic Imagination*, London, Methuen.

—— (1996) *Living Room Wars: Rethinking Media Audiences for a Postmodern World*, New York, Routledge.

Armstrong, M., Blakeney, M. and Watterson, R. (1988) *Media Law in Australia: A Manual*, Oxford, Oxford University Press.

Artel, L. and Wengraf, S. (1990) 'Positive Images: Screening Women's Films', in Erens, P. (ed.) *Issues in Feminist Film Criticism*, Bloomington, Indiana University Press, 9–12.

Arup, C. (2000) *The New World Trade Organisation Agreements: Globalising Law Through Services and Intellectual Property*, Cambridge, Cambridge University Press.

Atkinson, J. M. (1984) *Our Masters' Voices*, London, Methuen.

Atkinson, J. M. and Heritage, J. C. (eds) (1984) *Structures of Social Action: Studies in Conversation Analysis*, Cambridge, Cambridge University Press.

Aufderheide, P. (2002), "Competition and Commons: The Public Interest, in and after the AOLTW Merger", *Journal of Broadcasting and Electronic Media*, 46: 1.

Austin, J. L. (1962) *How to do Things with Words*, Oxford, Oxford University Press.

Bagrit, L. (1965) *The Age of Automation*, Harmondsworth, Penguin.

Baker, H., Diawara, M. and Lindeborg, R. (eds) (1996) *Black British Cultural Studies*, Chicago, University of Chicago Press.

Banks, J. (1998) 'Controlling Gameplay', *M/C: A Journal for Media and Culture*, 5. Found at *http: //english.uq.edu.au/mc/9812/game.html*.

Barker, M. and Petley, J. (2001) 'Introduction: From Bad Research to Good – A Guide for the Perplexed', in Barker, M. and Petley, J. (eds) *Ill Effects: The Media/Violence Debate*, London, Routledge, 1–26.

Barr, T. (2000) *newmedia.com.au*, Sydney, Allen & Unwin.

Barrell, J. (1986) *The Political Theory of Painting from Reynolds to Hazlitt: 'The Body of the Public'*, New Haven, Yale University Press.

Barret-Lennard, B. (2001) *Anti-globalisation*, Melbourne, Beach Box Books.

Barthes, R. (1973) *Mythologies*, St Albans, Paladin.

—— (1977) *Image – Music – Text*, London, Collins.

Beck, U. (1992) *The Risk Society*, London, Sage.

Beharrell, P. (1993) 'AIDS and the British Press', in Eldridge, J. (ed.) *Getting the Message: News, Truth and Power*, London, Routledge, 210–249.

Bell, D. (1980) 'The Social Framework of the Information Society', in Forrester, T. (ed.) *The Microelectronics Revolution*, London, Basil Blackwell, 500–549.

Bennett, T. (1979) *Formalism and Marxism*, London, Methuen.

—— (1992) 'Useful Culture', *Cultural Studies*, 6: 3, 395–408.

—— (1998) *Culture: A Reformer's Science*, Sydney, Allen & Unwin.

Bennett, T., Emmison, M. and Frow, J. (1999) *Accounting for Tastes*, Cambridge, Cambridge University Press.

Benton Foundation (2001) *Digital Divide Basics Fact Sheet*, Benton Foundation. Found at *http: //www.digitaldividenetwork.org/content/ stories/index.cfm?key=168*. Accessed 7 December 2001.

Berger, A. (2000) *Media and Communication Research Methods: An Introduction to Qualitative and Quantitative Approaches*, Thousand Oaks, California, Sage.

Berger, J. (1972) *Ways of Seeing*, Harmondsworth, Penguin/BBC.

Berkowitz, D. (ed.) (1997) *Social Meaning of News: A Text-Reader*, Thousand Oaks, California, Sage.

Biddiss, M. (1977) *The Age of the Masses*, Harmondsworth, Penguin.

Biddulph, S. (1994) *Manhood: A Book About Setting Men Free*, Sydney, Finch Publishing.

Bilton, T., Bonnett, K., Jones, P., Stanworth, M., Sheard, K. and Webster, A. (1987) *Introductory Sociology*, 2nd edition, Houndmills, Macmillan Education Ltd.

Birdwhistle, R. L. (1970) *Kinetics and Context*, London, Allen Lane.

Blumer, H. (1969) *Symbolic Interactionism: Perspective and Method*, Englewood Cliffs, New Jersey, Prentice-Hall.

Bogle, D. (1989) *Toms, Coons, Mulattoes, Mammies, and Bucks: An Interpretive History of Blacks in American Films*, New York, Continuum.

Bonney, B. and Wilson, H. (1983) *Australia's Commercial Media*, Melbourne, Macmillan.

Bordwell, D. and Thompson, K. (2001) *Film Art: An Introduction*, New York, McGraw-Hill.

Bourdieu, P. (1984) *Distinction: A Social Critique on the Judgement of Taste*, London, Routledge.

Boyle, J. (1996) *Shamans, Software, & Spleens: Law and the Construction of the Information Society*, Cambridge, Massachusetts, Harvard University Press.

Braithwaite, J. and Drahos, P. (2000) *Global Business Regulation*, Cambridge, Cambridge University Press.

Branscomb, A. (1994) *Who Owns Information? From Privacy to Public Access*, New York, Basic Books.

Branwyn, G. (1997) *Jamming the Media: A Citizens Guide: Reclaiming the Tools of Communication*, San Francisco, Chronicle Books.

Braudy, L. (1986) *The Frenzy of the Renown: Fame and Its History*, New York, Oxford University Press.

Brennan, M. (2001) 'Child(hood) Abuse: Constructing the Australian Public in Public Service Advertisements', *Media International Australia*, 99: 91–104.

Bronner, S. and Kellner, D. (eds) (1989) *Critical Theory and Society: A Reader*, New York, Routledge.

Brooker, W. (2002) *Using the Force: Creativity, Community and Stars Wars Fans*, New York, Continuum.

Bruzzi, S. (2001) 'Docu-Soap', in Creeber, G. (ed.) *The Television Genre Book*, London, BFI Publishing, 132–134.

Bruzzi, S. and Gibson, P. (eds) (2000) *Fashion Cultures: Theories, Explorations and Analysis*, London, Routledge.

Buckingham, D. (2000) *After the Death of Childhood*, London, Polity Press.

Butler, J. (1990) *Gender Trouble: Feminism and the Subversion of Identity*, London, Routledge.

Calabrese, A. (1999) 'Communication and the End of Sovereignty?', *Info*, 1: 4, 313–326.

Calabrese, A. and Borchert, M. (1996) 'Prospects for Electronic Democracy in the United States: Rethinking Communication and Social Policy', *Media, Culture & Society*, 18: 249–268.

Calhoun, C. (ed.) (1992) *Habermas and the Public Sphere*, Cambridge, Massachusetts, MIT Press.

Caporaso, J. and Levine, D. (1992) *Theories of Political Economy*, Cambridge, Cambridge University Press.

Carey, J. (1992) *The Intellectuals and the Masses*, London, Faber & Faber.

Carey, J. and Quirk, J. (1989) 'The Mythos of the Electronic Revolution', in Carey, J. (ed.) *Communication as Culture*, New York, Routledge, 113–141.

Carey, J. W. (1989) *Communication as Culture*, Boston, Unwin Hyman.

Carrington, B (2001) 'Decentering the Centre: Cultural Studies and its Legacy', in Miller, T. (ed.) *A Companion to Cultural Studies*, Malden, Massachusetts, Blackwell, 275–297.

Casey, B., Casey, N., Calvert, B., French, L. and Lewis, J. (2002) *Television Studies: The Key Concepts*, London, Routledge.

Cassell, J. and Jenkins, H. (eds) (1998) *From Barbie to Mortal Combat: Gender and Computer Games*, Cambridge, Massachusetts, MIT Press.

Cassell, J. and Jenkins, H. (1998a) 'Chess for Girls? Feminism and Computer Games', in Cassell, J. and Jenkins, H. (eds), 2–45.

Castells, M. (1996) *The Rise of the Network Society*, Malden, Massachusetts, Blackwell.

—— (1999) 'Flows, Networks, and Identities: A Critical Theory of the Informational Society', in Castells, M. (ed.) *Critical Education in the New Information Age*, Lanham, Rowman & Littlefield, 37–64.

—— (2000) 'Materials for an Exploratory Theory of the Network Society', in Hartley, J. and Pearson, R. (eds) *American Cultural Studies: A Reader*, Oxford, Oxford University Press, 414–426.

Castels, S., Kalantzis, M., Cope, B. and Morrissey, M. (1988) *Mistaken Identity: Multiculturalism and the Demise of Nationalism in Australia*, Sydney, Pluto Press.

Caughie, J. (ed.) (1981) *Theories of Authorship: A Reader*, London, Routledge.

Caves, R. (2000) *Creative Industries: Contracts between Art and Commerce*, London, Harvard University Press.

Cerulo, K. (1998) *Deciphering Violence: The Cognitive Structure of Right and Wrong*, New York, Routledge.

Clifford, J. (1986) 'Introduction: Partial Truths', in Clifford, J. and Marcus, G. (eds) *Writing Culture: The Poetics and Politics of Ethnography*, Berkeley, University of California Press, 1–26.

—— (1997) 'Diasporas', in Guibernau, M. and Rex, J. (eds) *The Ethnicity Reader: Nationalism, Multiculturalism and Migration*, Cambridge, Polity Press.

Cohen, R. (1997) *Global Diasporas*, London, Routledge.

Cohen, S. (1980) *Folk Devils and Moral Panics: The Creation of the Mods and Rockers*, Oxford, Blackwell.

Cohen, S. and Young, J. (eds) (1973) *The Manufacture of News: Social Problems, Deviance and the Mass Media*, London, Constable.

Collins, R. and Murroni, C. (1996) *New Media, New Policies*, Cambridge, Polity Press.

Cooper, J. and Mackie, D. (1986) 'Video Games and Children: Effects on Leisure Activities, Schoolwork and Peer Involvement', *Journal of Applied Social Psychology*,16: 726–744.

Cormack, M. (1992) *Ideology*, London, Batsford.

Corner, J. (1998) *Studying Media: Problems of Theory and Method*, Edinburgh, Edinburgh University Press.

Coulthard, M. and Montgomery, M. (eds) (1981) *Studies in Discourse Analysis*, London, Routledge & Kegan Paul.

Coyle, D. (1998) *The Weightless World*, Cambridge, Massachusetts, MIT Press.

Craik, J. (1994) *The Face of Fashion: Cultural Studies in Fashion*, London, Routledge.

Creed, B. (1990) '*Alien* and the Monstrous-Feminine', in Kuhn, A. (ed.) *Alien Zone: Cultural Theory and Contemporary Science Fiction Cinema*, London, Verso, 128–141.

Crompton, R., Devine, F., Savage, M. and Scott, J. (eds) (2000) *Renewing Class Analysis*, Oxford, Blackwell.

Croome, J. (1999) *Reshaping the World Trading System: History of the Uruguay Round*, The Hague, Kluwer Law International.

Culler, J. (1976) *Saussure*, London, Collins.

—— (1983) *Barthes*, London, Collins.

Culture, Media and Sport, Department of (2001) *Creative Industries: Mapping Document 2001*. Found at *http: //www.culture.gov.uk/creative/mapping.html*.

Cunningham, S. (1992) *Framing Culture: Criticism and Policy in Australia*, Sydney, Allen & Unwin.

—— (2000) *Floating Lives: The Media and Asian Diaspora*, Brisbane, University of Queensland Press.

Darley, A. (2000) *Visual Digital Culture: Surface Play and Spectacle in New Media Genre*, London, Routledge.

Davis, M. (1997) *Gangland: Cultural Elites and the New Generationalism*, Sydney, Allen & Unwin.

de Certeau, M. (1984) *The Practice of Everyday Life*, Berkeley, University of California Press.

DeFleur, M. and Ball-Rokeach, S. (1989) *Theories of Mass Communication*, New York, Longman.

DeRosa, D. (2001) *In Defense of Free Capital Markets: The Case Against a New Financial Architecture*, Princeton, Bloomberg Press.

Doty, A. (1995) 'There's Something Queer Here', in Creekmur, C. and Doty, A. (eds) *Out in Culture: Gay, Lesbian and Queer Essays on Popular Culture*, London, Duke University Press, 71–90.

Dovey, J. (2000) *Freakshow: First Person Media and Factual Television*, London, Pluto Press.

—— (2001) 'Reality TV', in Creeber, G. (ed.) *The Television Genre Book*, London, BFI Publishing, 134–137.

Drahos, P. (ed.) (1999) *Intellectual Property*, London, Ashgate.

During, S. (1993) 'Introduction', in During, S. (ed.) *The Cultural Studies Reader*, London, Routledge.

Dyer, G. (1982) *Advertising as Communication*, London, Methuen.

Dyer, R. (1987) *Heavenly Bodies: Film Stars and Society*, Houndmills, Macmillan Education Ltd.

—— (1993) *The Matter of Images: Essays on Representations*, London, Routledge.

—— (1997) *White*, London, Routledge.

—— (1998) *Stars*, New Edition, London, BFI Publishing.

Eagleton, T. (2000) *The Idea of Culture*, Oxford, Blackwell.

Easthope, A. and McGowan, K. (eds) (1992) *A Critical and Cultural Theory Reader*, Buckingham, Open University Press.

Eco, U. (1972) 'Towards a Semiotic Inquiry into the Television Message', *WPCS* 3: 103–21; reprinted in Corner, J. and Hawthorn, J. (eds) (1989) *Communication Studies: An Introductory Reader*, London, Edward Arnold.

Edgell, S. (1993) *Class*, London, Routledge.

Egan, B. L. (1991) *Information Superhighways: The Economics of Advanced Public Communication Networks*, Boston, Artech House.

Entwisle, J. (1997) ' "Power Dressing" and the Construction of the Career Woman', in Nava, M., Blake, A., MacRury, I. and Richards, B. (eds) *Buy This Book: Studies in Advertising and Consumption*, London, Routledge, 311–323.

Enzensberger, H. M. (1970) 'Constituents of a Theory of the Media', in McQuail, A. (ed.) (1972); see also Enzensberger, H. M. (1974) *The Consciousness Industry*, New York, Seabury Press.

Escobar, A. (2000) 'Place, Power and Networks in Globalisation and Postdevelopment', in Wilson, K. (ed.) *Redeveloping Communication for Social Change*, Lanham, Rowman & Littlefield, 163–174.

Fawcett, R. (1980) *Cognitive Linguistics and Social Interaction* Heidelberg, Julius Groos Verlag.

Featherstone, M. (ed.) (1990) *Global Culture: Nationalism, Globalisation and Modernity*, London, Sage.

Feldman, T. (1997) *An Introduction to Digital Media*, London, Routledge.

Ferguson, C. A. (1972) 'Diglossia', in Giglioli, P. P. (ed.) *Language and Social Context*, Harmondsworth, Penguin.

Ferguson, M. and Golding, P. (eds) (1997) *Cultural Studies in Question*, London, Sage.

Fischer, J. (2001) 'The Dot-Bomb Survivors Club', *US News & World Report*, 130: 11, 34–37.

Fiske, J. (1987) *Television Culture*, London, Routledge.

—— (1989a) *Understanding Popular Culture*, London, Unwin Hyman.

—— (1989b) *Reading the Popular*, London, Unwin Hyman.

—— (1990) *Introduction to Communication Studies*, 2nd edition, London, Routledge.

Fiske, J. and Hartley, J. (1978) *Reading Television*, London, Methuen.

Foucault, M. (1977) *Discipline and Punish: The Birth of the Prison*, Harmondsworth, Peregrine.

—— (1984) *The Foucault Reader*, ed. Paul Rabinow, New York, Pantheon and London, Penguin.

Fraser, N. (1992) 'Rethinking the Public Sphere: A Contribution to the Critique of Actually Existing Democracy', in Calhoun, C. (ed.) *Habermas and the Public Sphere*, Cambridge, Massachusetts, MIT Press, 109–142.

Friedman, J. (1990) 'Being in the World: Globalisation and Localisation', in Featherstone, M. (ed.) *Global Culture: Nationalism, Globalisation and Modernity*, London, Sage, 311–328.

Frow, J. (1995) *Cultural Studies and Cultural Value*, Oxford, Clarendon Press.

—— (1997) *Time and Commodity Culture: Essays in Cultural Theory and Postmodernity*, Oxford, Oxford University Press.

Fuller, M. and Jenkins, H. (1995) 'Nintendo and New World Travel Writing: A Dialogue', in Jones, S. (ed.) *Cybersociety: Computer-Mediated Communication and Community*, Thousand Oaks, California, Sage, 57–72.

Galtang, J. and Ruge, M. (1973) 'Structuring and Selecting News', in Cohen, S. and Young, J. (eds), 62–73.

Gansom, J. (1994) *Claims to Fame: Celebrity in Contemporary America*, Berkeley, University of California Press.

Garnham, N. (1986) 'The Media and the Public Sphere', in Golding, P., Murdock, G. and Schlesinger, P. (eds) *Communicating Politics*, Leicester, Leicester University Press, 45–53.

Gauntlett, D. (1998) 'Ten Things Wrong with the "Effects Model" ', in Dickinson, R., Harindranath, R. and Linné, O. (eds) *Approaches to Audiences: A Reader*, London, Arnold.

Gayle, D. and Goodrich, J. (eds) (1990) *Privatization and Deregulation in Global Perspective*, New York, Quorum Books.

Gelder, K. and Thornton, S. (eds) (1997) *The Subcultures Reader*, London, Routledge.

Giddens, A. (1993) *Sociology*, 2nd edition, Cambridge, Polity Press.

—— (1994) *Beyond Left and Right*, Cambridge, Polity Press.

—— (2000) *The Third Way and its Critics*, Cambridge, Polity.

Gillespie, M. (1995) *Television, Ethnicity and Cultural Change*, London, Routledge.

Gilroy, P. (1987) *There Ain't No Black in the Union Jack: The Cultural Politics of Race and Nation*, London, Routledge.

—— (1993) *The Black Atlantic: Modernity and Double Consciousness*, London, Verso.

Gimein, M. and Diba, A. (2001) 'Welcome to Silicon Valley's Twilight Zone', *Fortune*, 143: 6, 170–178.

Glasgow Media Group (1982) *Really Bad News*, London, Writers and Readers Publishing Co-operative.

Gledhill, C. (ed.) (1991) *Stardom: Industry of Desire*, London, Routledge.

Goggin, G. (2000) 'Pay Per Browse? The Web's Commercial Futures', in Gauntlett, D. (ed.) *Web.Studies: Rewiring Media Studies for the Digital Age*, London, Arnold, 103–112.

—— (2001) '"Mate! Mate!": Australian Telecommunications and its Consuming Subjects, 1988–201', in *Transdisciplinarity: Annual Conference of the Australian & New Zealand Communication Association*, ANZCA, Perth, Edith Cowan University.

Goldstein, J. (1998a) 'Introduction', in Goldstein, J. (ed.) (1998b), 1–6.

—— (ed.) (1998b) *Why We Watch: The Attractions of Violent Entertainment*, Oxford, Oxford University Press.

Gore, A. (1999) 'Putting People First in the Information Age', in Leer, A. (ed.) *Masters of the Wired World: Cyberspace Speaks Out*, London, Financial Times Management, 7–17.

Gramsci, A. (1971) *Extracts from Prison Notebooks*, London, Lawrence & Wishart.

Grant, B. (ed.) (1995) *Film Genre Reader 2*, Austin, University of Texas Press.

Gray, A. (1992) *Video Playtime: The Gendering of a Leisure Technology*, London, Routledge.

Gray, H. (2000) 'African-American Political Desire and the Seductions of Contemporary Cultural Politics', in Hartley, J. and Pearson, R.E. (eds) *American Cultural Studies: A Reader*, Oxford, Oxford University Press, 242–50.

Green, L. (1994) 'Introduction', in Green, L. and Guinery, R. (eds)

Framing Technology: Society, Choice & Change, Sydney, Allen & Unwin, xxvii–xxxvi.

Grice, H. P. (1975) 'Logic and Conversation', in Cole, P. and Morgan, J. L. (eds) *Syntax and Semantics*, Volume 3, New York, Academic Press.

Gripsrud, J. (1998) 'Television, Broadcasting, Flow: Key Metaphors in TV Theory', in Geraghty, C. and Lusted, D. (eds) *The Television Studies Book*, London, Arnold, 17–32.

Groenewegen, P. (1991) 'Deregulation: Some General Reflections', in Head, B. and McCoy, E. (eds) *Deregulation or Better Regulation? Issues for the Public Sector*, Melbourne, Macmillan, 9–20.

Grossberg, L. (1996) 'Identity and Cultural Studies – Is That All There Is?', in Hall, S. and du Gay, P. (eds) *Questions of Cultural Identity*, London, Sage, 87–107.

Grossberg, L., Nelson, C. and Treichler, P. (eds) (1992) *Cultural Studies*, London and New York, Routledge.

Gunter, B. (1997) *Measuring Bias on Television*, Luton, John Libbey Media.

Gurevitch, M., Bennett, T., Curran, J. and Woollacott, J. (eds) (1982) *Culture, Society and the Media*, London, Methuen.

Habermas, J. (1989) *The Structural Transformation of the Public Sphere: An Inquiry into a Category of Bourgeois Society*, Cambridge, Massachusetts, MIT Press.

—— (1996) *Between Facts and Norms: Contributions to a Discourse Theory of Law and Democracy*, Cambridge, Massachusetts, MIT Press.

Hacker, S. (2000) *MP3: The Definitive Guide*, Sebastopol, O'Reilly.

Hague, B. and Loader, B. (eds) (1999) *Digital Democracy: Discourse and Decision Making in the Information Age*, London, Routledge.

Halberstam, J. and Livingston, I. (eds) (1995) *Posthuman Bodies*, Indianapolis, Indiana University Press.

Hall, E. T. (1973) *The Silent Language*, Bishops Stortford, Anchor.

Hall, P. (2000) 'Creative Cities and Economic Development', *Urban Studies*, 37: 4, 639–650.

Hall, S. (1973) *Encoding and Decoding in the Television Discourse*, Birmingham, Centre for Contemporary Cultural Studies, University of Birmingham.

—— (1982) 'The Rediscovery of Ideology', in Gurevitch *et al.*

—— (1988) 'New Ethnicities', in *Identity: The Real Me*, Institute for Contemporary Arts Document 6, London, 27–31.

—— (1994) 'The Question of Cultural Identity', in *The Polity Reader in Cultural Theory*, Cambridge, Polity Press, 119–125.

—— (1997) 'What is This "Black" in Black Popular Culture?', in Smith, V. (ed.) *Representing Blackness: Issues in Film and Video*, London, Athlone Press, 123–133.

Hall, S., Hobson, D., Lowe, A. and Willis, P. (eds) (1980) *Culture, Media, Language*, London, Hutchinson.

Hall, S. and Jefferson, T. (eds) (1976) *Resistance Through Rituals*, London, Hutchinson.

Halliday, M. A. K. (1973) *Explorations in the Functions of Language*, London, Edward Arnold.

—— (1978) *Language as Social Semiotic*, London, Edward Arnold.

—— (1985) *Functional Grammar*, London, Edward Arnold.

Halliday, M. A. K. and Hasan, R. (1975) *Cohesion in English*, London, Longman.

Hannerz, U. (1990) 'Cosmopolitans and Locals in World Culture', in Featherstone, M. (ed.) *Global Culture: Nationalism, Globalisation and Modernity*, London, Sage, 237–252.

Hansen, A., Cottle, S., Negrine, R. and Newbold, C. (1998) *Mass Communication Research Methods*, Houndmills, Macmillan Press.

Haraway, D. (1990) 'A Manifesto For Cyborgs: Science, Technology, and Socialist Feminism in the 1980s', in Nicholson, L. J. (ed.), *Feminism/Postmodernism*, London, and New York, Routledge.

Hardt, H. (1992) *Critical Communication Studies*, London and New York, Routledge.

Hartley, J. (1982) *Understanding News*, London, Methuen.

—— (1992a) *Tele-ology: Studies in Television*, London, Routledge.

—— (1992b) *The Politics of Pictures: The Creation of the Public in the Age of Popular Media*, London, Routledge.

—— (1996) *Popular Reality: Journalism, Modernity and Popular Culture*, London, Arnold.

—— (1999) *Uses of Television*, London, Routledge.

Hartley, J. and Lumby, C. (2002) 'Working Girls or Drop Dead Gorgeous? Young Girls in Fashion and News', in Mallan, K. and Pearce, S. (eds) *Youth Cultures: Texts, Images and Identities*, Westport, Connecticut, Greenwood Press.

Hartley, J. and McKee, A. (2000) *The Indigenous Public Sphere: The Reporting and Reception of Aboriginal Issues in the Australian Media*, Oxford, Oxford University Press.

Hartley, J. and Montgomery, M. (1985) 'Representations and Relations: Ideology and Power in TV and Press News', in T. Van Dijk (ed.) *Discourse and Communication*, Berlin and New York, Walter de Gruyter.

Hawkes, D. (1996) *Ideology (The New Critical Idiom)*, London, Routledge.

Hawkes, T. (1977) *Structuralism and Semiotics*, London, Methuen.

Hawkins, G. (1993) *From Nimbin to Mardi Gras: Constructing Community Arts*, Sydney, Allen & Unwin.

—— (1999) 'Public Service Broadcasting in Australia', in Calabrese, A. and Burgelman, J. (eds) *Communication, Citizenship, and Social Policy: Rethinking the Limits of the Welfare State*, Lanham, Rowman & Littlefield, 173–187.

Hayles, N. (1999) 'The Condition of Virtuality', in Lunenfeld, P. (ed.) *The Digital Dialectic: New Essays on New Media*, Cambridge, Massachusetts, MIT Press, 69–94.

Hazen, D. and Winokur, J. (eds) (1997) *We the Media*, New York, The New Press.

Head, B. (1991) 'Regulation and Deregulation', in Head, B. and McCoy, E. (eds) *Deregulation or Better Regulation? Issues for the Public Sector*, Melbourne, Macmillan, 1–8.

Healey, J. (2001) 'Antitrust Probe of Music Firms Intensifies', *Los Angeles Times*, 15 October. Found at *www.latimes.com.business/la-000082195oct15.story*. Accessed 24 January 2002.

Hebdige D. (1979) *Subculture: The Meaning of Style*, London, Routledge.

—— (1988) *Hiding in the Light: On Images and Things*, London, Routledge.

Held, D. (1980) *Introduction to Critical Theory: Horkheimer to Habermas*, London, Hutchinson.

—— (2002) 'Is Globalisation New?', *Open Democracy*, 13. Updated 25 January, *www.opendemocracy.net*.

Hirst, P. (1996) *PERC Occasional Paper 11: Globalisation in Question*, Sheffield, University of Sheffield.

Hobson, D. (1982) *Crossroads: The Drama of a Soap Opera*, London, Methuen.

Hoggart, R. (1957) *The Uses of Literacy: Aspects of Working-class Life with Special Reference to Publications and Entertainments*, London, Chatto & Windus.

Hollinger, D. (2000) 'The Ethno-Racial Pentagon', in Steinberg, S. (ed.) *Race and Ethnicity in the United States*, Malden, Massachusetts, Blackwell, 197–210.

Hovland, C., Janis, I. and Kelly, H. (1961) *Communication and Persuasion*, New Haven, Yale University Press.

Hughes, A. and Trudgill, P. (1979) *English Accents and Dialects*, London Edward Arnold.

Jacobs, J. (1984) *Cities and the Wealth of Nations*, Harmondsworth, Viking.

Jakobson, R. (1960) 'Concluding Statement: Linguistics and Poetics', in Sebeok T. (ed.) *Style in Language*, Cambridge, Massachusetts, MIT Press.

Jenkins, H. (1992) *Textual Poachers: Television Fans and Participatory Culture*, New York, Routledge.

—— (2000) 'Art Form for the Digital Age', *Technology Review*, 103: 5, 17–120.

Jhally, S. and Lewis, J. (1992) *Enlightened Racism: The Cosby Show, Audiences and the Myth of the American Dream*, Boulder, Westview Press.

Joseph, R. (2001) 'Understanding the Digital Divide', *Prometheus*, 19: 4, 333–336.

Katz, R. L. (1988) *The Information Society: An International Perspective*, New York, Praeger.

Keane, J. (1991) *The Media and Democracy*, Cambridge, Polity Press.

Keenan, E. (1974) 'Conversational Competence in Children', *Journal of Child Language*, 1: 2, 163–183.

Kellner, D. (1990) *Television and the Crisis of Democracy*, Boulder, Westview Press.

—— (2001) 'Cultural Studies and Philosophy: An Intervention', in Miller, T. (ed.) *A Companion to Cultural Studies*, Malden, Massachusetts, Blackwell, 139–153.

Kelly, K. (1998) *New Rules for the New Economy: 10 Radical Strategies for a Connected World*, New York, Penguin.

Kirkup, G., Jones, L., Woodward, K. and Hovenden, F. (eds) (2000) *The Gendered Cyborg: A Reader*, London, Routledge.

Klein, N. (2000) *No Logo*, Toronto, Knopf Canada.

Kronig, J. (2000) 'Elite Versus Mass: The Impact of Television in an Age of Globalisation', *Historical Journal of Film, Radio and Television*, 20: 1, 43–49.

Krugman, P. (1997) *Pop Internationalism*, Cambridge, Massachusetts, MIT Press.

Kuhn, A. (1990) *The Power of the Image: Essays on Representation and Sexuality*, London, Routledge.

Kukathas, C. (1995) 'Are There Any Cultural Rights?', in Kymlicka, W. (ed.) *The Rights of Minority Cultures*, Oxford, Oxford University Press, 228–253.

Kymlicka, W. and Norman, W. (1994) 'Return of the Citizen: A Survey of Recent Work on Citizenship Theory', *Ethics*, 104: 352–381.

Laclau, E. (1977) *Politics and Ideology in Marxist Theory*, London: New Left Books.

Landry, C. and Bianchini, F. (1994) *The Creative City*, Working Paper 1: Key Themes and Issues, London, Comedia.

Landry, D. and Maclean, G. (eds) (1996) *The Spivak Reader*, New York, Routledge.

Lang, B. (ed.) (1987) *The Concept of Style*, New York, Cornell University Press.

Langer, J. (1998) *Tabloid Television: Popular Journalism and the 'Other News'*, London, Routledge.

Larrain, J. (1979) *The Concept of Ideology*, London, Hutchinson.

Lasn, K. (2000) *Culture Jam: How to Reverse America's Suicidal Consumer Binge – And Why We Must*, New York, HarperCollins.

Lawson, H. (1985) *Reflexivity: The Post-modern Predicament*, London, Hutchinson.

Leach, E. (1976) *Culture and Communication*, Cambridge, Cambridge University Press.

—— (1982) *Social Anthropology*, London, Collins.

Leadbeater, C. (1997) *Living on Thin Air: The New Economy*, London, Penguin.

Leadbeater, C. and Oakley, K. (1999) *The Independents: Britain's New Cultural Entrepreneurs*, London, Demos.

—— (2001) *Surfing the Long Wave: Knowledge Entrepreneurship in Britain*, London, Demos.

Lechner, F. J. and Boli, J. (eds) (2000) *The Globalisation Reader*, Malden, Massachusetts, Blackwell.

Lee, C., Miller, W., Hancock, M. and Rowen, H. S. (2000) '"The Silicon Valley Habitat", in Lee, C., Miller, W., Hancock, M. and Rowen, H. (eds) *The Silicon Valley Edge: A Habitat for Innovation and Entrepreneurship*, Stanford, Stanford University Press, 1–15.

Leech, G. (1966) *A Linguistic Guide to English Poetry*, London, Longman.

Leech, G. N. (1983) *Principles of Pragmatics*, London, Longman.

Leeds-Hurwitz, W. (1993) *Semiotics and Communication: Signs, Codes, Cultures*, New Jersey, Lawrence Erlbaum Associates.

Leiner, B. M., Cerf, V. G., Clark, D. D., Kahn, R. E., Kleinrock, L., Lynch, D. C., Postel, J., Roberts, L. and Wolf, S. (2000) *A Brief History of the Internet*, ISOC. Found at http: //www.isoc.org/internet/history/brief.shtml. Accessed 2 October 2001.

Leith, D. (1983) *A Social History of English*, London, Routledge.

Lessig, L. (1999) *Code and Other Laws of Cyberspace*, New York, Basic Books.

Levinson, S. (1983) *Pragmatics*, Cambridge, Cambridge University Press.

Leymore, V. L. (1975) *Hidden Myth: Structure and Symbolism in Advertising*, London, Heinemann.

Lotman, Y. (1990) *The Universe of the Mind: A Semiotic Theory of Culture*, Bloomington, Indiana University Press.

Lumby, C. (1997) *Bad Girls: The Media, Sex and Feminism in the 90s*, Sydney, Allen & Unwin.

—— (1999a) *Gotcha: Life in a Tabloid World*, Sydney, Allen & Unwin.

—— (1999b) 'Sex, Murder and Moral Panic: Coming to a Suburb Near You', *Meanjin*, 58: 4, 92–107.

Lyons, J. (1977) *Semantics*, Volume 2, Cambridge, Cambridge University Press.

—— (1981) *Language, Meaning and Context*, Glasgow, Collins.

McBride, J. and Wilmington, M. (1975) *John Ford*, New York, De Capo Press.

McGregor, B. (1997) *Live, Direct and Biased? Making Television News in the Satellite Age*, London, Arnold.

McGuigan, J. (1992) *Cultural Populism*, London, Routledge.

McKay, G. (ed.) (1998) *DIY Culture: Party and Protest in Nineties Britain*, London, Verso.

McKee, A. (2001) 'Stereotype', in Pearson, R. and Simpson, P. (eds) *Critical Dictionary of Film and Television Theory*, London, Routledge, 424–426.

McKie, D. (1994) 'Virtual Reality Fakes the Future: Cybersex, Lies and Computer Games', in Green, L. and Guinery, R. (eds) *Framing Technology: Society, Choice and Change*, Sydney, Allen & Unwin, 15–28.

McLuhan, M. (1962) *The Gutenberg Galaxy*, London, Routledge & Kegan Paul.

—— (1964) *Understanding Media: The Extensions of Man*, London, Routledge.

Macpherson, C. B. (1962) *The Political Theory of Possessive Individualism: Hobbes to Locke*, Oxford, Oxford University Press.

McQuail, D. (1987) *Mass Communication Theory: An Introduction*, Beverly Hills, Sage.

McRobbie, A. (1994) *Postmodernism and Popular Culture*, London, Routledge.

—— (1998) *British Fashion Design: Rag Trade or Image Industry*, London, Routledge.

—— (1999) *In the Culture Society: Art, Fashion and Popular Music*, London, Routledge.

Marshall, A. (1961) *Principles of Economics*, London, Macmillan & Co.

Marshall, P. D. (1997) *Celebrity and Power: Fame in Contemporary Culture*, Minneapolis, University of Minnesota Press.

Marshall, T. H. (1965) *Class, Citizenship and Social Development*, New York, Anchor.

Marx, K. (1977) *Karl Marx: Selected Writings*, ed. David McLellan, Oxford, Oxford University Press.

Meyer, L. (1987) 'Toward a Theory of Style', in Lang, B. (ed.), 21–71.

Miller, T. (1993) *The Well-tempered Self: Citizenship, Culture and the*

Postmodern Subject, Baltimore, Maryland, Johns Hopkins University Press.

—— (1998) *Technologies of Truth: Cultural Citizenship and the Popular Media*, Minneapolis, University of Minnesota Press.

Miller, V. (2000) 'Search Engines, Portals and Global Capitalism', in Gauntlett, D. (ed.) *Web.Studies: Rewiring Media Studies for the Digital Age*, London, Arnold, 113–121.

Milner, A. (1999) *Class*, London, Sage.

Mills, Q. (2001) 'Who's to Blame for the Bubble?', *Harvard Business Review*, 79: 5, 22–24.

Mills, S. (1997) *Discourse (The New Critical Idiom)*, London, Routledge.

Milroy, J. and Milroy, L. (1987) *Authority in Language*, London, Routledge.

Mirzoeff, N. (ed.) (2000) *Diaspora and Visual Culture: Representing Africans and Jews*, London, Routledge.

Mitchell, W. J. T. (1998) *The Last Dinosaur Book: The Life and Times of a Cultural Icon*, Chicago: Chicago University Press.

Montgomery, M. (1986) *An Introduction to Language and Society*, London, Methuen.

Moores, S. (1994) 'Texts, Readers and Contexts of Reading: Developments in the Study of Media Audiences', in Graddol, D. and Boyd-Barrett, O. (eds), *Media Texts, Authors and Readers: A Reader*, Cleveden, Open University, 256–272.

Morgan, J. (1994) 'We *Aren't* the World: A Farewell to Multiculturalism from a Sista Scorned', *Rebelle* (NY), premier issue, Summer: 32–35.

Morley, D. (1980) *The Nationwide Audience*, London, BFI Publishing.

—— (1986) *Family Television: Cultural Power and Domestic Leisure*, London, Comedia/Routledge.

—— (1996) 'Postmodernism: The Rough Guide', in Curran, D., Morley, D. and Walkerdine, V. (eds) *Cultural Studies and Communications*, London, Arnold, 50–65.

Morrison, D. E. (1998) *The Search for a Method: Focus Groups and the Development of Mass Communication Research*, Luton, University of Luton Press.

Mulgan, G. (1998) *Connexity: Responsibility, Freedom, Business and Power in the New Century*, London, Vintage.

Mulhauser, P. (1986) *Pidgin and Creole Linguistics*, Oxford, Blackwell.

Mulvey, L. (1990) 'Visual Pleasure and Narrative Cinema', in Erens, P. (ed.) *Issues in Feminist Film Criticism*, Bloomington, Indiana University Press, 28–40.

Murdock, G. (1992) 'Citizens, Consumers and Public Culture', in

Skovmand, M. and Schroder, K. *Media Cultures: Reappraising Transnational Media*, London, Routledge.

Myers, P. (2002) 'Follow the Napster Users', *MediaGuardian.co.uk*. Found at *www.media.guardian.co.uk/mediaguardian/story/0,7558,636559,00.html*. Accessed 24 January 2001.

Naficy, H. (1993) *The Making of Exile Cultures: Iranian Television in Los Angeles*, Minneapolis, University of Minnesota Press.

Neale, S. (1981) 'Genre and Cinema', in Bennett, T., Boyd-Bowman S., Mercer, C. and Woolacott, J. (eds) *Popular Television and Film*, London, BFI Publishing, 6–25.

—— (1990) 'Questions of Genre', *Screen*, 31: 1, 45–66.

Negroponte, N. (1995) *Being Digital*, Rydalmere, Hodder & Stoughton.

Nordenstreng, K. and Schiller, H. (eds) (1993) *Beyond National Sovereignty: International Communication in the 1990s*, New Jersey, Ablex.

Norris, C. (1982) *Deconstruction: Theory and Practice*, London, Methuen.

Norris, P. (2001) *Digital Divide: Civic Engagement, Information Poverty and the Internet Worldwide*, Cambridge, Cambridge University Press.

Office of the e-Envoy (2001) *UK Online: The Future of Broadband*, 01, London, Crown.

Ong, W. J. (1982) *Orality and Literacy*, London, Methuen.

O'Shaughnessy, M. (1999) *Media and Society: An Introduction*, Oxford, Oxford University Press.

Pakulski, J. and Waters, M. (1996) *The Death of Class*, London, Sage.

Parekh, B. (2000) *Rethinking Multiculturalism: Cultural Diversity and Political Theory*, London, Macmillan Press.

Parkins, W. (1997) 'Taking *Liberty's*, Breaking Windows: Fashion, Protest and the Suffragette Public', *Continuum*, 11: 3, 37–46.

Pearce, C. (1997) *The Interactive Book: A Guide to the Interactive Revolution*, Indianapolis, Macmillan Technical Publishing.

Pensky, M. (1997) 'Adorno's Actuality', in Pensky, M. (ed.) *The Actuality of Adorno: Critical Essays on Adorno and the Postmodern*, New York, State University of New York Press, 1–20.

Philo, G. (1990) *Seeing and Believing: The Influence of Television*, London, Routledge.

Porter, M. (1998) *The Competitive Advantage of Nations*, New York, The Free Press.

—— (1999) 'Clusters and the New Economics of Competition', in Margretta, J. (ed.) *Managing in the New Economy*, Boston, Harvard Business School Press, 25–48.

Poster, M. (2000) 'Cyberdemocracy: The Internet and the Public

Sphere', in Hartley, J. and Pearson, R. E. (eds) *American Cultural Studies*, Oxford, Oxford University Press, 402–413.

Price, M. (1995) *Television, the Public Sphere, and National Identity*, Oxford, Clarendon Press.

Provenzo, E. (1991) *Video Kids: Making Sense of Nintendo*, Cambridge, Massachusetts, Harvard University Press.

Putnam, R. (2000) *Bowling Alone: The Collapse and Revival of American Community*, New York, Simon & Schuster.

Quah, D. (1997) 'The Weightless Economy: Nintendo and Heavy Metal', *CentrePiece*, 2: 1.

Rajchman, J. (ed.) (1995) *The Identity in Question*, London, Routledge.

Rheingold, H. (1992) *Virtual Reality*, London, Mandarin.

—— (1994) *The Virtual Community: Homesteading on the Electronic Frontier*, New York, HarperPerennial.

Richardson, D. (1996) 'Heterosexuality and Social Theory', in Richardson, D. (ed.) *Theorising Heterosexuality*, Buckingham, Open University Press, 1–20.

Riffe, D., Lacy, S. and Fico, F. (1998) *Analyzing Media Messages: Using Quantitative Content Analysis in Research*, New Jersey, Lawrence Erlbaum Associates.

Robins, K. and Webster, F. (1988) 'Cybernetic Capitalism: Information, Technology, Everyday Life', in Mosco, V. and Wasco, J. (eds) *The Political Economy of Information*, Madison, University of Wisconsin Press, 44–75.

Rogers, E. M. (1995) *Diffusions of Innovations*, New York, The Free Press.

Rohde, G. and Shapiro, R. J. (2000) *Falling Through the Net: Toward Digital Inclusion (A Report on Americans' Access to Technology Tools)*, U.S. Department of Commerce, Economics and Statistics Administration, National Telecommunications and Information Administration. Found at *http: //www.ntia.doc.gov/ntiahome/fttn00/contents00.html*. Accessed 7 July 2001.

Ronell, A. (1996) 'A Disappearance of Community', in Moser, M. and Macleod, D. (eds) *Immersed in Technology: Art and Virtual Environments*, Cambridge, Massachusetts, MIT Press, 119–127.

Roscoe, J. (2001) 'Real Entertainment: New Factual Hybrid Television', *Media International Australia*, 100: 9–20.

Rose, N. (1999) *Powers of Freedom: Reframing Political Thought*, Cambridge, Cambridge University Press.

Ross, R. (1990) *Understanding Persuasion*, 3rd edition, Englewood Cliffs, New Jersey, Prentice-Hall.

Ryan, M. and Kellner, D. (1988) *Camera Politica: The Politics and Ideology of Contemporary Hollywood Film*, Bloomington, Indiana University Press.

Sahlins, M. (1976) *Cultural and Practical Reason*, Chicago, Chicago University Press.

Said, E. (1979) *Orientalism*, New York, Vintage.

—— (1985) 'Orientalism Reconsidered', *Cultural Critique*, 1: 89–107.

Salzer, J. H. (1999) ' "Open Access' is Just the Tip of the Iceberg'. Found at *http: //mit.edu/Salzer/www/publications/openaccess.html*. Accessed 3 October 2001.

Sassen, S. (1999) 'The State and the New Geography of Power', in Calabrese, A. and Burgelman, J. (eds) *Communication, Citizenship and Social Policy*, Lanham, Rowman & Littlefield, 17–31.

Saussure, F. de (1974) *Course in General Linguistics*, London, Collins. First published 1916.

Schlesinger, P. (1987) *Putting Reality Together*, London, Methuen.

Schultz, J. (1994) 'Universal Suffrage? Technology and Democracy', in Green, L. and Guinery, R. (eds) *Framing Technology: Society, Choice and Change*, Sydney, Allen & Unwin, 105–116.

Sclove, R. (1995) *Democracy and Technology*, New York, Guilford Press.

Sconce, J. (2000) *Haunted Media: Electronic Presence from Telegraphy to Television*, Durham, Duke University Press.

Searle, J. (1969) *Speech Acts*, Cambridge, Cambridge University Press.

Severin, W. and Tankard, J. (2001) *Communication Theories*, 5th edition, New York, Longman.

Shannon, C. and Weaver, W. (1949) *The Mathematical Theory of Communication*, Illinois, University of Illinois Press.

Shattuc, J. (1997) *The Talking Cure: TV Talk Shows and Women*, New York, Routledge.

Shuker, R. (1994) *Understanding Popular Music*, London, Routledge.

Skirrow, G. (1990) 'Hellovision: An Analysis of Video Games', in Alvarado, M. and Thompson, J. (eds) *The Media Reader*, London, BFI Publishing.

Smith, M. A. and Kollock, P. (eds) (1999) *Communities in Cyberspace*, London, Routledge.

Spender, D. (1995) *Nattering on the Net: Women, Power and Cyberspace*, Melbourne, Spinifex Press.

Sreberny, A. (2000) 'Media and Diasporic Consciousness: An Exploration Among Iranians in London', in Cottle, S. (ed.) *Ethnic Minorities and the Media: Changing Cultural Boundaries*, Buckingham, Open University Press, 179–196.

Stam, R. (2000) *Film Theory: An Introduction*, Malden, Massachusetts, Blackwell.

Stam, R., Burgoyne, R. and Flitterman-Lewis, S. (1992) *New Vocabularies in Film Semiotics*, London, Routledge.

Stone, A. (2001) 'Will the Real Body Please Stand Up?: Boundary Stories about Virtual Cultures', in Trend, D. (ed.) *Reading Digital Culture*, Oxford, Blackwell, 185–198.

Sturrock, J. (ed.) (1979) *Structuralism and Since*, Oxford, Opus.

Sunstein, C. (2001) *Republic.com*, Princeton, Princeton University Press.

Swingewood, A. (1977) *The Myth of Mass Culture*, London, Macmillan.

Tapscott, D. (1995) *The Digital Economy*, New York, McGraw-Hill.

Tassel, J. V. (2001) *Digital TV over Broadband: Harvesting Bandwidth*, Boston, Focal Press.

Taylor, L. and Willis, A. (1999) *Media Studies: Texts, Institutions and Audiences*, Oxford, Blackwell.

Thornton, S. (1994) 'Moral Panic, the Media and British Rave Culture', in Ross, A. and Rose, T. (eds) *Microphone Fiends: Youth Music, Youth Culture*, London, Routledge, 176–192.

—— (1995) *Club Cultures: Music Media and Subcultural Capital*, Cambridge, Polity Press.

Thwaites, T., Davis, L. and Mules, W. (1994) *Tools for Cultural Studies*, Melbourne, Macmillan Education Australia.

Todd, L. (1984) *Modern Englishes: Pidgins and Creoles*, Oxford, Blackwell.

Tsagarousianou, R., Tambini, D. and Bryan, C. (eds) (1998) *Cyberdemocracy: Technology, Cities and Civic Networks*, London, Routledge.

Tunstall, J. (1986) *Communications Deregulation: The Unleashing of America's Communications Industry*, Oxford, Blackwell.

Turner, G. (1990) *British Cultural Studies*, Boston, Unwin Hyman.

—— (1993) *Film as Social Practice*, 2nd edition, London, Routledge.

Turner, G., Marshall, D. and Bonner, F. (2000) *Fame Games*, Melbourne: Cambridge University Press.

Volosinov, V. (1973) *Marxism and the Philosophy of Language*, New York, Seminar Press.

Walzer, M. (1989) 'Citizenship', in Ball, T., Farr, J. and Hanson, R. (eds) *Political Innovation and Conceptual Change*, Cambridge, Cambridge University Press, 211–219.

—— (1997) *On Toleration*, New Haven, Yale University Press.

Wark, M. (1994) *Virtual Geography*, Bloomington, Indiana University Press.

—— (1999) *Celebrities, Culture and Cyberspace*, Sydney, Pluto Press Australia.

Watson, J. (1998) *Media Communication: An Introduction to Theory and Process*, Basingstoke, Macmillan.

Whorf, B.L. (1956) *Language, Thought and Reality*, Cambridge, Massachusetts, MIT Press.

Wiggershaus, R. (1994) *The Frankfurt School: Its History, Theories and Political Significance*, Cambridge, Polity Press.

Wilkins, K. G. (ed.) (2000) *Redeveloping Communications for Social Change*, Lanham, Rowman & Littlefield.

Williams, R. (1958) *Culture and Society 1780–1950*, London, Chatto & Windus.

—— (1968) *Communications*, Harmondsworth, Penguin.

—— (1981) *Culture*, London, Collins.

Williamson, J. (1978) *Decoding Advertisements: Ideology and Meaning in Advertising*, London, Marion Boyers.

Willis, J. and Wollen, T. (eds) (1990) *The Neglected Audience*, London, BFI Publishing.

Wilson, E. (1985) *Adorned in Dreams: Fashion and Modernity*, London, Virago.

Wise, R. (2000) *Multimedia: A Critical Introduction*, London, Routledge.

Wollf, R. P. (1970) *In Defense of Anarchism*, New York, Harper & Row.

Wyatt, S., Henwood, F., Miller, N. and Senker, P. (eds) (2000) *Technology and In/equality: Questioning the Information Society*, London, Routledge.

Wyckoff, A. (1999) *The Economic and Social Impact of Electronic Commerce: Preliminary Findings and Research Agenda*, Paris, Organisation for Economic Cooperation and Development.

Young, I. (1990) *Justice and the Politics of Difference*, Princeton, Princeton University Press.

Young, J. (1971) *The Drugtakers: The Social Meaning of Drug Use*, London, Paladin.

INDEX